Race, Gender, and Class in Criminology

CURRENT ISSUES IN CRIMINAL JUSTICE
VOLUME 19
GARLAND REFERENCE LIBRARY OF SOCIAL SCIENCE
VOLUME 1072

CURRENT ISSUES IN CRIMINAL JUSTICE
FRANK P. WILLIAMS III AND MARILYN D. MCSHANE
Series Editors

Race, Gender, and Class in Criminology
The Intersection

Edited by
Martin D. Schwartz
and Dragan Milovanovic

Garland Publishing, Inc.
New York and London
1996

Library of Congress Cataloging-in-Publication Data

Race, gender, and class in criminology : the intersection / edited by Martin D.
Schwartz and Dragan Milovanovic.
       p.   cm. — (Garland reference library of social science ; vol. 1072.
Current issues in criminal justice ; vol. 19)
    Includes bibliographical references and index.
    ISBN 0-8153-2136-8 (alk. paper)
    1. Criminology. 2. Social classes. 3. Social structure. 4. Sex role.
5. Race. I. Schwartz, Martin D. II. Milovanovic, Dragan, 1948–   .
III. Series: Garland reference library of social science ; v. 1072. IV. Series:
Garland reference library of social science. Current issues in criminal
justice ; v. 19.
HV6025.R34 1996
364.2'4—dc20   96–17322
                                                  CIP

Printed on acid-free, 250-year-life paper

Manufactured in the United States of America

SERIES EDITOR'S FOREWORD

This series is dedicated to creative, scholarly work in criminal justice and criminology. Moreover, we ask the authors to emphasize readability. In this anthology Martin Schwartz and Dragan Milovanovic have managed to produce a work that is a combination of both. They also did this in the face of difficulties presented by a variety of theoretical perspectives and methodologies.

The subject matter of this anthology—race, gender, and class—is a critical one for criminology. One cannot find a single theoretical perspective that does not incorporate race and class overtly and gender at least covertly. Yet, at the same time, there is no general agreement about the effect of those three critical variables. Many of the contributors are well-known criminologists whose academic careers have been dedicated to the study of race, class, and gender. What they have to say here is culled from years of thought and, therefore, is quite informative.

Unlike many anthologies, where the various chapters are connected by some tenuous thread, the authors of these chapters are serious in their attempt to provide the uniform focus asked for by Schwartz and Milovanovic. Indeed, because of this, readers can more easily compare the way in which the different perspectives of conflict, feminism, left realism, postmodernism, and peacemaking treat race, gender, and class. Actually, because this volume is unique in this respect, it may serve the field as a clarification of those perspectives.

The chapters that are more focused on specific criminal justice issues follow the same general scheme and assist the reader in understanding the way in which theoretically-oriented analyses take place. This, of course, reflects on the theoretical concepts themselves and provides even greater clarity. Moreover, the choice of topics is indicative of the criminological themes with which critical scholars are most concerned. Readers would do well to ask how these themes differ from traditional criminological concerns and application.

Schwartz and Milovanovic, and their chapter authors, have produced a volume that should assist understanding of critical theoretical perspectives. For this reason alone, we expect it to have great utility as a reference.

Frank P. Williams III
Marilyn D. McShane

CONTENTS

INTRODUCTION

It is commonplace for class to be a variable in mainstream criminology, and it is certainly not unusual for race to be examined. There have been times during the 20th century when gender has been investigated, although most of this work is recent, and done at the instigation of feminist criminologists. Generally, however, mainstream criminology has been the study of working class men and boys. Although radical criminologists have decried this fact, concrete study has been slow to follow.

Within the critical criminology literature, class, race and gender have each been given extensive attention. What has been conspicuously absent has been the investigation of their various intersections—the set of configurations that are more than the sum of the parts. As the authors in this book know well, it is difficult enough to simply discuss class, race and gender on a particular topic. It is much more difficult to locate the points of intersection, to discover how these intersections create manifestations of oppression. Such a method of inquiry poses challenging questions on how to discover the appearances and effects of such intersections, and how to produce strategies of social change designed to eradicate them.

The strategy of just mentioning each of these areas has even been named. Collins (1993) argues that "additive analyses" are often based on two fallacious premises: first, dichotomous thinking (i.e., black/white, man/woman, fact/opinion, and so on) which maintains opposition terms; and second, the assumption of a necessary ranked ordering (hierarchies) of the two stated premises. Both overlook the interlocking nature of these two assumed premises.

One fashionable recent attempt to overcome these problems has been through "standpoint epistemology," the early forms of which were heavily criticized by African American feminists as unilaterally offering a white female perspective. As a result, much contemporary critical analysis acknowledges a plurality of perspectives, of possible standpoints that can develop, each competing with others for ascendancy (see, for example, Grant, 1993; Kerruish, 1991). Today, the literature is replete with discussion, polemic, and synthesis of the various viewpoints on this matter. Yet, too often what has been overlooked in this literature, again, is the intersection (of race, class, and gender) question. If these three aspects are interlocking, then the challenge is to not only discover their configurations and repressive effects, but also to conceive ways of transcending these historical structures. Thus, the various chapters included in this anthology directly or indirectly address the question of existing structures of domination and the possibility of their eradication.

This book has its origins in the urging of Jean Belkhir, who suggested that the field of criminology needed to begin to look at these intersections. Belkhir began a new journal, *Race, Sex and Class*, in the fall of 1993, using for his philosophical preface ideas from Andersen and Collins (1992): this periodical "is not just another 'journal,' but a collecting point for all teachers and researchers on 'Integrating Race, Sex, Class Throughout Our Disciplines,' because 'race, sex , and class are interlocking categories of experiences that affect all aspects of human life...and are indeed the basis for many social problems.'" Under Belkhir's leadership, a new Section on Race, Gender, and Class has been established within the American Sociological Association.

Of course, just forming organizations is only a start. A great deal of scholarly work is beginning to appear, both in the modernist and postmodernist tradition. Henry and Milovanovic in *Constitutive Criminology* (1995), for example, have indicated how a postmodernist analysis must address the constitutive nature of the three aspects. Each aspect, they argue, already appears in the others. Analytical separations render each an independence that does not exist. A number of monographs, in addition to journal articles, are beginning to appear, as Belkhir and Ball (1993) point out: they list new anthologies and monographs that examine race, class and gender in the fields of education, historical analysis, social work, philosophy, political science, psychology, art, and biopsychosocial analysis.

THE ORGANIZATION OF THIS BOOK

Obviously, then, the authors of the articles in this book look at various facets of the intersection of class, gender and race in criminology. This field is brand-new, and the articles here should not be taken as the final word on these subjects. Much more likely is that the authors here took the challenge of the editors to try to formulate their *first* words on this subject, putting down in writing what they had not attempted to write before. Similarly, the editors have not attempted

x

to provide an exhaustive view of the terrain, but rather more of a call for further critical inquiry of the effects of the more insidious forms of domination and repression. The authors here hail from the United States, Canada, the United Kingdom, and Australia, and represent some of the better thinking on three continents.

In our opening chapter, Michael Lynch introduces the question of intersections of class, race and gender in critical criminology. The co-author of an important theoretical work in critical criminology (Lynch and Groves, 1989), Lynch takes this opportunity to lay out in some detail just why it is that it is important to undertake these studies. Bluntly, this essay is so good that we have decided to forego a lengthy editor's introduction to the subject in favor of just sending the reader directly to Lynch.

This ground-setting work is followed by two sections. Section 1 is specifically designed to cover positions that are theoretical and critical in nature. In previous works, we have argued that critical criminology is best divided into four major areas: feminist, left realist, postmodern and peacemaking (Schwartz, 1989). Newsmaking criminology, however, is also an important area of critical criminology. Authors who are well known representatives of each of these areas were persuaded to investigate how their particular theoretical orientation has and could look at these intersections.

The two perspectives that are the most theoretically advanced are feminism and left realism. To represent the first, Mona Danner takes a socialist-feminist perspective to examine women's crime rates across nations. She examines race, class and gender in the context of unequal power relations and the resulting multiple layers of domination. Thus, with poor and ethnic minority women often dominated by men of their own groups, they can be seen as the most vulnerable people in society.

Walter DeKeseredy takes on left realism, which has been important in critical criminology in the United Kingdom, Canada and Australia, and has begun to be taken seriously in the United States. The basic premise is that progressives need to avoid romantic views of street crime, and face up to the fact that most working class victims are victimized by other members of the working class. Within this "realist" perspective, DeKeseredy tries to show the value of the theoretical work that has been done before, and in some very original breakthrough work to locate where left realism needs to go in the future to complete this agenda.

There are, of course, a great many postmodernisms, but one of the most prolific postmodernist criminologists, Bruce Arrigo, here provides a critical inquiry highly informed by a psychoanalytic semiotic viewpoint developed from Jacques Lacan. Arrigo indicates how these conceptual tools may incorporate the three aspects and their specific manifested intersections in understanding how more omnipotent forms of domination exist and how they may be challenged.

Even among peacemaking criminologists the general argument is that this perspective has not yet progressed to the "school of thought" stage. Yet, Susan Caulfield argues that the intersection question can be better understood by developing the conceptual tools of peacemaking criminology, a perspective developed by Richard Quinney. A commitment to peace and to the alleviation of human suffering, she argues, should be at the root of dissections of these intersections.

Newsmaking criminology, to Gregg Barak, indicates how the media is instrumental in constructing images: the "social reality" of crime. The three aspects are often handled as if they were separate effects, and how often, when they are produced together, they are done so in "additive" form rather than in their interlocking, interpenetrating form. The analysis presented revolves around mass-mediated themes of crime and justice which have become staples of both entertainment and information communications.

In Section 2 the emphasis is away from broad theory, and into specific application. Here, each author takes on one topical area, and discusses how the specific or directive study has been or should be informed by attention to the intersection of race, class and gender. Each piece is an example of how to do research that includes race, class and gender. Of course, some of the pieces are more tentative than others, and some break newer ground than others. This is to be expected in any new area. There are few criminologists willing to explore these issues, let alone stand as complete experts in them. All of these authors see their works as first statements, designed to stimulate discussion and thought, and better work by the next wave of criminologists to tackle these subjects.

Meda Chesney-Lind shows us how the intersections manifest themselves in the form of discrimination. This bias often defies easy understanding if using only one of the aspects, or by using the three in additive form. Although much of the literature in the field only looks at the question of gender, Chesney-Lind indicates how it is not only gender, but also class and race that fuel discriminatory practices by the criminal justice system. She concludes with the question of how to reduce women's imprisonment.

David O. Friedrichs's essay is one of the pre-eminent statements in the literature on the intersection question as applied to white collar crime. He indicates that the three constitutive elements are "fluid social constructs" and still call for more precise operationalization in the literature. Emphasizing one, however, or two, without adequate attention to the other(s) may lead the researcher down a path that does not provide genuine answers. Thus Friedrichs reviews the literature concerning the nexus between each of these components and white collar crime, noting their deficiencies. He extrapolates, however, from the literature to conclude that the intersections of the three may structure criminal opportunities and indeed shape criminal behavior. The postmodern era, he continues, may see boundary blurring and new forms of intersections with effects as to white collar crime.

Suzanne E. Hatty, Nanette J. Davis, and Stuart Burke argue that homelessness cuts across gender, class, and race lines. They argue that varied subject positions occupied by the homeless are organized around "axes of differences." The intersection question, they tell us, is intimately connected with the politics of domination and hegemonic social structures that pervade the modern industrialized states. They are interested in how these subjectivities are colonized, silenced, and oppressed, but they include in their discussion the question of resistance to domination.

Rick Sarre applies the intersection theme to the plight of the aboriginal population in Australia. He indicates how the understanding of discriminatory practices by the criminal justice system can be better understood if we are more sensitive to how the three aspects have their interpenetrating effects. Additive analysis in the literature, including the critical literature, although convenient as a presentational style can easily overlook the subtleties of how in fact the three aspects have changing configurations with effects.

Jody Miller uses quantitative log linear analysis and qualitative analysis of case folders to look at the ways in which delinquent girls are adjudicated in county probation offices in California. She finds that race, gender and class are factors that weave through the decision-making process in a complex manner.

Victoria Pitts argues that homeless shelters and their inhabitants can be better understood when approaching the question with an acute sensitivity to how the three aspects, in combined form, are the basis of discriminatory practices by social control agencies. Her first-hand participant observation study provides several illuminating lines of possible analysis for future research as to how social control operates at the micro-level.

Jo Goodey, in our final essay, brings the intersection question to the sphere of adolescent concerns of crime. Based on her research in England, she argues that being afraid of crime, especially among adolescents, is a gendered position cutting across race and class. Her chapter examines the socialization of fear during childhood with its gender, class and racial connotations.

In sum, we find that the intersections of class, gender and race and their unique articulations in historical eras provide the basis for needed research into the questions of domination, repression, and social control. Critical criminology must become more sensitive to the more ubiquitous, be it more subtle forms, of discriminatory practices. In closing, we are at one with Jean G. Belkhir and Michael Ball's recent initiative with the new journal, now renamed *Race, Gender and Class*, and their stated objectives. Namely:

—to discuss how to use race, sex and class as the central categories of analysis in our respective disciplines.

—to develop strategies for understanding race, sex and class from an interdisciplinary perspective.

—to share resources and ideas for bringing race, sex and class to the center of our disciplines' undergraduate teaching.

—to enrich our disciplines with theoretical work from an interdisciplinary approach.

—to celebrate our human diversity while emphasizing racial, sexual, and class social equality.

—to struggle against racial, sexual and class inequality. (1993: 10)

Among the many people we would like to thank are Frank Williams and Marilyn McShane, our series editors, and David Estrin, our editor. Sue Logan did an enormous amount of work with the manuscripts, and Molly Leggett came flying in to save the day, and the index, at the very end.

Martin D. Schwartz
Dragan Milovanovic

REFERENCES

Andersen, Margaret L. and Patricia H. Collins. 1992. *Race, Class, and Gender: An Anthology.* Belmont, CA: Wadsworth.

Belkhir, Jean G. and Michael Ball. 1993. Integrating Race, Sex and Class in Our Disciplines. *Race, Sex and Class* 1(1): 3-11.

Collins, Patricia H. 1993. Toward a New Vision: Race, Class and Gender as Categories of Analysis and Connection. *Race, Sex and Class* 1(1): 3-11.

Grant, Judith. 1993. *Fundamental Feminism: Contesting the Core Concepts of Feminist Theory.* New York: Routledge.

Henry, Stuart and Dragan Milovanovic. 1995. *Constitutive Criminology.* London: Sage.

Kerruish, Valerie. 1991. *Jurisprudence as Ideology.* New York: Routledge.

Lynch, Michael and W. Byron Groves. 1989. *A Primer in Radical Criminology,* 2nd ed. Albany: Harrow and Heston.

Schwartz, Martin. 1989. The Undercutting Edge in Critical Criminology. *Critical Criminologist,* 1(2): 1-5.

SECTION I

THEORETICAL PERSPECTIVES

CHAPTER 1

Class, Race, Gender and Criminology: Structured Choices and the Life Course.*

Michael J. Lynch

INTRODUCTION

This chapter outlines the ways in which race, class and gender have been included within radical and critical criminology. We begin with the idea that the class-based perspective central to radical criminology has given way to a broader perspective (critical criminology) that makes a greater attempt to include race and gender issues along side class concerns. We attempt to build upon this transformation in criminological thought by: (1) linking race, class, and critical criminology to life course or life history research; (2) connecting race, class and gender to the types of choices that are structured into people's lives; (3) demonstrating life course and structured choice effects by reviewing data on income, wealth, and power disparities that arise from race, gender and class inequality; and (4) finally, by examining how race, class and gender intersect to affect the production of crime. Let us begin this journey with a brief history of radical/critical criminology.

* The author would like to thank Elizabeth S. Cass for her comments.

RACE, GENDER AND CLASS: TRANSFORMING RADICAL CRIMINOLOGY

Over the past several years there has been tremendous growth in the styles of thinking employed by radical or critical criminologists[1]. During its formative years (late 1960s - 1970s) radical criminology was most closely associated with class analysis and the work of Karl Marx (for overview see Lynch and Groves, 1989; Lynch, 1993a). And to be sure, class models were extremely important to the development of contemporary critical criminology. Early radical analyses of crime and justice used a class model to: expose the connections between power and privilege (Krisberg, 1975); critique traditional criminological perspectives (Taylor, Walton, and Young, 1973; Schwendinger and Schwendinger, 1972, 1970); pinpoint the causes of lower class crime (Gordon, 1971); and to expose class biases in law (Chambliss and Seidman, 1971; Tigar, 1971; Barak, 1974), including biases in the process of defining and labelling crime (Quinney, 1970), the enforcement of law (Quinney, 1974), and the penal process (Wright, 1973). Over the next decade, this view was expanded to include corporate crime (Reiman, 1979), state sponsored terrorism (Petras, 1987), the state as criminal (Frappier, 1985), and quantitative assessments of radical theory (Greenberg, 1977; Lynch, 1988).

Beginning in the mid-1980s, a number of new issues emerged in radical criminology. Among these were a variety of postmodern concerns (for review see: Milovanovic, 1994), feminist perspectives (Daly and Chesney-Lind, 1988; Caringella-MacDonald, 1988; Messerschmidt, 1986, 1993; Cain, 1990; Schwartz and DeKeseredy, 1991), and left-realism (Young, 1987) to name a few. Increasingly, issues related to race were also recognized as more relevant to the concerns radical criminologists were attempting to address (e.g., see MacLean and Milovanovic, 1990). This broadening of focus signalled the "shift" from radical (class models) to critical criminology.

What is most noteworthy about this shift for the purposes of this essay is the greater emphasis placed upon race and gender. Gender and race were once seen as unnecessary to the economic/class models radical scholars preferred. However, over time, radical criminologists expanded their view and began to understand race and gender (along with class) as **structuring forces** that affect: how people behave, how others react to and define that behavior, who has the power to define and label behaviors, and, how law and law enforcement are organized and focused to control behavior. In part, the inclusion of race and gender along side class concerns was connected to the types of political, social and economic struggles in which radical theorists became involved—issues that directly involved race and gender bias in addition to class bias. Further, the types of problems radical criminologists sought to solve theoretically became (or at least began to be thought of as) more complex, and required the addition of race and gender dimensions to class models (e.g., Messerschmidt, 1986; more generally see, Morrissey and Stoecker, 1994; Geschwender and Levine, 1994). To be sure, many of the new issues radical and critical criminologists addressed were class linked. But many issues could not be understood or fully solved without resort to other structuring social forces such as race and gender.

Thus, over the past decade, as radical/critical criminology matured, its scope has expanded to include a greater number of issues and a greater number of voices[2]. In short, it is only recently that issues and voices that had been repressed to the margins of the radical approach[3] have become more central to the development of critical criminology. Clearly, forms of theory that place race and gender center stage along side class issues are increasingly offered by critical theorists, and have been welcomed into the center of radical thought. The next section addresses the need for such inclusion by way of reviewing the sociology of the life course.

THE LIFE COURSE

Over the past several years, sociologists and criminologists have advanced the idea that a person's "life course of events" or "life history" is important in determining behavior (Granovetter, 1985, 1974; Hagan, 1993; Sampson and Laub, 1993, 1990). There appear to be two ways to interpret this idea.

In the first view, described in criminology as the "propensity" or "kinds of people" approach (e.g., Gottfredson and Hirschi, 1990), there is an attempt to predict individual behavior from specific information drawn from a person's life course of events (e.g., Hagan, 1993; Sampson and Laub, 1990). Some attempt is made to discuss the effect of context, and certain approaches seem capable of including facts beyond those that relate strictly to the individual (Sampson and Laub, 1993).

Although the use of aggregated data gives this view the appearance of being situated in a macro-perspective, the "kinds of people" approach is a very traditional micro-sociological perspective, repackaged in modern form (for critique of this view relative to racism see, Carnoy, 1994:6-12). Mills (1959) criticized such individual-level perspectives over 35 years ago, arguing that "kinds of people" approaches examine the "abstract individual," which Mills defined as the person separated from the social context[4] in which they live and act. In Mills' view, the social context (which he called the social "milieux"), constrained an individual's actions. This meant that if we want to understand how and why people act as they do, we must think about how people are connected and affected through and by the social context. In short, an individual's behavior, the problems s/he faced, and the issues that affected her/him could not be understood once we disassociate the individual and the social environment (e.g., class location, connections to others, etc.).

The second, more radically oriented life course view follows Mills' logic more closely, and attempts to situate individuals within the social context in which they live and act. This view, which we will call the **structured life course** perspective, is concerned with the sociologically, economically and politically relevant forces that either enhance or limit the probability of an outcome in a life-course (e.g., Granovetter, 1974, 1985). Rather than view each individual separately or as a person abstracted from the social context, here individuals are examined as similarly situated groups of people affected by social structures that enhance or constrain outcomes. The idea is to call attention to characteristics which people share that structure their life-course and guide them into similar life courses.

The structured life course view makes sense to the extent that individuals are constrained by factors such as class, race and gender, and to the extent that we can demonstrate that these similarities have a relatively constant effect across a group of persons who share a set of characteristics. The first view or "kinds of people" approach is useful to the extent that people are individuals, unaffected by social, economic and political structures. The logic behind the "kinds of people" approach is questionable, though well received in our society, supported by free-market ideologies (Carnoy, 1994: 6) as well as ideologies of individualism (O'Connor, 1986: 1-23; Ryan, 1982; Henry, 1965: 1-44).

Race, gender and class are extremely important concerns in the structured life course approach. Each of these factors, on its own and in combination, shapes or structures the life-course of an individual. Gender, race and class location, in other words, function to enhance or limit access to economic and political power in the U.S., which in turn, shapes the choices people have at their disposal (Groves and Frank, 1993; for summary see also, Lynch, 1993b). In general, for example, men have more choices than women; whites more choices than minorities; and, the wealthy more choices than the poor. Combining these factors, we can see that wealthy, white, males have access to the greatest number of choices in their life course, while poor, minority women would appear to have the fewest choices.

Within criminology, the intersection of race, class and gender and the effects of these factors upon life course and choices has rarely been employed. The only existing work which draws upon this view is Groves and Frank's (1993) argument that class and race affect the types of choices an individual has at his or her disposal. From this, they argue that those with a greater number of choices should be held more accountable for their behaviors. Their argument is compelling, and stands in direct contrast to actual criminal justice and legal practices which tend to hold the powerless more accountable for their behavior (i.e., sentences, measured as length or type, are more serious for powerless people compared to powerful people; see, Frank and Lynch, 1992; Reiman, 1979). After reviewing information relevant to race, class, gender and life choices, and demonstrating how each affects the types of opportunities for success a person has in American society, we will turn to an analysis of how crime and justice are affected by structured choice and life course.

THE IMPORTANCE OF RACE, CLASS AND GENDER TO CRIMINOLOGISTS AND TO LIFE COURSE

As noted above, the importance of race and gender as key organizing concepts was by no means readily accepted by the majority of radical criminologists when they were first introduced. Early on, many radical criminologists clung tightly to a class model despite appeals to included race and gender issues, and over time race and gender issues were merged slowly with the class theory that formed the heart of the radical approach. To their credit, and through their inclusion of race and gender issues, radical criminologists have seen the wisdom of adapting their theoretical views to the realities of the world around them[5].

The importance of race, class and gender to contemporary social, political and economic life cannot be denied nor overstated. Following decades of struggle for equality in these areas, race, class and gender still matter in American society (e.g., Davis, 1983; West, 1994; Morrison, 1992; Carnoy, 1994). Each of these identifiers is a means of differentiation or stratification in American society. As a means of differentiation, race, class and gender operate by structuring access to chances for success and failure that make up an individual's life course of events. On its own and in combination with the other dimensions of differentiation, each of these identifiers establishes a stratification mechanism that shapes life experiences.

At different points in history, each of the identifiers noted above has a different effect. And, while the degree of the effect differs, to date there has been no era in human history where social, political and economic differentiation was not affected by race, class and/or gender. For example, prior to "emancipation," race had a much different impact upon African Americans than it does today. Though African Americans continue to reside under a system designed to exclude or oppress them even today (see for example, Close and Jones, 1995; Davis, 1983), their exclusion and oppression was at least ideologically different under slavery (Genovese, 1975; Hawkins and Thomas, 1991).

For generations, most societies have been based upon a gendered division of labor and a patriarchical system of power and control (Messerschmidt, 1986, 1993; French, 1992). In comparison to this history, American women have made great strides in the latter half of this century alone. While women have yet to attain "equal rights" with men, they are in some ways better off today than at the turn of the century when they were considered chattel and male property (French, 1992). However, being "better off" is relative, and women still lack the economic and political clout men can access.

Of the three identifiers discussed here, the most inflexible effects seem to be class related. Class effects have changed little in reality, even though today's workers appear better off than 19th century laborers (Perlow, 1988; O'Connor, 1986: 24-51). The class into which a person is born limits social mobility, and is correlated with occupational choices, and class location as an adult.

The irony of the discussion presented thus far is that it completely contradicts the prevalent ideology in American society—the one many

Americans believe or would like to believe—which rejects the view that race, class, and gender matter. The typical American believes (or wants to) that each individual is judged upon his/her merits; that working hard gets you ahead (for critique of these views see Ryan, 1982). What the typical American does not want to believe, and what traditional criminology does not speak to, are the many ways in which class, gender and race affect the life course of individuals, their access to crime, the criminal justice system's response to people, and the chances that a person will be labelled as a criminal.

It is important to remember that race, class and gender effects are not simply additive forces (Anderson and Collins, 1995:xi-xiii). If, for instance, someone is a lower class, African American woman, this person does not experience the simple negative additive effects of being "female," "African American" and "lower class." Rather, her experience is an outcome of how these forces intersect with each other through the social and economic structure (Anderson and Collins, 1995: xii). In other words, the effect is contextual, not mathematical. To "live as" a lower class, African American woman means something different that "adding together" the effects of being a woman, being African American, and being lower class. Understanding such experiences goes beyond statistics, and requires either personal knowledge, or familiarity with ethnographic and biographical materials that attempt to deal with what it means to "live as" (e.g., Williams, 1991; Lerner, 1992).

Materials that allow us to grasp the idea of "living as" are difficult to present within the confines of a chapter designed to serve as an introduction to race, gender, class and criminology. Yet, we need to be somewhat familiar with the effects of race, class and gender as structures that act upon individuals. Consequently, the next few sections review some statistical materials that demonstrate how race, class and gender structure an individual's life course. This material is designed to show how race, gender and class affect the types of choices available to people, their income, occupations, and the types of power they wield or to which they are subjected.

LIFE COURSE, STRUCTURED CHOICES, AND THE EFFECTS OF RACE, CLASS AND GENDER

In this section, we review enough evidence to demonstrate the ways in which gender, race and class structure a life course and constrain or enhance the types of choices individuals can make. It is necessary to review this information before the relevance of these factors for a gender, race and class conscious criminology can be discussed.

Gender

Many Americans assume that the effect of gender has been eliminated or at least greatly reduced at this point in history. Many point to the positive effects of affirmative action for women (and minorities), and the negative effects of "reverse" discrimination upon men as a means of bolstering this view . But, no such evidence can be found when the political and economic power of women (or minorities) is reviewed (for critique of the impact of affirmative action programs see, Ryan, 1982:147-158).

Historically, women have been deprived of equal political and economic power when compared to men. The situation is worse for women of color. On average across all occupations, women earn approximately 70 percent of what men make (Ruth, 1995:309; Rotella, 1995; Sklar, 1995). And, while statistics from recent years show that women are gaining on men economically, these gains are the result of a **decline in male wages** rather than an increase in wages paid to women (Amott, 1995:207). About 80 percent of all women are employed in service, clerical and sales positions—low wage, low status, relatively powerless positions. For example, nearly 98 percent of all secretaries are women. And, within a given occupation, even those dominated by women, women earn less than men (Ruth, 1995). Ruth (1995:309) notes, for instance, that the average weekly income for full-time clerical work varies by gender: women earn approximately $370 per week, while male clerical assistants earn $404 per week. Ruth also notes that income disparities are found in high status professions, such as the legal and medical fields. Female physicians, for instance, earn approximately $240 less per week than male physicians, while female lawyers and judges earn $270 less than their male counterparts (Ruth, 1995:309).

The apologists' argument for such disparities is that women earn less because: (1) they don't work as hard as men, and are less ambitious than men, which is why they accept low status, low paying jobs; and/or, (2) they have less experience than men; and/or, (3) they have less education than men; and/or, (4) many women have husbands who are the primary bread winners, and therefore they need less income when they work. None of these apologies for gendered income or occupational disparities holds water. For example, consider these facts:

1. Over the past two decades, women have made great educational gains; for the past few years more women than men have graduated from colleges and universities. Yet, income and occupational disparities are still evident for women who have recently entered the workforce.

2. Thirty-four percent of all families living under the poverty-line are headed by single female wage earners (see, Rotella, 1995; Sklar, 1995; Kozol, 1995);

3. Sixty-five percent of the female labor force is either single, widowed, divorced[6], separated, or married to men earning less than $15,000 per year (Ruth, 1995: 309);

4. Women are less likely to receive promotions than men, and are also less likely to be placed in positions that net the necessary experience required for promotion (Schur, 1984; for discussion relevant to policing careers, see, Lynch et al., 1992).

These facts completely contradict the apologists' argument; women have increased their educational skills, and they need the money they earn as single heads of households, and as women married to men with insufficient incomes. At the same time, however, they have not been placed in positions conducive to career advancement. They also work as hard as men, but in occupations where upward mobility is limited.

In fact, studies suggest that relative to men, women are more likely to experience downward mobility (Payne and Abbott, 1990).

In short, the facts reviewed above point out how women's economic and occupational life course is determined by gender. Women are channelled into occupations that fit the nurturing stereotype our society has assigned to women (e.g., teachers, day-care workers, nursing, waitressing, etc., see, Schur, 1984; French, 1992; Ruth, 1995). Women's life courses are also affected by a variety of factors outside of the workplace. Women, more often than men, are channelled into "wife" and "homemaker" careers that revolve around the home (Oakley, 1976; Ruth, 1995: 211-222) and are defined as "nonproductive" (Waring, 1990). Child-bearing "concerns" (i.e., the "biological" clock) and responsibilities (child-care), differential education and teacher attention, male-domination (patriarchy), and female-devaluation (Schur, 1984) all structure the path women take.

Race

The effects of racial identification have a clear impact upon life course. Half of all African American children in America, for example, grow up in poverty (Carnoy, 1994: 3), meaning that their access to opportunities for success will be limited. They will receive substandard educations, grow up in unhealthy, polluted environments, have little access to health care, be more likely to die in infancy and in childhood than whites, and generally die at a younger age than whites. They will also learn about racism early in life, and will be avoided because of their appearance and stereotypes that are attached to "how they look." These early, negative conditions have an equally negative impact on the life course of African Americans in the context of U.S. society.

Blacks earn approximately 64 percent of what whites earn (calculated as a percentage of all workers, full and part time, see, Carnoy, 1994: 15). This is an increase from early to mid-1980 figures, but lower than income comparisons from the late 1960s and early 1970s (Carnoy, 1994:15). Average real income for black families has been relatively constant for the past 25 years, and is currently around $19,000 per year (Carnoy, 1994:18). White families have experienced a small increase in real income, and currently earn approximately $34,000 per year or about 80 percent more than the average black family (see, Carnoy, 1994: 18-19). Relative to median white family income, black median income has decreased slightly since 1967, and is currently about 57 percent of the white family average (Carnoy, 1994: 19). Interestingly, black family incomes fell relative to white family incomes at the same time a greater number of black families were joining the middle class (Carnoy, 1994: 13-14, 17-18, 22-24). This was due to a large increase in the percent of blacks earning wages at the lowest end of the economic spectrum (Carnoy, 1994: 22). Thus, while the percent of African American families earning more than $100,000 tripled by 1989 (1 percent of all African American families by 1989), the percent and number of African American families living in poverty also increased (to over 30 percent by 1989; Carnoy, 1994: 23). And, for the poorest black families (bottom 40 percent of black families), average annual family income decreased nearly $800 between 1970 and 1990 in constant dollars (Carnoy, 1994: 23).

During the past several years, getting an education also seems to be failing to help African Americans get ahead. Between 1939 and 1949, wages paid to young, African American, male college graduates rose compared to their white counterparts. Black/white wage ratios remained relatively constant until 1969, when black wages rose relative to those of whites until 1985 (Carnoy, 1994: 25). Since 1985, however, there has been a decrease in wages for African American males, marking the "beginning of an era of tough times" for young, African American, male college graduates that is likely to persist throughout their life course (see, Carnoy, 1994: 25-27).

Other factors influence the life course of African Americans. Chief among these are race-linked stereotypes and expectations held by many people in society (West, 1994), which affect the way people react to African Americans (particularly young, African American males) and the way African Americans react to the labels placed upon them. African American males in particular face forms of criminal justice discrimination (Lynch and Patterson, 1991; Lynch, 1990; Lynch and Patterson, 1990; Patterson and Lynch, 1991) that impact their life course. Young black males are: more likely to be retained by police for processing than young white males; more likely to receive differential bail, even where bail schedules are employed; and more likely to receive longer and more severe types of sentences than whites (see especially Farnworth et al. 1991; on disparities in misdemeanor processing, see Nelson, 1991; on juveniles, see Tollet and Close, 1991). Consider, too, that there are more African American males in prison than in universities and colleges in the U.S. (Irwin and Austin,

1994:5), and that "the biggest single killer of young minority males is gunshot wounds" (Carnoy, 1994:3), and we can begin to comprehend the grim life course that faces many African Americans.

There are apologies for these facts, too, just as there are apologies for why women remain so far behind men. Once again, the attempt is to: (1) blame the individual for not working hard enough to get ahead (Carnoy, 1994: 6-9, 58-68); (2) employ general stereotypes of blacks as "lazy"; (3) lay blame on the welfare system for creating welfare cheats, frauds, and welfare career families (Langston, 1995; Sklar, 1995); and, (4) employ the blatantly biased "blacks are inferior to whites" thesis. Again, these apologies are hard to swallow—they simply are not true—not a single apology noted above can be proven by available data. What is true is that there is an ingrained form of racism in American society that affects African Americans: all African Americans. Cornel West, Professor of Afro-American Studies at Harvard University, and formerly a Professor of Religion at Princeton, relates the following stories of the types of everyday treatment he receives:

> [In 1993], I left my car…in a safe parking lot on the corner of 60th street and Park Avenue to catch a taxi…I waited and waited and waited. After the ninth taxi refused me, my blood began to boil. The tenth taxi refused me and stopped for a kind, well-dressed, smiling female fellow citizen of European decent. As she stepped into the cab, she said, "This is really ridiculous, is it not?"

> Years ago, while driving…to teach at Williams College, I was stopped on fake charges of trafficking cocaine. When I told the police officer I was a professor of religion, he replied, "Yeah, and I'm the Flying Nun. Let's go nigger!" I was stopped three times in my first ten days in Princeton for driving too slowly on a residential street with a speed limit of twenty-five miles per hour (West, 1994:xv).

These excerpts from West's recent book provide fine examples of what it means to "live as" an African American in the U.S.

Class

Americans are both preoccupied with and unclear about the idea of social class. When asked, most Americans will tell you they are "middle class," yet, there are clear differences between the tastes and habits of those who earn $20,000 per year and those who earn $70,000 per year (Fussell, 1984). People will not admit that these differences exist because, it seems, they are acutely aware that their class position has clear implications for the amount of status and respect they receive. In addition, they may be aware but unwilling to admit, that the class into which they are born either enhances or limits their choices and life course. This idea is clearly anathema in terms of American ideology and the idea that hard work gets you ahead (for critique, see Ryan, 1982). As C. Wright Mills (1963:305-306) noted:

> Each ranking or stratum in a society may be viewed as a stratum by virtue of the fact that all of its members have similar chances to gain things and experiences that are generally valued, whatever they may be: things like cars, money, toys, houses, etc.; experiences, like being given respect, being educated to certain levels, being treated kindly, etc. To belong to one stratum or to another is to share with the other people in this stratum similar chances to receive such values.

America has always had a lopsided class structure. Over the past decade, between class economic disparities, linked to Reagan's and Bush's administration economic policies and tax plans, **increased** (Ehrenreich, 1995; Carnoy, 1994). As Ehrenreich (1995: 121) notes, "9 out of 10 Americans now face higher taxes than before Reagan. It's just the top 10 percent that pay lower taxes. This from a decade in which the rallying cry was 'no new taxes.'" The rich are keeping more, while the middle and lower classes are coughing up the difference.

Increasingly, the American class structure is polarized, with increases in the number of wealthy and the number of poor (Ehrenreich, 1995). For example, the wealthiest 1 percent of people in the U.S. own approximately 42 percent of the wealth (Perlow, 1988: 52). Such wealth is not typically earned but is handed down from generation to generation. Millionaires are not made (and when they are, its seems there is a state lottery jackpot involved!)—they are born. At the same time, there were increases in a number of poverty measures: increased long-term unemployment, increased number of people living below poverty, an increase in the feminization of poverty, and a decrease in real wages (see Carnoy, 1994).

To make a long story short, class matters in America. Class affects income and wealth, and chances for success later in life. It affects where you grow up, how you grow up, and the quality of the schools you attend, from elementary school through college. It affects your occupational choices, your career path, whom you marry, and, some studies suggest, even when you have children (Sklar, 1995). It affects your ability to enter politics, and your ability to influence politics and politicians. It affects everyday, mundane decisions, from where you shop, to where you eat, and sometimes, whether you eat at all. Class affects the resources that you have at your disposal. Such resources are useful, for example, both for committing certain types of crimes (e.g., white collar, corporate, and governmental crimes, see, Frank and Lynch, 1992; Simon and Eitzen, 1993), and avoiding the criminal justice process (Reiman, 1979; Lynch and Groves, 1989).

Having discussed three forces that structure life course and choices, we now turn to a discussion of crime and justice. The following section will attempt to integrate the various points discussed above as they relate to crime and justice in American society.

RACE, CLASS, GENDER, CRIME AND JUSTICE

Criminologists attempt to answer four general questions about crime and its control: (1) motivations toward crime; (2) opportunities for crime; (3) bonds that prevent crime; (4) official reactions towards crimes and criminals (Frank and Lynch, 1992). Each element is a necessary component of a "good" theory of crime causation. Certain of these elements directly address the way justice is carried out. Other elements address the "criminal," the structure of society, and the location of the person defined as "criminal" within a social structure. Each element needed to discuss crime and its control is connected to the complex set of class, race and gender relations that have become part of modern social structure. Motivations, for example, may vary by gender, race and class, or the intersection of these structuring forces. Bonds, opportunities and official reactions toward those accused of crime and defined as criminal may also vary according to race, class and gender intersections. In short, to intelligently discuss and understand crime and justice we need to relate opportunities, bonds, motivations and reactions to gender, race and class intersections.

This way of looking at crime and justice contains a VERY BIG problem. That very big problem, simply put, is that few people think about crime in this way. Some criminologists have examined bonds (e.g., social bonding theory, Travis Hirschi); while others examine the structure of motivation (e.g., anomie, Robert Merton), opportunities (e.g., differential opportunity, Cloward and Ohlin) and official reactions to crime (e.g., labelling theory, Richard Quinney). Few, if any, criminologists have examined the ways in which class, gender and race intersections affect the way the four dimensions of crime and justice come together in the process of creating crime.

We are, in other words, only at the beginning of a long process of attempting to understand crime and justice in relation to gender, race and class intersections. The various chapters in this book begin to move us further in this direction. Much more work is needed, however, because many criminologists do not think about or understand the ways in which bonds, opportunities, motivations and reactions combine to create crime. Criminologists know even less about the ways in which race, class and gender intersect, and even less about how class, gender and race impact bonds, opportunities, motivations and reactions to crime. It seems beyond our criminological imaginations at this point in history, then, to connect crime, justice, gender, class and race.

While it may be beyond us to completely understand these issues and how they connect, we can still see the necessity in undertaking such a task. Below, I will offer my modest and initial contribution to such a discussion. This model is offered as a guideline to thinking about these issues, and should not be seen as a completed discussion of the process involved in creating crime.

After making a few preliminary comments, an example of the structure of crime and justice as it relates to gender, class, and race will be provided. This discussion will initially focus upon crimes women experience, such as rape, sexual harassment, and wife battering in order to discuss the structure of justice where gender alone **appears** to be the main issue. This issue has also been selected because of its importance, and to keep the discussion within manageable limits.

THE STRUCTURE OF CRIME AND JUSTICE

Race, class and gender affect what you do, how you do it, how you are perceived by others, and the reactions of others. Race, class and gender taken as statuses or structures act as "codes"; repositories of behavioral cues, possibilities and choices (see Thomas, 1991). The socialization process you pass through as you grow up, from the cradle to the school house, teaches you how to behave so that you conform to your statuses, and also how to react to the statuses of others. For example, African American men react to white men differently than they react to other African American men; upper class women react to upper class women differently than they do to women they perceive as being from classes below them, and so on. These socialized reactions differ from person to person because people from different structural locations (defined by their race, class and gender) are taught different lessons.

Although behaviors, reactions and expectations are affected by structural locations, in American society certain reactions and behaviors seem to be more highly valued than others. Typically, critical criminologists have argued that those with economic power also have access to political power, and thus to the ability to influence the scope and shape of law (Quinney, 1980; Reiman, 1979). This mean that the values found in law will generally be most consistent with the interests of the upper class. As we saw above, race, gender and class have a strong impact on economic power, and from this flows the idea that the dominant race, class and gender will be more likely than other groups to control the political and legal process. Crime, which is a political-legal phenomenon, will reflect gender, race and class power. The less powerful a person in terms of race, class and gender, the more likely that person is to be subjected to the controlling power of the law (and vice versa). And, the less powerful the class, gender and race to which a person belongs, the more likely behaviors common to that group will be treated as criminal (and vice versa).

To be "subjected to the controlling power of the law," the powerless do not have to be arrested, tried or convicted at greater rates than other groups (for discussion see Lynch, 1990). Women, for example, are controlled by a variety of laws that attempt to limit/affect how they use their bodies (e.g., prostitution, abortion, surrogate motherhood, divorce laws, see, Schur, 1984). In addition, women are controlled by the law's failure to address many of the "crimes" that affect women (French, 1992; Schur, 1984; Messerschmidt, 1986). In particular, women are controlled by the lack of an appropriate response to rape, spouse abuse and sexual harassment (DeKeseredy and Kelly, 1993; DeKeseredy and Schwartz, 1993; McKay, 1992; Crenshaw, 1992; Brownmiller, 1975; Box, 1983; Messerschmidt, 1986, 1993). Compared to men, women are relatively powerless economically, which may help explain their lack of influence over law, and the many ways in which law and its enforcement favors males over females.

Adding to this discussion, we must recognize that while gender matters in the process of creating crime, so, too does race (e.g., see: Farnworth et al., 1991; Patterson and Lynch, 1991). And, we must see these effects as simultaneous. Gary LaFree (1988), for example, shows how race of victim and defendant affects the outcome of rape cases controlling for legally relevant criteria (see also, LaFree, 1985, 1980). His "sexual stratification" thesis holds that black women are less likely to be protected by the law when the offender is white, other circumstances held constant (e.g., use of weapon; type of evidence, etc.). Thus, we cannot simply say that women are less powerful than men, or that it is women's relative powerlessness that affects the way women are treated in and by the legal process. Rather, gender and race interact, so that white women, black women, black men and white men are all afforded different degrees of legal protection, and different forms of legal reaction. And further, the degree of protection and legal reaction is not simply a consequence of being a "black female," or "white male." Rather, the effect is relative to the interaction of the race **and** gender of the victim **and** the offender.

As noted earlier, class enters our discussion when considering who shapes the law. The amount of economic and political power people wield is, in turn, correlated with race and gender. Economically powerful (white) males, for example, can use their resources to provide for their defense in rape, sexual harassment or spouse abuse cases to a greater extent than economically deprived (minority) males. Further, wealthy males have a relative advantage over women, who as we saw earlier, have less economic wealth and income than men. And, since race is a correlate of wealth and income, we also know that black males will be disadvantaged as defendants relative to white males; that black women will be disadvantaged as victims relative to white women; and so on[7].

In short, who the law reacts to as offender and victim, who the law protects and discriminates against, both as statute and as a process[8], depends upon the race, class and gender of the parties involved. This is not to say that decisions are made on an individual or case by case basis. While race, class and gender are characteristics of individuals, the importance of these characteristics comes into play at the level of the group; people who belong to a group (e.g., white males) are treated similarly, and are assigned stereotypical characteristics associated with the group to which they belong (LaFree, 1989). When we react to a person, we react to the group we identify that person as belonging to, and to our assumptions about that group rather than to that person as an individual. Crime and justice are structured by assumptions made about groups, their power and ways in which we assume groups relate to one another.

CONCLUSION

Increasingly, criminologists are seeing the wisdom of developing theory that addresses race, class and gender. It is important that such theory and research examines race, class and gender as interrelated; contextually situates the problem of crime relative to race, class and gender; and views the making of crime as a process bound to race, class and gender differentiation and stereotyping. Such views are relatively new to criminology and criminal justice, and much work remains to be done in this area.

Critical criminologists have been very concerned with this issue over the past few years, and have taken the lead in providing integrated race-gender-class explanations of crime, criminal justice processes, and law. Similar integrated models are lacking in more traditional criminological theory, which may explain the stagnation in traditional criminology, and its continued inability to understand or adequately address the problem of crime in our society.

At this point in history, we can only look forward to the day when race, gender and class no longer affect people's life histories. For now, race, gender and class do matter, and it is incumbent upon us to create explanations that help us understand how and why these attributes affect crime and justice. Without exposing, exploring and understanding these affects, there is little hope that they will be eradicated. They certainly do not seem to disappear on their own, as any history of criminology sensitive to race, gender and class would reveal. The next few years will include many exciting theoretical developments that will affect our understanding this problem. A few short years ago, this book itself would not have been possible. One hopes that it is only one of many to come, and one of many that will help us understand how justice and crime are affected by and relate to class, gender and race.

NOTES

1. There are a number of ways of distinguishing "radical" and "critical" criminology." For ease of presentation, these differences have been simplified. Radical criminology is more closely linked to Marx and Marx's economic analysis of society and bears strong similarities to radical economics (on radical economics, see Ward, 1979). In contrast, critical criminology is more squarely situated in the Frankfurt tradition, emphasizing an integration of diverse theoretical approaches such as Marx and Freud (for discussion of critical theory generally see Horkheimer, 1989; for a discussion of critical theory and criminology see, Groves and Sampson, 1986). Both views owe a debt to Marx, and the main difference is the extent to which a view strictly adheres to Marx's model.

2. By "voices," I mean "situated perspectives," or approaches that attempt to be sensitive to views of the world that are non-mainstream and offered by persons generally considered to be "powerless." This includes various perspectives offered by women, women of color, African Americans, Hispanic, etc....It may also include various works by privileged authors that attempt to give exposure to omitted voices and their spoken concerns and issues.

3. Compared to mainstream criminology, critical theory is light years ahead in terms of the inclusion of gender and race related theory. See for example, Lynch et al., 1992; Barak 1991.

4. The term "social context" is not limited to social relationships alone but also includes economic and political relationships as important and necessary forces that shape the environment of society.

5. The same conclusion cannot be reached with regard to mainstream (traditional) criminological approaches. In those views, race and gender (as well as class) remain marginal to theorizing about the world around us, and, for our purposes theorizing about how that world relates to crime and its control. And clearly, the realities of everyday life speak to the wisdom of adopting a radical/critical voice as opposed to the views that dominate traditional criminological perspectives.

6. For those who would argue that divorced women are not economically disadvantaged, consider that the majority of such women are in worse financial shape after their divorce (Schur, 1984; French, 1992), and that only 16 percent of divorced women receive alimony (Ruth, 1995: 309).

7. In all, there are some 36 possible race, gender and class victim-offender interactions that can be discussed here if we restrict ourselves to a three class, two gender, two race (white, nonwhite) model. It is beyond the scope of this paper to be able to analyze the complexity of these interactions completely.

8. This is the same as the classical sociology of law distinction between "law on the books" and "law in action."

REFERENCES

Amott, Teresa. 1995. Shortchanged: Restructuring Women's Work. In M. L. Anderson and P. H. Collins (eds.) *Race, Class and Gender: An Anthology*. Belmont, CA: Wadsworth.

Anderson, Margaret L. and Patricia Hill Collins. 1995. *Race, Class and Gender*. (2nd Ed.) Belmont, CA: Wadsworth.

Barak, Gregg. 1991. Cultural Literacy and a Multicultural Inquiry into the Study of Crime and Justice. *Journal of Criminal Justice Education*, 2(2): 173-192.

Barak, Gregg. 1974. In Defense of the Rich: The Emergence of the Public Defender. *Crime and Social Justice*, 3:2-14.

Brownmiller, Susan. 1975. *Against Our Will: Men, Women and Rape*. NY: Simon and Schuster.

Cain, Maureen. 1990. Towards Transgression: New Directions in Feminist Criminology. *International Journal of the Sociology of Law,* 18(1): 1-18.

Caringella-MacDonald, Susan. 1988. Marxist and Feminist Interpretations on the Aftermath of Rape Reforms. *Contemporary Crises,* 12(2): 125-143.

Carnoy, Martin. 1994. *Faded Dreams: The Politics and Economics of Race in America.* NY: Cambridge University Press.

Chambliss, William and Robert Seidman. 1971. *Law, Order and Power.* Reading, MA: Addison-Wesley.

Close, Billy R., and William Jones. 1995. Oppression and Criminal Justice. In M.J. Lynch and E. B. Patterson (eds.), *A Further Look at Race and Criminal Justice.* New York: Harrow and Heston.

Cloward, Richard, and Lloyd Ohlin. 1960. *Delinquency and Opportunity.* NY: The Free Press.

Cohen, Albert K. 1955. *Delinquent Boys.* NY: The Free Press.

Crenshaw, Kimberle. 1992. Whose Story Is It Anyway? Feminist and Antiracist Appropriations of Anita Hill. In T. Morrison (ed.), *Race-ing Justice, En-gendering(ing) Power.* NY: Pantheon.

Daly, Kathleen, and Meda Chesney-Lind. 1988. Feminism and Criminology. *Justice Quarterly.* 5(4): 497-538.

Davis, Angela Y. 1983. *Women, Race and Class.* NY: Vintage.

DeKeseredy, Walter, and Katharine Kelly. 1993. The Incidence and Prevalence of Woman Abuse in Canadian University and College Dating Relationships. *Canadian Journal of Sociology.* 18(2): 137-159.

DeKeseredy, Walter, and Martin D. Schwartz. 1993. Male Peer Support and Women Abuse: An Expansion of Dekeseredy's Model. *Sociological Spectrum.* 13: 393-413.

Ehrenreich, Barabra. 1995. Are You Middle Class? In M. L. Anderson and P. H. Collins (eds.), *Race, Class and Gender.* Belmont, CA: Wadsworth.

Farnworth, Margaret, Raymond H.C. Teske, and Gina Thurman. 1991. Ethnic, Racial, and Minority Disparity in Felony Court Processing. In M.J. Lynch and E. B. Patterson (eds.), *Race and Criminal Justice.* NY: Harrow and Heston.

Frappier, D. O. 1985. Above the Law: Violations of Inter-National Law by the U.S. Government from Truman to Reagan. *Crime and Social Justice.* 21-22: 1-36.

French, Marilyn. 1992. *The War Against Women.* NY: Ballantine.

Fussell, Paul. 1984. *Class.* NY: Ballantine.

Genovese, Eugene D. 1975. *Roll, Jordan, Roll: The World the Slaves Made.* NY: Random House.

Geschwender, James A., and Rhonda F. Levine. 1994. Classical and Recent Theoretical Developments in the Marxist Analysis of Race and Ethnicity. In P. McGuire and D. McQuire (eds.), *From The Left Bank to the Mainstream: Historical Debates and Contemporary Research in Marxist Sociology.* Dix Hills, NY: General Hall.

Gordon, David M. 1971. Class and the Economics of Crime. *The Review of Radical Political Economy.* 3(3): 51-72.

Gottfredson, Michael, and Travis Hirschi. 1990. *A General Theory of Crime.* Stanford, CA: Stanford University Press.

Granovetter, Mark. 1985. Economic Action and Social Structure: The Problem of Embeddedness. *American Journal of Sociology.* 91: 481-510.

Granovetter, Mark. 1974. *Getting A Job: A Study of Contacts and Careers.* Cambridge, MA: Harvard University Press.

Greenberg, David. 1977. The Dynamics of Oscillatory Punishment Processes. *Journal of Criminal Law and Criminology.* 68(4): 643-651.

Groves, W. Byron, and Nancy Frank. 1993. The Sociology of Structured Choice. In G. Newman, M.J. Lynch and D. Galaty (eds.), *Discovering Criminology.* NY: Harrow and Heston.

Groves, W. Byron, and Robert J. Sampson. 1986. Critical Theory and Criminology. *Social Problems.* 33(6): s58-s80.

Hagan, John. 1993. The Social Embeddedness of Crime and Unemployment. *Criminology.* 31(4): 465-491.

Hawkins, Homer, and Richard Thomas. 1991. White Policing of Black Populations: A History of Race and Social Control in America. In E. Cashmore and E. MacLaughlin (eds.), *Out of Order.* London: Routledge.

Henry, Jules. 1965. *Culture Against Man.* NY: Vintage.

Hirschi, Travis. 1969. *The Causes of Delinquency.* Berkeley: University of California Press.

Horkheimer, Max. 1989. *Critical Theory*. NY: Continuum.

Kozol, Jonathan. 1995. Homeless in America. In S. Ruth (ed), *Issues in Feminism*. Palo Alto, CA: Mayfield.

Krisberg, Barry. 1975. *Power and Privilege*. Englewood Cliffs, NJ: Prentice Hall.

LaFree, Gary. 1989. *Rape and Criminal Justice: The Social Construction of Sexual Assault*. Belmont, CA: Wadsworth.

LaFree, Gary. 1985. Official Reactions to Hispanic Defendants in the Southwest. *Journal of Research in Crime and Delinquency*. 22: 213-237.

LaFree, Gary. 1980. The Effect of Sexual Stratification by Race on Official Reactions to Rape. *American Sociological Review*. 45: 842-854.

Langston, Donna. 1995. Tired of Playing Monopoly? In M.L. Anderson and P. H. Collins (eds.), *Race, Class and Gender*. Belmont, CA: Wadsworth.

Lerner, Gerda. 1992. *Black Women in White America: A Documentary History*. NY: Vintage.

Lynch, Michael J. 1993a. Discovering Criminology: Lessons from the Radical Tradition. In P. Maguire and D. McQuarie (eds.), *From the Left Bank to the Mainstream*. Dix Hills, NY: General Hall.

Lynch, Michael J. 1993b. The Radical Groves. In G. Newman, M.J.Lynch and D. Galaty (eds.), *Discovering Criminology*. NY: Harrow and Heston.

Lynch, Michael J. 1990. Racial Bias and Criminal Justice: Methodological and Definitional Issues. In B. MacLean and D. Milovanovic (eds.), *Racism, Empiricism and Criminal Justice*. Vancouver: Collective Press.

Lynch, Michael J. 1988. Surplus Value, Crime and Punishment: A Preliminary Assessment. *Contemporary Crises*. 12: 329-344.

Lynch, Michael J. and W. Byron Groves. 1989. *Primer in Radical Criminology*. NY: Harrow and Heston.

Lynch, Michael J., Jacklyn Huey, Billy R. Close, J. Santiago Nunez, and Carolyn Johnston. 1992. Cultural Literacy, Criminology, and Female Gender Issues: The Power to Exclude. *Journal of Criminology and Criminal Justice*. 3(2): 183-202.

Lynch, Michael J., and E. B. Patterson. 1991. Introduction: Race and Criminal Justice, An Overview. In M. J. Lynch and E. B. Patterson (eds.), *Race and Criminal Justice*. NY: Harrow and Heston.

Lynch, Michael J., and E. Britt Patterson. 1990. Racial Discrimination in the Criminal Justice System: Evidence from Four Jurisdictions. In B. Maclean and D. Milovanovic (eds.), *Racism, Empiricism and Criminal Justice*. Vancouver: Collective Press.

MacLean, Brian, and Dragan Milovanovic (eds.). 1990. *Racism, Empiricism and Criminal Justice*. Vancouver: Collective Press.

McKay, Nellie Y. 1992. Remembering Anita Hill and Clarence Thomas: What Really Happened When One Black Woman Spoke Out. In T. Morrison (ed.), *Race-ing Justice, En-gendering(ing) Power*. NY: Pantheon.

Messerschmidt, James. 1993. *Masculinities and Crime*. Totowa, NJ: Rowman, Littlefield.

Messerschmidt, James. 1986. *Capitalism, Patriarchy and Crime*. Totowa, NJ: Rowman, Littlefield.

Merton, Robert K. 1968. Social Structure and Anomie. *American Sociological Review*. 3: 677-682.

_____. 1968. *Social Theory and Social Structure*. NY: The Free Press.

Mills, C. Wright. 1963. The Sociology of Social Stratification. In I. L. Horowitz (ed.), *C. Wright Mills: Power, Politics and People*. NY: Ballantine.

Mills, C. Wright. 1959. *The Sociological Imagination*. NY: Oxford.

Milovanovic, Dragan. 1994. *A Primer in the Sociology of Law*. NY: Harrow and Heston.

Morrison, Toni (ed.). 1992. *Race-ing Justice, En-gender(ing) Power: Essays on Anita Hill, Clarence Thomas, and the Construction of Social Reality*. NY: Pantheon.

Morrissey, Marietta, and Randy Stoecker. 1994. Marxist Theory and the Oppression of Women. In P. McGuire and D. McQuire (eds.), *From The Left Bank to the Mainstream: Historical Debates and Contemporary Research in Marxist Sociology*. Dix Hills, NY: General Hall.

Nelson, James F. 1991. Disparity in the Incarceration of Minorities in New York State. In M. J. Lynch and E. Britt Patterson (eds.), *Race and Criminal Justice*. NY: Harrow and Heston.

Oakley, Annie. 1976. *Women's Work: The Housewife, Past and Present*. NY: Vintage.

O'Connor, James. 1986. *Accumulation Crisis*. NY: Basil Blackwell.

Patterson, E. Britt, and Michael J. Lynch. 1991. The Biases of Bail: Race Effects on Bail Decisions. In M. J. Lynch and E. Britt Patterson (eds.), *Race and Criminal Justice*. NY: Harrow and Heston.

Payne, G., and P. Abbott. 1990. *The Social Mobility of Women*. London: Falmer.

Perlow, Victor. 1988. *Super Profits and Crises*. NY: International.

Petras, James. 1987. The Political Economy of State Terrorism. *Crime and Social Justice*. 27-28: 88-109.

Quinney, Richard. 1980. *Class, State and Crime*. NY: Longman.

Quinney, Richard. 1974. *Critique of Legal Order*. Boston: Little, Brown.

Quinney, Richard. 1970. *The Social Reality of Crime*. Boston: Little, Brown.

Reiman, Jeffrey. 1979. *The Rich Get Richer and the Poor Get Prison*. NY: Wiley.

Rotella, Elyce J. 1995. Women and the American Economy. In S. Ruth (ed.), *Issues in Feminism*. Palo Alto, CA: Mayfield.

Ruth, Shelia. 1995. *Issues in Feminism*. Palo Alto, CA: Mayfield.

Ryan, William. 1982. *Equality*. NY: Vintage.

Sampson, Robert J., and John Laub. 1993. *The Making of Crime*. Cambridge, MA: Harvard University Press.

Sampson, Robert J., and John Laub. 1990. Stability and Change in Crime and Deviance over the Life Course: The Salience of Adult Social Bonds. *American Sociological Review*. 56: 609-627.

Schwartz, Martin D., and Walter S. DeKeseredy. 1991. Strengths, Weaknesses and the Feminist Critique. *Law, Crime and Social Change*. 15(1): 51-71.

Schwendinger, Herman, and Julia Schwendinger. 1972. The Continuing Debate on the Legalistic Approach to the Definition of Crime. *Issues in Criminology*. 7(1): 71-81.

Schwendinger, Herman, and Julia Schwendinger. 1970. Defenders of Order or Guardians of Legal Rights? *Issues in Criminology.* 113-146.

Simon, David R., and D. Stanley Eitzen. 1993. *Elite Deviance.* Boston: Allyn and Bacon.

Sklar, Holly. 1995. The Upper Class and Mothers in the Hood. In M. L. Anderson and P. H. Collins (eds.), *Race, Class and Gender: An Anthology.* Belmont, CA: Wadsworth.

Taylor, Ian, Paul Walton, and Jock Young. 1973. *The New Criminology.* London: Routledge and Kegan Paul.

Thomas, Jim. 1991. Racial Codes in Prison Culture: Snapshots in Black and White. In M. J. Lynch and E. B. Patterson (eds.), *Race and Criminal Justice.* NY: Harrow and Heston.

Tigar, Michael. 1971. *Law Against the People.* NY: Random House.

Tollet, Ted, and Billy R. Close. 1991. The Over-representation of Blacks in Florida's Juvenile Justice System. In M. J. Lynch and E. B. Patterson (eds.), *Race and Criminal Justice.* NY: Harrow and Heston.

Ward, Benjamin. 1979. *The Radical Economic View.* NY: Basic.

Waring, Marylin. 1990. *If Women Counted: A New Feminist Economics.* San Francisco: Harper-Collins.

West, Cornel. 1994. *Race Matters.* NY: Vintage.

Williams, Patricia J. 1991. *The Alchemy of Race and Rights: Diary of a Law Professor.* Cambridge, MA: Harvard University Press.

Wright, Erik Olin. 1973. *The Politics of Punishment: A Critical Analysis of Prisons in America.* NY: Harper and Row.

Young, Jock. 1987. The Task Facing a Realist Criminology. *Contemporary Crises.* 11: 337-356.

CHAPTER 2

Gender Inequality and Criminalization: A Socialist Feminist Perspective on the Legal Social Control of Women

Mona J.E. Danner

INTRODUCTION

Women, who comprise more than half of the world's population, account for only about 15% of criminal arrests on average, and great variance exists in the arrests of women across nations where women represent from just 4% to nearly 30% of all arrests (Bowker, 1978; Marshall, 1982). Scholars have long struggled to understand both the curious underrepresentation of women among those arrested for crime and the striking cross-national variance in women's arrest rates. Unfortunately, most theoretical perspectives adopt sexist, racist, and class-based notions of women as explanations for women's crime specifically or women's responsibility for juvenile and adult male crime generally (Klein, 1973; Smart, 1976).

Here I offer a socialist feminist perspective informed by the work of Women of Color regarding women's crime rates across nations. Socialist feminist theory provides an excellent foundation to consider previous explanations of women's crime and to explore the implications for criminological theory of the intersections of gender, race/ethnicity, class, and nation. Socialist feminists recognize that gender, class, and race/ethnicity are socially constructed according to power relations. Unequal power between classes, ethnic groups, and between women and men, results in social and political arrangements which allow domination. Two precepts form the core of socialist feminism

(Danner, 1991). Firstly, the mode and relations of production and reproduction are inter-connected, indeed, inseparable. The sexual division of labor results in differences in the work performed by women and men. Work commonly done by men (i.e., production) is more highly valued than work commonly done by women (i.e., biological and social reproduction), but neither persons nor whole societies can exist long without each type of work. And secondly, in large part due to the writings of Women of Color, socialist feminists recognize that gender, class, race/ethnicity, and nation interact in fundamental ways that result in important differences in life experiences for groups and persons. Specifically, most women live with fewer advantages than do most men within their class and ethnic group. Poor and ethnic minority women are especially vulnerable because they may experience domination by men of their own class and ethnic group as well as by elite persons who may exercise their domination with impunity.

Early theorists interested in issues pertaining to women and crime located the low rates of women's arrests in their adjustment to the "proper" domestic roles of subservient wife and doting mother (Klein, 1973). They assumed that all women possessed an inherent and universal nature and that women's varied reactions to this "nature" in the areas of sexuality, reproduction, and domestic work comprised the roots of female behavior and misbehavior; changes in women's "proper" roles would inevitably lead to increases in women's crime. In short, these early criminologists contended that women's liberation from domesticity and involvement in publicly visible life clashes with women's essential nature and causes increases in women's crime.

Some criminologists continue to advance liberation-causes-crime arguments to understand the rates of women's arrests, although not in the clearly sexist manner of earlier writers. Rather, they assert that increases in women's status, particularly women's employment rates, bring increases in their criminal opportunities (Simon, 1975) and/or proclivities (Adler, 1975); as women become liberated from the home, enter into the public world and secure paid employment, they also venture into the criminal world.[1]

A socialist feminist stance alerts us to problems in the liberation-causes-crime argument. Recent heralders of the liberation thesis fail first to recognize the inter-relationship between production and reproduction. They interpret correlations between women's rates of employment and crime at the macro level to mean that paid employment replaces unpaid household labor. In fact, research throughout the world clearly shows that employment simply adds to household responsibilities (Dwyer and Bruce, 1988). In addition, the liberation model neglects the differences among women and speaks only to a minority of women: middle- and upper-class professional (often) white women in the Northern/Western world. Poor and working-class white women, Women of Color, and Third World women have always been "liberated" to work outside of their own homes due to economic necessity. Finally, Steffensmeier, Allan and Streifel (1989) note that the underlying causes of women's criminality posited by liberation theorists (i.e., increased opportunities in employment and education) are exactly opposite those generally associated with men's criminality (i.e., lack of opportunity in education and employment).[2]

The time appears ripe for a new thesis, one rooted in the material reality of women's lives within social structures around the world. I propose an alternative conceptualization regarding the criminalization of women. Rather than focusing on the "causes" of women's criminality, this thesis addresses the rate of women's arrests and recognizes that criminalization is foremost a mechanism of social control. Mechanisms of social control maintain the existing social order to the benefit of the materially powerful in a society; the criminal law is the state's ultimate formal or legal mechanism of control, its most fundamental function. The criminal justice system assists in the maintenance of inequality through the process of criminalization whereby the law is selectively applied in a manner detrimental to those groups and persons most disadvantaged in unequal relations. Thus, an inverse relationship exists between gender inequality in the distribution of socially valued resources and the rate of legal social control of women; where gender inequality is great, the criminalization of women is less than in places where gender inequality is less.

The thesis takes seriously both critiques of the liberation hypothesis (to which liberation theorists do not respond) and feminist insights to the realities and complexities of women's lives especially women who experience multiple oppressions (Collins, 1990). Beginning from women's disadvantaged positions within the social structure and the social control nature of the criminalization process, I consider how inequality in the distribution of material resources may explain rates of women's arrests. The thesis represents an alternative explanation of women's criminalization in the aggregate.

CONCEPTUALIZING THE RELATIONSHIP BETWEEN GENDER INEQUALITY AND SOCIAL CONTROL

My thoughts about gender inequality and social control are founded upon the premise that relations are socially constructed, primarily on a material base with ideological consequences. I recognize that those groups in possession of the greatest material resources—men as a group, as well as members of the dominant classes, nations, and the ruling racial/ethnic groups—also possess the greatest political and ideological power to define and enforce their definition of reality. The existing patterns in the distribution of women and men across socially valued positions, and in the distribution of wealth, demonstrate that men as a group possess the greatest material resources. Around the world, nations continue to distribute nutritional, health, educational, economic, and political resources to male citizens in greater quantity and quality than to female citizens (United Nations, 1991).[3] Unequal resource distribution allows men as a group to maintain their economic, political and social advantages—and construct new ones—over women as a group. Men, therefore, benefit both materially and ideologically from the subordination of women. Clearly, men control social life as a result of their superior allocation of resources, and they exercise that control in ways that maintain gender inequality and male domination.

Structural inequality—the relatively constant, stable, and ideologically legitimized pattern of distribution of socially valued material and symbolic resources, "the things that count in a given society" (Heller, 1987: 5)—endures as one of the most obvious aspects of gender in societies worldwide (United Nations, 1991; Seager and Olson, 1986). Throughout much of the world and across historical time, gender stratification has meant that women as a group have been disadvantaged while men as a group have been advantaged. Such advantage fuels various mechanisms for maintaining control over women, many of which differ little from mechanisms used by members of any powerful group to maintain their position. The various means of social control which enable dominant groups to maintain their position include violence and force or their threat, ideology, propaganda and socialization, the distribution of resources, and criminalization, or some combination of these. Criminalization offers a unique opportunity to exercise control because it articulates the various mechanisms of control. Criminalization also represents the formal and most powerful means of social control for any advantaged group.[4]

Criminalization refers to "the process whereby criminal law is selectively applied to social behavior" (Beirne and Messerschmidt, 1991: 24). The criminalization process includes the definition and legislation of certain behaviors as criminal, and the surveillance, policing and punishment of so identified behavior. Crime is socially defined, and that definition enforced by the state to the benefit of the materially powerful through a process with at least two paths. First, actions in which the powerful engage are less likely to be labeled criminal, regardless of social harm, than are harmful behaviors of less powerful groups. More important in maintaining social inequality, however (and more common than the process of defining criminal behavior), is the selective surveillance, policing and punishment of criminal behavior—that is, the normal discretion accorded agents of the state working within the criminal justice system. Arrest represents the point of entry to the criminal justice system; it also endures as the moment encompassing the greatest number of persons and affording the state and its agents the greatest degree of discretion with the least amount of oversight.

With respect to gender inequality and criminalization, I suggest that where women as a group are already heavily controlled, the state's most formal mechanism of social control—the criminal justice system—is less frequently invoked. Women experience much repression due to their lack of material resources, especially when combined with their care of dependent others. Thus, where there exists relatively high fertility and inequality relative to men in the distribution of socially valued resources, there is little need for additional control of women relative to men. And, under these conditions we would expect to see a lower rate of criminalization of women. In contrast, where these conditions are less severe and women are less subordinated to men, primarily because of lower fertility and less gender inequality in the distribution of resources, there is a greater need for additional control—to maintain superior male advantage—which the state apparatus assumes; this results in a higher rate of criminalization of women.

Not all women experience the criminalization of their behavior to the same extent because of inequality across race/ethnicity and class in the distribution of socially valued resources to women. Poor and ethnic minority women remain even less likely to receive health, education, employment, and political resources than do class and ethnic advantaged women. Aída Hurtado (1989) relates differences among women rooted in race/ethnicity to their differing positions to elite men which, I also argue, results in differences in the distribution of material resources and thereby differences in rates of criminalization. The subordination of ethnic- and class-elite women as a group comes through *seduction* as they are raised to be partners (albeit unequal) to elite men; as partners they must receive resources which make them valuable and enable them to resist some intrusions from the state. Disadvantaged women as a group are subordinated through *rejection* by elite men who do not require them as public partners; the miserly distribution of resources to them means that they remain relatively powerless to resist criminalization. It is not relatively elite women whom the criminal justice system captures, but poor and ethnic minority women.

It is essential to note that this is a distributional process on a macro scale and at a structural level. I am not proposing a micro explanation about why some specific individuals are arrested while others, engaged in the same behaviors, avoid arrest, nor am I suggesting that all group members arrested exhibit the characteristics of the group at large. I am interested in the *structure* of women's arrests and my conceptualization suggests that the distribution of women and men across key dimensions of social life influences the extent of formal social control—the rate of criminalization—of women.

THE SOCIAL CONTROL OF WOMEN

Historically, the law has done little or nothing to compel the leading major social institutions to serve women. "For most of legal history, law restricted women from obtaining both material and human capital resources and prevented their participation in lawmaking and other important establishment institutions" (Epstein, 1988: 121). In essence, the law operated to enforce elite male supremacy (Bartlett, 1993). Because men as a group have been and continue to be in power, they presumably may make and enforce definitions in line with their interests, and their interests resemble those of any dominant group—maintaining their superior position.

One way in which "the legal system of a patriarchal society enforces and maintains a male supremacist social order" (Polan, 1982: 295) is located in the ideology surrounding public and private spheres. Convictions regarding the proper place for women's influence—the home—collude with beliefs about the sacredness of private relations and the law's inaccessibility to sacred space (Taub and Schneider, 1982; Polan, 1982). This belief system helps to convince middle- and upper-class women to stay home bearing and caring for children and remain out of the public workplace. The ideology also serves to justify the legal exclusion of women from certain occupations. Further, by restricting the operation of the law to public space, it legitimizes the law's exclusion from the very place—the home—in which many women spend most of their time. Girls' and womens' resistance to victimization in the home begins a cycle of structural dislocation from important social institutions (the family, school, work) which, in turn, makes criminal activity a rational survival strategy (Chesney-Lind, 1989; Arnold, 1990, 1994). But privacy is not equally distributed to women and separate spheres ideology with its nuclear family ideal does not describe the experiences of Women of Color (Higginbotham, 1983). Poor, minority, and disabled women have been forced to acquiesce to legal demands that they give up control over their fertility, children, or futures in order to obtain state assistance in times of need. Thus, the law has not been a reliable vehicle for aiding women (Smart, 1989).

The maintenance of the existing social order occurs, in part, through the caretaking activities done most often by women which also act as mechanisms of informal/extralegal social control (Heidensohn, 1985: 163-195). In the home, women socialize their own or other's children, care for and control the behavior of other dependents (e.g., elderly parents, handicapped relatives), and limit the deviant proclivities of their male partners. The failure of women to undertake these activities is blamed as the source of a host of social ills. Women's responsibilities as quasi-social control agents extend beyond the home to the community where they are responsible for much of the community care work, (under)paid and unpaid, as teachers, social workers, and public service volunteers. However, women's role in social control—carried out in structures dominated by men—is largely limited to children, the elderly and disabled, and pales in comparison to the forces of control to which women are subject (Heidensohn, 1985: 173-174).

The social control of women may be undertaken at the micro or macro level, by persons acting as individuals or as agents of the state either informally or formally through the use of force, ideological socialization, or the distribution of material resources. Feminist scholars analyze the control of women within the family by the use of violence and how the state fails to prevent such violence (Dobash and Dobash, 1979; Russell, 1982), and the efficacy of the fear of violence to constrain women's movements (Stanko, 1988; Riger and Gordon, 1981; Smart and Smart, 1978a, 1978b). In fact, Dahl (1978: 22-23) suggests that the conditions of social life under which many women live—especially the double burden of wage and domestic labor as well as ideological socialization—operate, in effect, as a private prison that checks women as effectively as violence or the threat and fear of violence.

Maureen Cain's (1989) edited collection examining the official policing and unofficial control of girls in Europe demonstrates how limited and socially structured alternatives constrain the choices young women may make. The authors illustrate the manner in which gender operates in every venue of a girl's life. Whether girls are at home, out with friends, on the streets, or in prison, and no matter whether they are with family, friends, a boyfriend, pimp, or pusher, girls quickly learn the very real social and economic benefits that accompany a relationship with a male. The enforcement of societal expectations of domestic life by informal relationships and formal control agencies, in combination with job segregation by sex and wage discrimination, make marriage appear a necessary addition or alternative to the paid work world. The girls whom the authors write about do not expect great futures; their realism about their lack of opportunities because of class, ethnic, and gender oppression is stunning. With few exceptions, these girls commit crimes mainly for economic reasons precisely because they lack material resources.

Thus, while force and ideology remain important in the social control of women, the distribution of material resources emerges as central in my understanding of the legal social control of women. Financial dependency due to inadequate education or employment skills combined with domestic responsibilities and accentuated by racial/ethnic oppression can be as effective a means of social control as a fist. But, how do we conceptualize and measure women's situation in a way which sheds light on social relations surrounding gender and criminalization?

Gender Inequality

Gender endures as a basic organizing category in societies. The gender system includes systems of gender differentiation, categorization, valuation, segregation, the gender division of labor, and gender stratification. Perhaps the most obvious aspect of gender is gender stratification and inequality. Gender stratification, synonymous with gender inequality:

> refers to the extent to which males and females who are otherwise social equals (e.g., in terms of age, social class, race/ethnicity, and religion) are equal in their access to the scarce and valued resources of their society. The higher the level of gender stratification, the greater the inequality between males and females as general categories. Empirically, gender stratification has always meant some degree of female disadvantage. (Chafetz, 1990: 29)

Materialist theorists of gender stratification emphasize the centrality of differential access to and control over material resources for maintaining unequal relations between women and men (Blumberg, 1988, 1984; Chafetz, 1990). Gender operates in key arenas of social life and leads to different outcomes for women and men in the attainment of socially valued resources. That is:

> gender operates in nutritional and *health* systems to lead to different outcomes for women and men in physical well-being; in *political* systems to lead to different outcomes in terms of public power to ensure control over personal existence; in *economic* systems to lead to different outcomes in terms of access to productive activities and control of resources; in *educational* systems to lead to different outcomes in the acquisition of knowledge and skills; in *family* systems to lead to different outcomes in the value of women and men as well as their relative control of reproduction. (Young, Fort, and Danner, 1994: 57)

The concept of gender inequality and its measures reveal the issue of differential and relative (women to men) distribution. Gender inequality is the departure from parity in the representation of women and men in key dimensions of social life (Young, Fort, and Danner, 1994). A uniquely comparative concept, gender inequality indicates discrepancies between women and men which exist in various dimensions and social locations. Gay Young, Lucía Fort and I (1994) identify 21 social indicators which comprise five dimensions of gender inequality: physical well-being, public power, economic activity, education, family formation. Most of the indicators are ratios of sex- (and, in some cases, age-) specific rates and so control for the sex (and age) distribution of the population. The value of an indicator is read as the number of women per 100 men. For example, a value of 75 for enrollment in first level education indicates that only 75 females have been or are enrolled in the first level for every 100 males so enrolled. The strategy of calculating ratios of rates allows us to actually see the outcomes of processes of distribution of material resources to women and men.[5]

The departure from parity in the distribution of resources does not simply reveal inequality, however, but also maintains it since "inequality refers to the unequal distribution of valued resources between persons that leads one party to dominate the other" (Horwitz, 1990: 36). Dominance begets advantages that can be used to maintain dominant-subordinate relationships. While dominance need not be used in this way, that it can be demonstrates power and control. In this way, the distribution of socially valued positions and resources represents both a key indicator of social control and a mechanism for maintaining control. Changes in the distribution of valued resources which alter social relations may call the basic organization of social life into question and threaten the advantaged positions of dominant groups. In such times, the increased criminalization of subordinated groups represents another mechanism for maintaining control and the extant social order.

GENDER INEQUALITY AND CRIMINALIZATION

My thesis regarding gender inequality and criminalization hypothesizes an inverse relationship between the two concepts: where women are already heavily controlled due to great inequality in the distribution of material resources, formal/legal control mechanisms are used to a lesser extent than in places where the distributional process approaches equality. In other words, lower women's arrest rates are found in places with higher inequality between women and men than in places with less gender inequality.

There is considerable support for such a relationship in the literature on social control. For example, Black's (1976, 105) proposition that "law varies inversely with other social control" supports my assertion that the state apparatus assumes the task of controlling the behavior of women where superior male advantage is threatened. More support is provided by Horwitz who writes:

> The degree of tolerance for female deviance is shaped by the extent of informal social control over women. When this control is strong, female deviance is accorded higher tolerance....When, however, women are not subject to male control, there is less tolerance for their behavior. (Horwitz, 1990: 115-116)

Horwitz thus posits a link between strategies in the social control of women, and this relationship to women's treatment by the state within the criminal justice system. Hartjen also sees linkages among various strategies of social control in India:

> regardless of criminality rates, rates of criminalization are likely to be relatively low in those societies in which (or among the members of those groups within them for whom) alternative, informal mechanisms of control are most available. In this context, women and children are not subjected to legal control in India only because they are less criminal, but because they are more subject to other forms of control.... (Hartjen, 1986: 52-53)

What none of these researchers address, however, is *why* a need exists to control women or who benefits from such control.

By focusing on the *rate* of criminalization, my thesis makes irrelevant the question of why individual women are brought into the criminal justice system. Earlier researchers studying women and crime assumed little more than that women are arrested because they offend and that higher arrest rates indicate more women committing more crimes. In contrast, I recognize the highly discretionary nature of the actions of agents of the state which result in recording an arrest. I do not deny that women harm others nor that they are often victims of men. The thesis simply recognizes that criminalization is foremost a mechanism of social control and posits that gender inequality is an important explanatory factor in the rate of legal social control initiated against women.

It lies beyond the scope of this paper to fully detail empirical tests of the hypothesis that gender inequality is inversely related to, and a significant explanatory factor in the rate of women's criminalization. In cross-national analysis it appears that several factors underlie gender inequality, one of which, the personal-societal connection factor, has a statistically significant and inverse effect on the dependent variable of women's arrest rate (Danner, 1993). Nations with lower rates of women's arrests are those nations with *higher* fertility rates, maternal mortality rates, and female/male age differences at marriage, and *lower* ratios of women to men in the formal labor force and holding seats in the national legislature. The results support my thesis; they indicate that greater inequality between women and men in the personal-societal connection factor seems to *decrease* the legal social control of women, while less inequality in that domain appears to *increase* women's criminalization.

The manner in which indicators generally thought of as only private or only public load on the same factor provides empirical confirmation of feminist challenges to the concept of separate spheres. Proponents of separate spheres ideology hold that women's world is (or should be) limited to family and household, and men's to paid work outside the home, at least for white, Northern/Western, middle-class women.

The false dichotomy ignores the interconnections of private and public in women's lives. Reproductive work occurring in the domestic unit reproduces the labor force in the bearing and rearing of children, and the sustaining of adult workers in food gathering, preparation, and home maintenance; reproductive work also maintains the society in the managing of social and cultural responsibilities. In turn, the wage (and any benefits) paid to the worker by the employer in productive work sustains the current and future labor force. The wage also sustains production by maintaining consumption and reproducing the society.

In sum then, the association of greater rates of fertility and maternal mortality, coupled with greater age differences at marriage, apparently maintains a social structure which restricts women's presence in the labor force and national legislature. In this way, the personal/private and the social/public worlds connect to control the distribution of socially valued resources and positions. Where the distribution of resources results in less inequality between women and men in the domain of life encompassed by the personal-societal connection, the rate of women's criminalization is higher. As women's responsibilities for the care of dependent others decreases and their share of valued positions and resources distributed within the state increases, women gain interpersonal and group power which makes them potentially challenging to existing male advantage. At these times, the state's ultimate mechanism of social control, the criminalization process, escalates its authority to identify women and bring them into the criminal justice system through arrest.

What about the intersection of class, race/ethnicity, and gender in nations? As we understand gender, race/ethnicity, and class as "relational, interlocking, socially constructed systems" (Glenn, 1992: 35), we begin to take seriously both the differences among women and the socially structured relationship between disadvantage and privilege. The division of labor is not only gendered, but raced and classed in reproductive as well as productive work (Glenn, 1992). Although women's share of public resources such as education and employment may increase, it does not increase equally or even randomly across all groups of women nor does their responsibility for maintaining home and family decrease. Since home work still must be completed, it is less advantaged women who do so at the (low) wage the relatively privileged women offer to pay. As societies undergo social upheaval due to increased urbanization, industrialization, and articulation in the global marketplace, the accompanying dislocations in social relations threaten the whole existing order including relationships of advantage and privilege. During such times, the state, supported by the materially powerful and dominant ideology but operating with relative autonomy, increases the rate of criminalization of groups which potentially threaten the status quo. Not all group members are equally vulnerable to criminalization, however. It is not relatively privileged women (according to class or race/ethnicity) whom the system captures, but poor and ethnic minority women since the former are in closer relationships to and are more valued by elite men and, therefore, the state.

CONCLUSION

The theoretical work presented here was initially motivated by the quantitative cross-national literature on women and crime. Many of the researchers within that tradition approach the issue conceptually by employing some variant of the liberation hypothesis. My theoretical approach and empirical analysis investigating the effect of gender inequality on the criminalization of women offers a new avenue for understanding the relationship between inequality and legal social control. Of course, I do not mean to suggest a conscious operation nor a conspiracy theory. Rather, the thesis describes a process which operates at the macro and structural level and applies to aggregate groups.

What are the implications of this thesis for men who, after all, comprise the majority of arrests? With respect to men, as the distribution of socially valued resources to poor and minority men increases, advantaged groups (wealthier and racial/ethnic majority men) may feel their privileged positions threatened. At these times, the state's system of social control may be activated to increase the criminalization of poor and minority men.

Unfortunately, empirical tests of this thesis remain challenging. There is simply far too much data missing in social and crime databases and substantial measurement problems exist. Women and the work we do, whether at home, in field, factory, or school or hospital room, are far too frequently not valued and so not counted or not included in final data reports. Data, especially international data, are rarely desegregated by gender and almost never further desegregated by those social divisions—social class, race/ ethnicity—pertinent to theoretical formulations. Precisely because of data limitations, the measurement of gender inequality advanced here remains flawed due to its inability to reveal the manner in which class and race/ethnicity operate in combination with gender. Thus, while the theoretical contribution presented here represents a class/race/gender analysis and "signal(s) a way that theory and research *ought* to be done," inadequate data limit empirical analysis and in this instance reduce class/race/gender to a "popular buzzword" (Daly, 1995: 449) since only gender can be exposed. Cross-national crime databases are also problematic in that while many nations regularly report data for the categories of crimes known to police and total arrests, far fewer record the numbers of women arrested. It seems that even *criminal* women don't count.

Unfortunately, criminologists remain largely untouched by feminist theory and methodology (Daly and Chesney-Lind, 1988). For too long, criminologists, like other social and physical scientists, have conducted research limited to unrepresentative samples of (usually oppressed) men and then generalized to all peoples. Or, we approach the study of women and crime laden with unrecognized sexist, racist, and classist assumptions and proceed to explain women's behavior with reference to expressive desires rather than to material realities. Too often, criminologists fail to appreciate the social control nature of the criminal justice system and so act as though crime is an objective fact; we assume without question that an increase in a group's arrest rate means little more than that its members are committing more crimes. A more complex reality exists. The reformulation of existing theories and methodologies, as well as the creation of new ones, can only be accomplished with attention to literature which points us in anti-sexist, -racist, and -classist ways to the lives of real women and men in all their intricacies recognizing differences as well as commonalities. This work advances that project by employing the insights of socialist feminists and Women of Color to challenge the predominant paradigm of the liberation hypothesis, explore the relationship between inequality and social control, advance a new conceptualization and operationalization of gender inequality, and propose a new thesis regarding the rate of women's arrest.

NOTES

1. Recent general criminological theorists may also be placed in the liberation-causes-crime category. Miller and Burack (1993) deftly demonstrate that the general theory of crime (Gottfredson and Hirschi 1990) blames poor mothering for low self-control (the primary cause of crime), masks a preference for traditional family structures, and assumes that women's employment means unsupervised children who become delinquent. Routine activity theory (Cohen and Felson 1979) links women's labor force participation to less guardianship of the home, thereby increasing the likelihood of burglary. And the power-control theory of delinquency (Hagan, Simpson, and Gillis 1987) essentially blames mothers' work for daughters' delinquency (Chesney-Lind 1989).

Thus, the liberation hypothesis indicts women's employment for men's and juvenile's crime as well as for women's arrest rates.

2.   For additional critiques of the liberation-causes-crime hypothesis, see Heidensohn (1985), Smart (1979), and Steffensmeier (1978, 1980).

3.   The authors of the Report of the World Conference, United Nations Decade for Women 1980 write that: "Women and girls are 1/2 the world's population, do 2/3 of the world's work, receive 1/10 of the world's income and own less than 1/100 of the world's property."

4.   For discussions of theory and research surrounding the concept of social control, see: Bridges and Myers (1994), Danner (1993), Liska (1992), Horwitz (1990), Cohen (1985), Coser (1982), Turk (1982), Smart and Smart (1978b).

5.   See Young, Fort, and Danner (1994) for discussion of the conceptualization of gender inequality, list and definition of the 21 social indicators, values for 70 nations, and empirical analysis of the relationship of national income to gender inequality.

REFERENCES

Adler, Freda. 1975. *Sisters in Crime*. New York: McGraw-Hill.

Arnold, Regina A.   1990.   Processes of Victimization and Criminalization of Black Women. *Social Justice* 17: 153-166.

_____. 1994. Black Women in Prison: The Price of Resistance. Pp. 171-184 in *Women of Color in U.S. Society,* edited by Maxine Baca Zinn and Bonnie Thornton Dill. Philadelphia: Temple University Press.

Bartlett, Katharine T. 1993. *Gender and Law: Theory, Doctrine, Commentary.* Boston: Little, Brown & Co.

Beirne, Piers, and James Messerschmidt. 1991. *Criminology*. San Diego: Harcourt Brace Jovanovich.

Black, Donald. 1976. *The Behavior of Law.* New York: Academic Press.

Blumberg, Rae Lesser. 1984. A General Theory of Gender Stratification. In *Sociological Theory*, edited by Randall Collins. San Francisco: Jossey-Bass.

_____. 1988. Income Under Female Versus Male Control. *Journal of Family Issues* 9: 51-84.

Bowker, Lee H. 1978. International Perspectives on Female Crime and Its Correction. Pp. 261-275 in *Women, Crime, and the Criminal Justice System* by Lee H. Bowker. Lexington, Mass: Lexington Books.

Bridges, George S., and Martha A. Myers, eds. 1994. *Inequality, Crime, and Social Control.* Boulder: Westview Press.

Cain, Maureen, ed. 1989. *Growing up Good: Policing the Behavior of Girls in Europe.* London: Sage.

Chafetz, Janet Saltzman. 1990. *Gender Equity: An Integrated Theory of Stability and Change.* Newbury Park, CA: Sage.

Chesney-Lind, Meda. 1989. Girls' Crime and Woman's Place: Toward a Feminist Model of Female Delinquency. *Crime & Delinquency* 35: 5-29.

Cohen, Lawrence E., and Marcus Felson. 1979. Social Change and Crime Rate Trends: A Routine Activity Approach. *American Sociological Review* 44: 588-608.

Cohen, Stanley. 1985. *Visions of Social Control: Crime, Punishment and Classification.* Cambridge: Polity Press.

Collins, Patricia Hill. 1990. *Black Feminist Thought: Knowledge, Consciousness, and the Politics of Empowerment.* Boston: Unwin Hyman.

Coser, Lewis A. 1982. The Notion of Control in Sociological Theory. Pp. 13-22 in *Social Control: Views from the Social Sciences* edited by Jack Gibbs. Beverly Hills: Sage.

Dahl, Tove Stang. 1978. The Coercion of Privacy: A Feminist Perspective. Pp. 8-26 in *Women, Sexuality and Social Control*, edited by Carol Smart and Barry Smart. London: Routledge and Kegan Paul.

Daly, Kathleen. 1995. Looking Back, Looking Forward: The Promise of Feminist Transformation. Pp. 443-457 in *The Criminal Justice System and Women: Offenders, Victims, and Workers*, 2nd Ed. edited by Barbara Raffel Price and Natalie J. Sokoloff. NY: McGraw-Hill.

Daly, Kathleen, and Meda Chesney-Lind. 1988. Feminism and Criminology. *Justice Quarterly* 5: 497-538.

Danner, Mona J.E. 1991. Socialist Feminism: A Brief Introduction. Pp. 51-54 in *New Directions in Critical Criminology,* edited by Brian D. MacLean and Dragan Milovanovic. Vancouver, Canada: The Collective Press.

_____. 1993. *Gender Inequality and Criminalization: A Cross-National Analysis of the Legal Social Control of Women,* Ph.D. Dissertation. Washington, DC: American University.

Dobash, R. Emerson, and Russell Dobash. 1979. *Violence Against Wives: A Case Against the Patriarchy.* New York: Free Press.

Dwyer, Daisy, and Judith Bruce, eds. 1988. *A Home Divided: Women and Income in the Third World.* Stanford: Stanford University Press.

Epstein, Cynthia Fuchs. 1988. *Deceptive Distinctions: Sex, Gender, and the Social Order.* New Haven: Yale University Press.

Glenn, Evelyn Nakano. 1992. From Servitude to Service Work: Historical Continuities in the Racial Division of Paid Reproductive Labor. *Signs: Journal of Women in Culture and Society* 18: 1-43.

Gottfredson, Michael R., and Gravis Hirschi. 1990. *A General Theory of Crime.* Stanford, CA: Stanford University Press.

Hagan, John, John Simpson, and A.R Gillis. 1987. Class in the Household: A Power-Control Theory of Gender and Delinquency. *American Journal of Sociology,* 92: 788-816.

Hartjen, Clayton A. 1986. Crime and Development: Some Observations on Women and Children in India. *International Annals of Criminology,* 24: 39-57.

Heidensohn, Frances. 1985. *Women and Crime.* London: Macmillan.

Heller, Celia S, ed. 1987. *Structured Social Inequality: A Reader in Comparative Social Stratification,* 2nd Edition. New York: Macmillan.

Higginbotham, Elizabeth. 1983. Laid Bare by the System: Work and Survival for Black and Hispanic Women. Pp. 200-215 in *Class, Race, and Sex: The Dynamics of Control,* edited by Amy Smerdlow and Hanna Lessinger. Boston: G. K. Hall.

Horwitz, Allan V. 1990. *The Logic of Social Control.* New York: Plenum Press.

Hurtado, Aída. 1989. Relating to Privilege: Seduction and Rejection in the Subordination of White Women and Women of Color. *Signs: Journal of Women in Culture and Society,* 14: 833-855.

Klein, Dorrie. 1973. The Etiology of Female Crime: A Review of the Literature. *Issues in Criminology,* 8 (2): 3-30.

Liska, Allen E., ed. 1992. *Social Threat and Social Control.* Albany: State University of New York Press.

Marshall, Ineke Haen. 1982. Women, Work and Crime: An International Test of the Emancipation Hypothesis. *International Journal of Comparative and Applied Criminal Justice,* 6: 25-38.

Miller, Susan L., and Cynthia Burack. 1993. A Critique of Gottfredson and Hirschi's General Theory of Crime: Selective (In)Attention to Gender and Power Positions. *Women & Criminal Justice,* 4: 115-134.

Polan, Diane. 1982. Toward a Theory of Law and Patriarchy. Pp. 294-303 in *The Politics of Law: A Progressive Critique* edited by David Kairys. New York: Pantheon.

Riger, Stephanie, and Margaret T. Gordon. 1981. The Fear of Rape: A Study in Social Control. *Journal of Social Issues,* 37(4): 71-92.

Russell, Diana. 1982. *Rape in Marriage.* New York: Macmillan.

Seager, Joni, and Ann Olson. 1986. *Women in the World: An International Atlas.* London: Pan and Pluto Press.

Simon, Rita James. 1975. *Women and Crime.* Lexington, Mass.: D.C. Heath and Co.

Smart, Carol. 1976. *Women, Crime and Criminology: A Feminist Critique.* London: Routledge & Kegan Paul.

_____. 1979. The New Female Criminal: Reality or Myth? *British Journal of Criminology* 19 (1): 50-59.

_____. 1989. *Feminism and the Power of Law.* London: Routledge.

Smart, Carol, and Barry Smart. 1978a. Accounting for Rape: Reality and Myth in Press Reporting. Pp. 89-103 in *Women, Sexuality and Social Control,* edited by Carol Smart and Barry Smart. London: Routledge and Kegan Paul.

_____. 1978b. Women and Social Control: An Introduction. Pp. 1-7 in *Women, Sexuality and Social Control,* edited by Carol Smart and Barry Smart. London: Routledge and Kegan Paul.

Stanko, Elizabeth A. 1988. Fear of Crime and the Myth of the Safe
    Feminist Critique of Criminology. Pp. 75-88 in *Feminist
    Perspectives on Wife Abuse,* edited by Kersti Yllo and Michele
    Bograd. Newbury Park, CA: Sage.
Steffensmeier, Darrell J. 1978. Crime and the Contemporary Woman:
    An Analysis of Changing Levels of Female Property Crime,
    1960-1975. *Social Forces,* 57: 566-584.
_____. 1980. Sex Differences in Patterns of Adult Crime, 1965-
    77. *Social Forces,* 58: 1080-1109.
Steffensmeier, Darrell, Emilie Allan, and Cathy Streifel. 1989.
    Development and Female Crime: A Cross-national Test of
    Alternative Explanations. *Social Forces,* 68: 262-283.
Taub, Nadine, and Elizabeth M. Schneider. 1982. Perspectives on
    Women's Subordination and the Role of Law. Pp. 117-139 in
    The Politics of Law: A Progressive Critique edited by David
    Kairys. New York: Pantheon.
Turk, Austin. T. 1982. Social Control and Social Conflict. Pp. 249-
    264 in *Social Control: Views from the Social Sciences,* edited by
    Jack P. Gibbs. Beverly Hills: Sage.
United Nations. 1991. *The World's Women 1970-1990.* New York:
    United Nations.
Young, Gay, Lucia Fort, and Mona Danner. 1994. Moving from
    'The Status of Women' to 'Gender Inequality':
    Conceptualisation, Social Indicators and an Empirical
    Application. *International Sociology,* 9: 55-85.

CHAPTER 3

The Left Realist Perspective on Race, Class, and Gender[1]

Walter S. DeKeseredy

INTRODUCTION

Prior to the early 1980s, most critical criminologists[2] focused primarily on two issues: (1) the extent, sources, and control of crimes of the powerful (e.g., white-collar and corporate crime) and (2) the influence of class relations on definitions of crime and the administration of justice. Their empirical and theoretical work on these problems played a key role in sensitizing the broader criminological community to the fact that "suite crime" is much more economically, physically, and environmentally harmful than any type of street crime, such as mugging, armed robbery, and stranger-to-stranger assault.[3] These scholars have also demonstrated that there is no "justice for all." For example, a large empirical literature clearly shows that First Nations people and African Americans are much more likely to be arrested, convicted, and incarcerated than members of the dominant culture who commit the same crimes (DeKeseredy and MacLean, 1990; Lynch and Patterson, 1991; Mann, 1993; Stevens, 1991).

Some critical criminologists assert that the above problems warrant more empirical, theoretical, and political attention. However, for the "truly disadvantaged" (Wilson, 1987) and other disenfranchised people, there are other major problems that require equal, if not more, attention. These are predatory street crime, woman abuse in intimate and public settings, racial/ethnic harassment, and the consumption and distribution of "hard" drugs (e.g., heroin and crack-cocaine).

It is also important to note that due in part to the fact that many crimes of the powerful (e.g., the dumping of toxic waste and other types of pollution) are invisible or difficult to recognize and do not cause immediate harm,[4] some conservative criminologists such as James Q. Wilson (1985) cheerfully dismiss those who emphasize the pain and suffering caused by suite crime by pointing out that people do not bar and nail shut their windows during heat waves, avoid public parks, stay in at night, harbor deep suspicions of strangers, and in general watch the social fabric of society be ripped apart because of unsafe working conditions, the clear-cutting of trees, or massive consumer fraud.

Indeed, due in large part to the devastating effects of economic problems caused by North American Free Trade Agreement, deindustrialization, and a vicious Republican attack on the welfare state, many inner-city U.S. citizens are currently experiencing what Elliott Currie (1993) refers to as "the American nightmare." In his path-breaking analysis of inner-city drug use, Currie correctly points out that:

> Americans living in the worst-hit neighborhoods still face the reality of dealers on their doorstep and shots in the night; many fear for their lives, or their children's lives, and sense that their communities have slid downward into a permanent state of terror and disintegration. Even those fortunate enough to live in better neighborhoods cannot pick up a newspaper or watch the news without confronting story after story about the toll of drugs and drug-related violence on communities and families. For most of us, the drug plague seems to have settled in, become a routine feature of an increasingly frightening and bewildering urban landscape (1993: 9).

What is to be done about these and other inner-city crime problems? Before the early 1980s, less than a handful of critical criminologists adequately answered this question. In fact, except for a few critical scholars who focused on violence against women, children and ethnic groups (e.g., Breines and Gordon, 1983; Dobash and Dobash, 1979; Pearson, 1976; Russell, 1982, 1984, 1986; Schechter, 1982), most critical criminologists completely ignored the extent and brutal nature of interpersonal crimes in the street and domestic settings. Unfortunately, the failure to address these harms allows right-wing politicians to manufacture ideological support for "law and order" policies that will never lower the rates of predatory street crime, racial harassment, and male-to-female victimization in family/household settings. For example, the U.S. is probably the most punitive country in the world and yet it is the most violent advanced industrial nation (E. Currie, 1985; Irwin and Austin, 1994). In sum, if left-wing criminologists refuse to take disenfranchised people's concerns seriously, for many people the right-wing approach is deemed better than none at all.

Since the early 1980s, British left realists have tried to break the left-wing silence on inner-city working-class crime, racial harassment, and domestic violence by providing a critical discourse that attempts to theorize these problems and proposes short-term socialist strategies to curb them. The main objective of this chapter is to evaluate left realist theory's treatment of race, gender, and class and to offer suggestions for further theorizing. Before I address these issues, however, it is necessary to first describe the most important principles of British left realism.

THE CENTRAL PRINCIPLES OF BRITISH LEFT REALISM

In the United Kingdom, left realism was not formally articulated until the publication of John Lea and Jock Young's (1984) *What Is to Be Done About Law and Order?* Since both the history and the major tenets of this important school of thought have been thoroughly described elsewhere,[5] only a summary of some of its basic principles will be repeated here.

First, unlike "left idealists" and "progressive minimalists" who downplay the extent and brutal nature of inner-city street crime for fear of "whipping up" public support for conservative, draconian crime control strategies such as longer prison sentences (E. Currie, 1992),[6] left realists contend that street crime is a serious problem for the working class. They further argue that it exemplifies values similar to those adhered to by corporate offenders and other affluent or powerful criminals. According to Lea and Young (1984: 72), working class crime:

> ...represents the ultimate in antisocial behaviour. It is palpable proof of the harshness of our system and the political impotence of the poor. It is ideologically significant and it has a considerable material effect on working-class people.

It should be noted in passing that just because British left realists take working class street crime seriously does not mean that they trivialize the extent of and the harm done by affluent offenders. Rather, they argue that working class people are victimized from all directions and that a "double thrust" against both street and suite crime is necessary. Jock Young, for example, argues that:

> [Left realism]...notes that the more vulnerable a person is economically and socially the more likely it is that both working class and white collar crime will occur against them; that one sort of crime tends to compound another, as does one social problem another. Furthermore, it notes that crime is a potent symbol of the antisocial nature of capitalism and is the most immediate way in which people experience other problems, such as unemployment or competitive individualism (1986: 23-24).

Second, left realists use both quantitative and qualitative methods to elicit rich data that can be used to challenge erroneous right-wing interpretations of both street crime and domestic violence and ineffective conservative means of curbing these problems (e.g., imprisonment). They have conducted local crime surveys on various types of victimization, fear of crime, and perceptions of the police (Kinsey et al., 1986; Jones et al., 1986; Crawford et al., 1990; Mooney, 1993). These surveys include questions that are generally considered irrelevant by the police, conservative politicians, and most middle-class members of the general public, such as the incidence and prevalence of woman abuse in intimate, heterosexual relationships, police deviance, corporate crime, and racial harassment.

The data generated by these and other questions provide inner-city communities with a "clearer picture" of what they are facing than they are able to get from police statistics and most state-sponsored victimization surveys (Lea and Young, 1984). For example, based on responses to questions such as how safe do you feel walking alone in your neighborhood at night, state-sponsored surveys such as the British Crime Survey, the Canadian Urban Victimization Survey, and the National Crime Survey have consistently found that women's level of fear of crime is approximately three times that of men even though their victimization rates are much lower (e.g., Hindelang et al., 1978; Skogan and Maxfield, 1981; Maxfield, 1984; Research and Statistics

Group, 1985). These results have led several criminologists and policy analysts to contend that personal experience with crime can play only a limited role in explaining the general incidence of women's fear of crime (Skogan and Maxfield, 1981; Warr, 1984, 1985).[7]

Left realists respond to this inaccurate conclusion by asking in-depth questions on gender issues, such as intimate violence. For example, in the first sweep of the Islington Crime Survey (ICS), Jones et al. (1986) used measures of: perceptions of risk; fear of crime; avoidance behaviors (e.g., precautions taken to reduce the risk of victimization); rates of criminal and noncriminal violence (e.g., sexual harassment); and the impact of domestic assault and rape. Based on the data generated by these measures, Jones et al. contend that:

> The ICS has shown that not only are women more fearful than men but they have very good reason for this. An examination of the criminal forms of violence directed specifically against women showed that there was a high level of both physical and psychological injury sustained by women very frequently. This survey illustrates that women receive very little institutional support of a satisfactory nature and must take responsibility for their own protection as a consequence. This means that they must engage in more avoidance behaviors than men which restricts them in their activities more often, especially at night (1986: 182-183).

In sum, local crime surveys informed by left realism provide a better understanding of woman abuse and other crimes against the powerless than most large-scale, state-sponsored surveys. Certainly there are some exceptions to this broad and sweeping generalization, chief among them being the two Canadian national surveys on woman abuse sponsored by Health Canada (DeKeseredy and Kelly, 1993; Rogers, 1994). Although national surveys are antithetical to the main objectives of left realism (see MacLean, 1992), in order to overcome the methodological limitations of previous Canadian surveys on woman abuse in university/college dating, challenge campus administrators' assertion that female students' fear of crime is irrational, and assist in feminist struggles to mobilize resources to curb dating abuse, Katharine Kelly and I developed and conducted a national representative sample survey heavily informed by left realist discourse.

For example, we used a broad definition of abuse, conducted preparatory research, asked questions that are sensitive to the experiences of the disenfranchised, and we obtained partnership funding (DeKeseredy, 1995). These are some of the key principles of local crime survey research advocated by left realists such as Brian MacLean (1992).

Third, left realists propose short-term anticrime strategies that both challenge the right-wing law and order campaign and take seriously working class communities legitimate fear of street crime. Examples of these initiatives are: demarginalization; preemptive deterrence; democratic control of policing; and community participation in crime prevention and policy development (Lea and Young, 1984).

Fourth, British left realists provide a theoretical perspective on crime to which the *square of crime* is a central component (see Figure 1). The square consists of four interacting elements: victim, offender, state agencies (e.g., the police), and the public. Young describes the social relationships between each point on the square:

> It is the relationship between the police and the public which determines the efficacy of policing, the relationship between the victim and the offender which determines the impact of crime, the relationship between the state and the offender which is a major factor in recidivism (1992: 27).

FIGURE 1: THE SQUARE OF CRIME

POLICE MULTI-AGENCIES		OFFENDER
		THE CRIMINAL
SOCIAL CONTROL		ACT
THE PUBLIC		VICTIM

If the square of crime is a major component of the left realist perspective, then so are the concepts of relative deprivation and subculture. For example, left realists' substantive theory of crime argues that "sheer poverty" or the absence of "glittering prizes" (e.g., car, house, color television, etc.) do not motivate working-class people to commit crime (Young, 1992). Rather, it is:

... poverty experienced as unfair (relative deprivation when compared to someone else) that creates discontent; and discontent where there is no political solution leads to crime. The equation is simple: relative deprivation equals discontent; discontent plus lack of political solution equals crime (Lea and Young, 1984: 88).

The relation between one's position in the broader social structure and crime is, according to left realists, mediated by subjective experiences. For example, in advanced capitalist societies, many people lack the legitimate means to achieve culturally defined goals (e.g., houses, cars, and other symbols of material success). Some respond to the strain induced by the disjunction between these goals and means by becoming "retreatists" (Merton, 1957). In other words, they "drop out" of the race for success and become either drug addicts, alcoholics, homeless, etc. (Merton, 1957; E. Currie, 1993).

However, other frustrated people may come into contact with those with similar status problems and form a subculture as a way of dealing with their problems of adjustment. A subculture is a collective solution to the problems created by broader social forces such as patriarchy and capitalism. According to Young (1992: 38), "[c]rime is one form of subcultural adaptation which occurs where material circumstances block cultural aspirations and where non-criminal alternatives are absent or less attractive."

This argument constitutes an attempt to link macro- and micro-levels of analysis. Although Marxist thought plays a key role in realist thinking, obviously, this school of thought is also heavily influenced by other theoretical perspectives, such as subcultural and strain theories (Matthews, 1987).

Obviously, the central concern of this book is the intersection of race, class, and gender. Unfortunately, like most of the other perspectives discussed in this book, British left realist theory has not yet adequately addressed this concern. Nevertheless, it does contribute to a sociological understanding of the ways in which crime and its control are influenced by each of these important concepts. Thus, in the discussion that follows, I will describe and critique left realism's consideration of race, class, and gender.

LEFT REALISM AND THE ISSUE OF RACE

Most critical and liberal criminologists contend that both the British and North American criminal justice systems are racist. For example, in the U.S., Irwin and Austin (1994) found that African American inmates are nearly twice as likely to receive a habitual sentence even when controlling for their offenses and prior criminal records. Data obtained by these researchers also show that (1994: 4-5)[8]:

- Close to one in four (23 percent) African American men in the age group 20-29 is either in prison, jail, probation, or parole on any given day.
- Sixty years ago, less than one-fourth of prison admissions were nonwhite. Today, nearly half are nonwhite.
- Over one out of every ten Hispanic men (10.4 percent) in the same age group is either in prison, jail, probation, or parole on any given day.
- For white men the ration is considerably lower — one in 16 (or 6.2 percent).
- The number of young African American men under control of the criminal justice system (609,960) is greater than the total number of African American men of all ages enrolled in college as of 1986 (436,000).

In sum, the above and other data demonstrate that African American people are incarcerated, arrested, and charged out of proportion to their numbers for the kinds of street crime disenfranchised people often commit, such as burglary, robbery, etc. Moreover, very few African American people have the opportunity to commit white-collar and corporate crimes, offenses typically committed by white males (Reiman, 1990; Messerschmidt, 1993). For these and other reasons, some critical criminologists such as Bridges and Gilroy (1982:35) argue that any relationship between crime rates and race/ethnicity is solely a function of racist policing and that any challenge to this argument provides "intellectual support to racist stereotypes of the black community as socially and politically disorganized."

There is no doubt that African American men and members of other visible minority groups are more likely to end up in prison than members of the dominant culture. This does not mean that crime is not "a pressing problem" for inner-city black communities. For example, in the U.S., homicide is the leading cause of death for African American men between the ages of fifteen and twenty-four (Mann, 1993; Reiss and Roth, 1993). Some researchers regard this problem as a major public health issue (O'Carroll and Mercy, 1986), while others refer to black homicide as a "form of black genocide, since the victim of homicide is most often another black person and the incidence of this crime is so pervasive" (Mann, 1993: 46). Such data hardly support those who trivialize the extent and severity of inner-city black criminality.

Left realists recognize both the racist nature of the criminal justice system and the high rates of *intra-racial* (e.g., black on black) victimization, and they use a subcultural approach to explain the relationship between race and crime. For example, blacks and Asians are not viewed as innately criminal. Rather, economic marginalization coupled with a high level of relative deprivation generate youth subcultures which represent collective solutions to the problems created by their race/ethnic position (Lea and Young, 1984; Young, 1992). Crime, then, is one type of subcultural adaptation employed by some members of visible minority groups.

Left realists' substantive theory of crime explains why both poor white and disenfranchised ethnic people commit predatory street crimes. However, it has not yet been applied to the problem of female criminality, a shortcoming shared by conservative and liberal subcultural theorists (e.g., Cohen 1955). As Chesney-Lind and Sheldon (1992) point out in their critique of strain-subcultural theories, so far, it is unclear how a subcultural perspective would explain the situation of young women in poor, inner-city communities.

LEFT REALISM AND THE ISSUE OF CLASS

Obviously class is a major concern for left realists. Realists could hardly be *left* realists if they did not devote a substantial amount of attention to this major determinant of inner-city, predatory street crime. Since the way in which realists theorize the relationship between class-related factors and crime was briefly described earlier, it will not be repeated here. Instead, I will discuss three central criticisms of their class analysis.

First, heavily informed by Leadbeater's (1987) typology of the British workforce in the late 1980s, Taylor (1992) argues that left realists have not paid close attention to the recomposition of the working class that has taken place since this time. Rather, realists tend to view working class people as members of a united group, one that has a "unitary orientation" toward crime and its control. According to Taylor (1992: 107), left realists have made:

> no serious attempt to try and identify the *many and various*
> kinds of *stressed social relations* as such that now go to
> make up the structured and complex totality that is British
> society, articulated, as these are, in and through inequalities
> of gender, race, position within the labor market, and
> position on the map of regional inequality, and *then* to
> analyse the relation of these different fractions of the social
> formation to fears and/or experiences of something they
> may call "crime."

In sum, the question of "what the working class is now" needs to be addressed because the working class is fractionalized. For example, even though many women and blacks are economically and politically marginalized, it is incorrect to view them as "core" members of the working class (Taylor, 1992). Many inner-city communities are characterized by considerable racial tension between black and white working class people. Also, many working class men physically, economically, and psychologically brutalize working class women, especially their marital/cohabiting partners (Schwartz, 1988; Smith, 1990). Furthermore, many white working class women have considerably more power than their black male counterparts (Morra and Smith, 1993).

Second, left realist theory does not explain how patriarchy perpetuates and legitimates woman abuse within working class families (Taylor, 1992). According to two prominent feminists (Gelsthorpe and Morris, 1988: 103), this is a "startling omission."

Third, while realists such as Frank Pearce (1992)[9] have collected victimization survey data on various crimes of the powerful, so far there has been no attempt to theorize "suite crime." Perhaps this theoretical gap will be filled soon; however, according to Pearce and Tombs (1992), in order to do so left realists must modify their conceptual categories and broaden their field of interest. For example, left realism's theoretical framework is restricted to interpersonal relations between working class individuals. Thus, it cannot adequately explain the "anonymous relationship" between a deviant company and its disenfranchised victims, such as those who are injured in the workplace or who are harmed by dangerous products. Furthermore, in its present form, left realism cannot:

> capture the extent to which acts of omission are what cause harm in many such cases or in those involving dangerous pollution, nor that it is the failure of employers to fulfil their statutory managerial duties that lead to many workplace injuries and deaths (Pearce and Tombs, 1992:71).

LEFT REALISM AND THE ISSUE OF GENDER

Before the early 1990s, like the bulk of their conservative and liberal counterparts, most "new," "critical," or "radical" criminologists, especially men, ignored the importance of gender and relied mainly on class-based analyses of crime and its control. One of the most salient examples of such a "gender-blind" approach is Taylor, Walton, and Young's (1973) *The New Criminology*, a path-breaking book which "contains absolutely nothing about women" (Valverde, 1991: 239). Some critical scholars may assert that since this book was published in 1973, attacking it for ignoring women, gender, and sexuality is tantamount to critiquing a "straw man." This point is well taken, but many recent critical publications still demonstrate "an appalling ignorance about the character and content of feminist studies" (Menzies and Chunn, 1991: 64), despite significant attempts by feminist scholars to sensitize the critical criminological community to the gender-blind nature of their empirical and theoretical work. As Renzetti (1993) correctly points out, "[t]hey *still* don't get it, do they?"

The one major exception to this dominant tendency is research on male violence against women (Daly and Chesney-Lind, 1988). Various types of feminist discourse, especially the radical variant, are evident in the theoretical and empirical literature on the victimization of women, and these feminist concerns had an impact on British left realism. In fact, according to Thomas and O'Maolchatha (1989), left

realists were among the first critical criminologists to recognize the
importance of feminist inquiry.   The influence of feminist studies on
male-to-female victimization on left realism is articulated below by two
of its main proponents, Matthews and Young (1986b: 2):

> The limits of the romantic conception of crime and the
> criminal were brought home forcibly by the growing
> feminist concern during the 1970s. Discussions around this
> issue served to reintroduce into radical criminology
> discourse neglected issues of aetiology, motivation and
> punishment.

What type of feminism has influenced left realism?   It appears
that this school of thought embraces elements of both radical and
socialist feminism. For example, like radical feminists such as Stanko
(1990) and Kelly (1988), left realists use broad definitions of violence.
For them, mental cruelty, threats, sexual abuse, physical violence and
other forms of patriarchal control and domination "are all domestic
violence, serious and merit individual investigation" (Mooney, 1993:
8).   What causes men to commit these crimes?   Taking a socialist
feminist approach, Jones et al. (1986) contend that the results of this
type of victimization raise "immediately the problems of a patriarchal
social criss-cross cutting the problems of class."
        Unfortunately, as I and Martin Schwartz (1991) have noted, the
influence of these two and other variants of feminist thought never
penetrated to the deeper levels of discourse, and at times seemed even
worse—extensive lip service only. We also argue that left realists have
not adequately integrated feminist concerns into their empirical work
on woman abuse.   Instead, their empirical and theoretical agenda is
dominated by a class-based analysis which views female victims as
"honorary members of the core working class" (Taylor, 1992: 106).
Realists also avoid the question of how ethnicity is related to woman
abuse in intimate contexts.
        Since suggestions for overcoming these and other pitfalls
concerning left realism's treatment of woman abuse have been well
covered elsewhere (see DeKeseredy, 1992; DeKeseredy and Schwartz,
1991), they will not be repeated here.   Instead, I will briefly turn to
another key problem raised by several feminist scholars—women's
experiences of crime as suspects, offenders, defendants, and inmates
(Carlen, 1992). To the best of my knowledge, like most contemporary

critical feminist criminology, left realism is still mainly concerned with the victimization of women (Schwartz, 1991). To date, left realists have not attempted to theorize both why women's offences are distinct from men's and the sexist nature of the criminal justice system. Needless to say, then, conspicuously absent from left realist theory is an attempt to show how female crime and its social control simultaneously reflect race, gender, and class relations.

In sum, the above discussion shows that the intersection of race, class, and gender is apparently not a central concern for British left realism. Even so, because I am a strong advocate of the realist endeavour, I agree with Dawn Currie (1992) who asserts that however important the above and other criticisms of left realism appear, they do not present a major challenge to its major academic and political goals. Despite my support for left realism, some proponents of this critical discourse may contend that my criticisms "misconstrue the realist project and in so doing set an agenda that probably exceeds original intentions—for example, the failure of realism to develop and test theories, especially of patriarchy (D. Currie, 1992: 221). Perhaps this is true; however, like some of the recent developments in masculinity theory (see Messerschmidt, 1993), I believe that the realist perspective, to a certain extent, can be enhanced by explicitly articulating the relationship among race/ethnicity, class and gender in the social construction of crime and its control. It is to a few brief suggestions for achieving this goal that I now turn.

SUGGESTIONS FOR FURTHER THEORIZING

In 1987, Desmond Ellis called for a kind of sociological theory that includes a theory of the state and that focuses simultaneously on deviant behavior or action and on societal, including state, reactions to it. Left realism answers this call by taking into account the dynamic relationships between the offender, victim, police and community (MacLean, 1991). The relationship or interaction between these four parties is described diagrammatically in the square of crime (see Figure 1).

The square of crime was developed to show that crime rates are the outcome of four interrelated causes: (1) the causes of offending (e.g., relative deprivation); (2) factors that make victims vulnerable (e.g., lifestyle/routine activities); (3) the social conditions that influence public levels of control and tolerance, and the social forces that propel agents of social control (e.g, police) (Young, 1992: 30). According to Lea (1992), the square of crime, like any theoretical model, is subject to elaboration. Space limitations preclude a detailed discussion of how the intersection of the "holy trinity" (e.g., race, class, and gender) can be situated within each point in this model. For example, John Lea (1992) devotes approximately 25 pages to explaining the complex relations between the various components of this theoretical framework. One hopes, then, others will either expand on or critique the following suggestions.

The square of crime perspective gives the above four major causes of crime rates equal weight and realists state that changes in the broader social structure affect all of these factors. For example, according to Young (1992: 55-56):

1. Increased gentrification affects the number of victims and also by increasing relative deprivation, the number of offenders;

2. Increased population mobility affects the social solidarity of the area and hence the strength of public control of crime;

3. Changes in the age structure, particularly of young males, affects the number of offenders;

4. Changes in employment and economic marginalization affects the number of offenders;

5. Changes in lifestyle by increasing, for example, the number of evenings out made by members of the public would affect the victimization rate, both in terms of risks in public space and the risks of homes unattended.

The above realist view of the world as an "open system *par excellence*" is diagrammatically described in Figure 2 (Young, 1992: 55). Nothing precludes this model from being modified to take into account how changes in broader race/ethnic, class, and gender relations affect all of the factors in the square. For example, consider the modified version presented in Figure 3. It diagrammatically shows that crime rates are the outcome of the ways in which the above three variables may affect the social relationships between each point on the square.

FIGURE 2: THE SQUARE OF CRIME AS AN OPEN SYSTEM

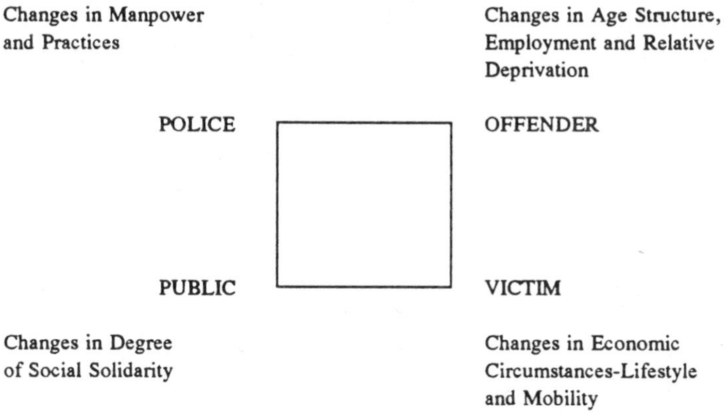

Changes in Manpower
and Practices

Changes in Age Structure,
Employment and Relative
Deprivation

POLICE ⸻⸻⸻ OFFENDER

PUBLIC ⸻⸻⸻ VICTIM

Changes in Degree
of Social Solidarity

Changes in Economic
Circumstances-Lifestyle
and Mobility

FIGURE 3: MODIFIED SQUARE OF CRIME

Changes in the Race/Ethnic, Class,
and Gender Composition of the Police and
the Ways in Which these Demographic Changes
affect Police Practices

Changes in Age, Gender,
Race/Ethnic, and Class
Position, Employment and
Relative Deprivation

POLICE ⸻⸻⸻ OFFENDER

PUBLIC ⸻⸻⸻ VICTIM

Changes in Degree of Respect and Support for
Racial/Ethnic, Class, and Gender/Sexual
Diversity

Changes in Economic and
Social Circumstances/
Lifestyle and Mobility

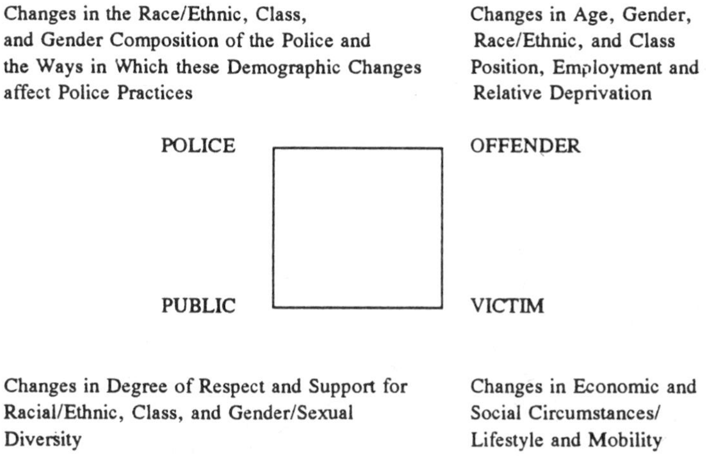

Below are examples of hypotheses derived from Figure 3. Unfortunately, like Figure 2, because this modified square of crime is also an open system, it is difficult, if not impossible, to precisely pinpoint cause and effect (Young, 1992):

1. Increased race/ethnic, class, and gender inequality would affect the number of victims and also by increasing relative deprivation, the number of offenders.

2. Increased population mobility would affect the respect and support for racial/ethnic, class, and gender/sexual diversity and hence the public control of crime.

3. Changes in the age, race/ethnic, class, and gender position would affect the number of offenders.

4. Changes in employment and economic, social, and political marginalization would affect the number of offenders.

5. Changes in economic and social circumstances/lifestyle would affect the victimization rate, both in terms of risks in public and private spaces and the risks of homes unattended.

CONCLUSIONS

In its current form, Figure 3 constitutes little more than a preliminary attempt to introduce race/ethnicity, class, and gender into the square of crime. Because left realists are constantly revising their academic and political agendas, they will probably develop a new square of crime, one that is superior to Figure 3. One hopes they will address several other theoretical questions, such as why do people commit corporate and white collar crimes? As I stated previously, in order to adequately answer this question, realists will have to address the anonymous relationship between criminal companies and their victims. Furthermore, according to Ruggiero (1992), a left realist theory of corporate and white collar crime should take into account theories that focus on learning processes (e.g., differential association theory) and those that go beyond the explanation of street crime.

As several scholars have pointed out (e.g., D. Currie, 1992; Ruggiero, 1992), future attempts to modify the square of crime should also add one more factor—the researcher. For example, according to Ruggiero, realists attribute a high degree of subjectivity to victims and offenders but these theorists do not attribute the same subjectivity to themselves. He further argues that they need to take into account how their own subjectivity and their own role as criminologists may influence their 'realistic' portrayal of crime and other social problems.

Perhaps, then, the square should evolve into a *"pentagon*, the fifth vertex being occupied by the *observers"* (1992: 136).

NOTES

1. I would like to thank Martin Schwartz, Dragan Milovanovic, Barry Wright, Dennis Forcese, and the anonymous reviewers for their helpful comments and criticisms.

2. For the purpose of this chapter, critical criminology is defined as a perspective which views the sources of crime as the class, race/ethnic, and patriarchal relations endemic in North American society and which regards major change as required to reduce criminality. This formulation is a modified version of Young's (1988) definition of radical criminology.

3. See DeKeseredy and Schwartz (in press) and Ellis and DeKeseredy (1995) for comprehensive reviews of the literature on the extent and distribution of corporate crime in North America.

4. For example, Chenier (1982) and DeKeseredy and Goff (1992) show that it is difficult to determine the frequency of congenital malformation and childhood developmental problems caused by daily work conditions because these afflictions often remain unnoticed by victims, their relatives, and medical professionals for months, or years. Many people are also unaware that stillbirths, spontaneous abortions, lactation problems, and other reproductive disorders are the product of dangerous work conditions.

5. See Kinsey et al. (1986), Lea and Young (1984), Lowman and MacLean (1992), Matthews and Young (1986a, 1992), Schwartz and DeKeseredy (1991), Young (1986), and Young and Matthews (1992).

6. See Young (1986) and E. Currie (1992) for more detailed critiques of left idealism and progressive minimalism.

7.   See Kelly and DeKeseredy (1994) for a comprehensive overview of the empirical and theoretical literature on women's fear of crime.

8.   The following data are derived from a study conducted by Mauer (1991).

9.   Despite his contribution to a left realist understanding of corporate crime, Frank Pearce no longer identifies himself with the left realist school of thought.

REFERENCES

Breines, Winni, and Linda Gordon. 1983. "The New Scholarship on Family Violence." *Signs: Journal of Women in Culture and Society*, 8: 491-553.

Bridges, L., and Paul Gilroy. 1982. "Striking Back." *Marxism Today*, 34-35.

Carlen, Pat. 1992. "Women, Crime, Feminism, and Realism," in John Lowman and Brian D. MacLean, eds., *Realist Criminology: Crime Control and Policing in the 1990s*. Toronto: University of Toronto Press.

Chenier, Nancy. 1982. *Reproductive Hazards at Work: Men, Women and the Fertility Gamble*. Ottawa: Canadian Advisory Council on the Status of Women.

Chesney-Lind, Meda, and Randall G. Shelden. 1992. *Girls, Delinquency and Juvenile Justice*. Pacific Grove, CA: Brooks/Cole.

Cohen, Albert K. 1955. *Delinquent Boys*. New York: Free Press.

Crawford, Adam, Trevor Jones, Tom Woodhouse and Jock Young. 1990. *Second Islington Crime Survey*. London: Centre for Criminology, Middlesex Polytechnic.

Currie, Dawn H. 1992. "Feminism and Realism in the Canadian Context," in John Lowman and Brian D. MacLean, eds., *Realist Criminology: Crime Control and Policing in the 1990s*. Toronto: University of Toronto Press.

Currie, Elliott. 1985. *Confronting Crime: An American Challenge*. New York: Pantheon.

Currie, Elliott. 1992. "Retreatism, Minimalism, Realism: Three Styles of Reasoning on Crime and Drugs in the United States," in John Lowman and Brian D. MacLean, eds., *Realist Criminology: Crime Control and Policing in the 1990s*. Toronto: University of Toronto Press.

Currie, Elliott. 1993. *Reckoning: Drugs, the Cities, and the American Future*. New York: Hill and Wang.

Daly, Kathleen, and Meda Chesney-Lind. 1988. "Feminism and Criminology." *Justice Quarterly*, 5: 497-538.

DeKeseredy, Walter S. 1992. "Confronting Woman Abuse in Canada: A Left-Realist Approach," in John Lowman and Brian D. MacLean, eds., *Realist Criminology: Crime Control and Policing in the 1990s*. Toronto: University of Toronto Press.

DeKeseredy, Walter S. 1995. "Left Realism and Woman Abuse in Dating," in Brian D. MacLean, ed., *Crime and Society: Readings in Critical Criminology*. Missisauga, Ontario: Copp Clark Longman.

DeKeseredy, Walter S., and Colin Goff. 1992. "Corporate Violence Against Canadian Women: Assessing Left-Realist Research and Policy." *The Journal of Human Justice*, 4: 55-70.

DeKeseredy, Walter S., and Katharine Kelly. 1993. "The Incidence and Prevalence of Woman Abuse in Canadian University and College Dating Relationships." *The Canadian Journal of Sociology*, 18: 137-159.

DeKeseredy, Walter S., and Brian D. MacLean. 1990. "Discrimination Against Native Peoples in the Canadian Parole Process," in Brian D. MacLean and Dragan Milovanovic, eds., *Racism, Empiricism and Criminal Justice*. Vancouver: Collective Press.

DeKeseredy, Walter S., and Martin D. Schwartz. 1991. "British Left Realism on the Abuse of Women: A Critical Appraisal," In Harold E. Pepinsky and Richard Quinney, eds., *Criminology as Peacemaking*. Bloomington: Indiana University Press.

DeKeseredy, Walter S., and Martin D. Schwartz. 1996. *Contemporary Criminology*. Belmont, CA: Wadsworth.

Dobash, R. Emerson, and Russell P. Dobash. 1979. *Violence Against Wives*. New York: Free Press.

Ellis, Desmond. 1987. *The Wrong Stuff: An Introduction to the Sociological Study of Deviance*. Toronto: Macmillan.

Ellis, Desmond, and Walter S. DeKeseredy. 1995. *The Wrong Stuff: An Introduction to the Sociological Study of Deviance* (2nd ed.). Toronto: Allyn and Bacon.

Gelsthorpe, Lorraine, and Allison Morris. 1988. "Feminism and Criminology in Britain." *British Journal of Criminology*, 28: 93-110.

Hindelang, Michael J., Michael R. Gottfredson, and James Garofalo. 1978. *Victims of Personal Crime: An Empirical Foundation for a Theory of Personal Victimization*. Cambridge, MA: Ballinger.

Irwin, John, and James Austin. 1994. *It's About Time: America's Imprisonment Binge*. Belmont, CA: Wadsworth.

Jones, Trevor, Brian MacLean, and Jock Young. 1986. *The Islington Crime Survey*. London: Gower.

Kelly, Katharine D., and Walter S. DeKeseredy. 1994. "Women's Fear of Crime and Abuse in College and University Dating Relationships." *Violence and Victims*, 9: 17-30.

Kelly, Liz. 1988. *Surviving Sexual Violence*. Minneapolis: University of Minnesota Press.

Kinsey, Richard, John Lea, and Jock Young. 1986. *Losing the Fight Against Crime*. London: Basil Blackwell.

Lea, John. 1992. "The Analysis of Crime," in Jock Young and Roger Matthews, eds., *Rethinking Criminology: The Realist Debate*. London: Sage.

Lea, John, and Jock Young. 1984. *What Is to Be Done About Law and Order?* New York: Penguin.

Leadbeater, Charles. 1987. *The Politics of Prosperity*. London: Fabian Society Pamphlet No. 523.

Lowman, John, and Brian D. MacLean (eds.). 1992. *Realist Criminology: Crime Control and Policing in the 1990s*. Toronto: University of Toronto Press.

Lynch, Michael J., and E. Britt Patterson (eds.). 1991. *Race and Criminal Justice*. New York: Harrow and Heston.

MacLean, Brian D. 1991. "Introduction: The Origins of Left Realism," in Brian D. MacLean and Dragan Milovanovic, eds., *New Directions in Critical Criminology*. Vancouver: Collective Press.

MacLean, Brian D. 1992. "A Program of Local Crime Survey Research for Canada," in John Lowman and Brian D. MacLean, eds., *Realist Criminology: Crime Control and Policing in the 1990s*. Toronto: University of Toronto Press.

Mann, Coramae Richey. 1993. *Unequal Justice: A Question of Color*. Bloomington: Indiana University Press.

Matthews, Roger. 1987. "Taking Realist Criminology Seriously." *Contemporary Crises*, 11: 371-401.

Matthews, Roger, and Jock Young (eds.). 1986a. *Confronting Crime*. London: Sage.

Matthews, Roger, and Jock Young. 1986b. "Editors' Introduction: Confronting Crime," in Roger Matthews and Jock Young, eds., *Confronting Crime*. London: Sage.

Matthews, Roger, and Jock Young (eds.). 1992. *Issues in Realist Criminology*. London: Sage.

Mauer, Marc. 1991. *Americans Behind Bars: A Comparison of International Rates of Incarceration*. Washington, D.C.: The Sentencing Project.

Maxfield, Michael. 1984. *Fear of Crime in England and Wales*. Home Office Research Study No. 78. London: HMSO.

Menzies, Robert, and Dorothy E. Chunn. 1991. "Kicking Against the Pricks: The Dilemmas of Feminist Teaching in Criminology," in Brian D. MacLean and Dragan Milovanovic, eds., *New Directions in Critical Criminology*. Vancouver: Collective Press.

Merton, Robert K. 1957. *Social Theory and Social Structure*. Toronto: The Free Press of Glencoe.

Messerschmidt, James W. 1993. *Masculinities and Crime: Critique and Reconceptualization of Theory*. Lanham, MD: Rowman and Littlefield.

Mooney, Jayne. 1993. *The Hidden Figure: Domestic Violence in North London*. London: Centre for Criminology, Middlesex University.

Morra, Norman, and Michael D. Smith. 1993. "Men in Feminism: Theorizing Sexual Violence." *The Journal of Men's Studies*, 2: 15-28.

O'Carroll, Patrick W., and James A. Mercy. 1986. "Patterns and Recent Trends in Black Homicide," in Darnell F. Hawkins, ed., *Homicide Among Black Americans*. Lanham, MD: University Press of America.

Pearce, Frank. 1992. "The Contribution of "Left Realism" to the Study of Commerical Crime," in John Lowman and Brian D. MacLean, eds., *Realist Criminology: Crime Control and Policing in the 1990s*. Toronto: University of Toronto Press.

Pearce, Frank, and Steve Tombs. 1992. "Realism and Corporate Crime," in Roger Matthews and Jock Young, eds., *Issues in Realist Criminology*. London: Sage.

Pearson, Geoff. 1976. "Paki-Bashing in a North-East Lancashire Cotton Town," in Geoff Mungham and Geoff Pearson, eds., *Working Class Youth Culture*. London: Routledge and Kegan Paul.

Reiman, Jeffrey. 1990. *The Rich Get Richer and the Poor Get Prison* (3rd ed.). New York: Macmillan.

Reiss, Albert J., and Jeffrey A. Roth (eds.). 1993. *Understanding and Preventing Violence*. Washington, D.C.: National Academy Press.

Renzetti, Claire M. 1993. "On the Margins of the Malestream (Or, They Still Don't Get It, Do They?): Feminist Analyses in Criminal Justice Education." *Journal of Criminal Justice Education*, 4: 219-234.

Research and Statistics Group. 1985. *Female Victims of Crime*. Canadian Urban Victimization Survey Bulletin No. 4. Ottawa: Solicitor General of Canada.

Rogers, Karen. 1994. *Wife Assault: The Findings of a National Survey*. Ottawa: Canadian Centre for Justice Statistics.

Ruggiero, Vincenzo. 1992. "Realist Criminology: A Critique," in Jock Young and Roger Matthews, eds., *Rethinking Criminology: The Realist Debate*. London: Sage.

Russell, Diana. 1982. *Rape in Marriage*. New York: Macmillan.

Russell, Diana. 1984. *Sexual Exploitation: Rape, Child Sexual Abuse, and Workplace Harassment*. Beverly Hills: Sage.

Russell, Diana. 1986. *The Secret Trauma: Incest in the Lives of Girls and Women*. New York: Basic Books.

Schechter, Susan. 1982. *Women and Male Violence*. Boston: South End Press.

Schwartz, Martin D. 1988. "Ain't Got No Class: Universal Risk Theories of Battering." *Contemporary Crises*, 12: 373-392.

Schwartz, Martin D. 1991. "The Future of Critical Criminology," in Brian D. MacLean and Dragan Milovanovic, eds., *New Directions in Critical Criminology*. Vancouver: Collective Press.

Schwartz, Martin D., and Walter S. DeKeseredy. 1991. "Left Realist Criminology: Strengths, Weaknesses and the Feminist Critique." *Crime, Law and Social Change*, 15: 51-72.

Skogan, Wesley, and Michael Maxfield. 1981. *Coping with Crime*. Beverly Hills: Sage.

Smith, Michael D. 1990. "Sociodemographic Risk Factors in Wife Abuse: Results from a Survey of Toronto Women." *The Canadian Journal of Sociology* 15: 39-58.

Stanko, Elizabeth. 1990. *Everyday Violence: How Women and Men Experience Sexual and Physical Danger*. London: Pandora.

Stevens, Sam. 1991. "Aboriginal People and the Canadian Criminal Justice System," in Les Samuelson and Bernard Schissel, eds., *Criminal Justice: Sentencing Issues and Reform*. Toronto: Garamond.

Taylor, Ian. 1992. "Left Realist Criminology and the Free Market Experiment in Britain," in Jock Young and Roger Matthews, eds., *Rethinking Criminology: The Realist Debate*. London: Sage.

Taylor, Ian, Paul Walton, and Jock Young. 1973. *The New Criminology*. London: Routledge and Kegan Paul.

Thomas, Jim, and Aogan O'Maolchatha. 1989. "Reassessing the Critical Metaphor: An Optimistic Revisionist View." *Justice Quarterly*, 2: 143-172.

Valverde, Mariana. 1991. "Feminist Perspectives on Criminology," in Jane Gladstone, Richard Ericson and Clifford Shearing, eds., *Criminology: A Reader's Guide*. Toronto: Centre of Criminology, University of Toronto.

Warr, M. 1984. "Fear of Victimization: Why Are Women and the Elderly More Afraid?" *Social Science Quarterly*, 65: 681-702.

Warr, M. 1985. "Fear of Rape Among Urban Women." *Social Problems*, 32: 328-350.

Wilson, James Q. 1985. *Thinking About Crime* (Revised ed.). New York: Vintage.

Wilson, William J. 1987. *The Truly Disadvantaged: The Inner City, the Underclass, and Public Policy*. Chicago: University of Chicago Press.

Young, Jock. 1986. "The Failure of Criminology: The Need for a Radical Realism," in Roger Matthews and Jock Young, eds., *Confronting Crime*. London: Sage.

Young, Jock. 1988. "Radical Criminology in Britain: The Emergence of a Competing Paradigm." *British Journal of Criminology*, 28: 159-183.

Young, Jock. 1992. "Ten Points of Realism," in Jock Young and Roger Matthews, eds., *Rethinking Criminology: The Realist Debate*. London: Sage.

Young, Jock, and Roger Matthews (eds.). 1992. *Rethinking Criminology: The Realist Debate*. London: Sage.

CHAPTER 4

Postmodern Criminology on Race, Class, and Gender

BRUCE A. ARRIGO

INTRODUCTION

Criminal justice studies addressing the intersecting categories of race, class, and gender are now regarded as important, though under-examined, domains of ideological and experiential investigation. As the theme of this book suggests, critical criminology is perhaps best suited to explore these matters of convergence, given their local sites of production. The theoretical context in which this production manifests itself is the source of considerable scrutiny for Part One of this text. Contributing to this more philosophical enterprise, the present study considers what insights, if any, the postmodern perspective offers to advance integrative studies of race, class, and gender in criminology. On this latter notion, we interpret the discipline of criminology broadly to include such areas as: law and social control; criminal justice practice; the sociology of deviance and mental illness; penology; and social problems.

As a point of clarification and departure, some general comments regarding the postmodern perspective, its relationship to criminology, and our approach to both are in order. The postmodern perspective is robust and diverse in orientation. Canvassing the full breadth of such varying approaches in criminology (and law) is decidedly beyond the scope of this article. For purposes of our analysis, we embrace several trends in post-Foucauldian (1980) theory on power-knowledge/truth discursive formations or disciplinary practices (see also Habermas, 1975 on *steering mechanisms*). This vastly emerging tradition encompasses the wisdom of: psychoanalytic semiotics and chaos theory (Milovanovic, 1992, 1993, 1994; Arrigo, 1996, 1995a, 1994a); constitutive ideology (Henry and Milovanovic, 1995; Henry and Milovanovic, 1991; Hunt, 1993); postmodern feminist jurisprudence (Arrigo, 1992, 1993a); and linkages from discourse analysis (Baudrillard, 1981, 1988; Deleuze and Guattari, 1987, 1977; Lecercle, 1985; Derrida, 1976, 1981; Benveniste, 1971; Lacan, 1977), including selected works of lucid application (Arrigo, 1993b; Voloshinov, 1986; Bakhtin, 1981).

The overall intellectual approach lacing our analysis together, however, borrows heavily from the more psychotropian scholarship of Jacques Lacan and his epigones. Many of today's more highly regarded postmodernists were known to have attended and/or to have participated in Lacan's famous seminars delivered in Paris, France, during the early 1950s to the late 1970s. Such notables included Jacques Derrida, Roland Barthes, Luce Irigaray, Michel Foucault, Jean Baudrillard, and Julia Kristeva. Accordingly, our investigation will emphasize several Lacanian schematizations to advance our postmodern critique of race, class, and gender in criminology and criminological theory.

Although still regarded as a heterodox and esoteric strain of inquiry within social theory, postmodernism is increasingly recognized as an intellectual force to be reckoned with among many academic communities. In the overlapping fields of law and criminology, however, acknowledgement of this more radical perspective has been slow in developing. By now, criticisms levied against this school of thought have been clearly documented and are well known. Postmodernism, in dismissing all essentialist truths, promotes subjectivism, relativism, and anti-foundationalism. Postmodernism, in deconstructing (*"trashing"*) the formation of social phenomena without offering something more or something other in their place, symbolizes pessimism, fatalism, and nihilism. Postmodernism, by categorically insisting upon the use of its own idiosyncratic and specialized vocabulary, communicates elitism, solipsism, and separatism.

Our position is that these summary statements, frequently expressed in the form of virulent attack, fail to remember, otherwise ignore, or altogether dismiss what the aim of any legitimate postmodern investigation is. In short, the postmodern critique endeavors to reveal how dominant discourses or language systems (e.g., law), and the coordinates used to define them (i.e., legalese), exclude and silence the voice of those who do not convey meaning from within the privileged (juridical) code in use. In other words, postmodernism concerns itself with linguistic production and circulation, with discursive ideological domination, and with the covert/overt form(s) of speech typifying symbolic violence (Henry and Milovanovic, 1991: 303-305; Schwartz and Friedrichs, 1994: 229-232) or, more insidiously, underlying social oppression (Arrigo, 1995b).

Clearly, the postmodern theoretical position presents many justice-based implications. Criminal justice and sociolegal scholars have demonstrated the magnitude and scope of these effects when examining such diverse application topics as: punishment (Arrigo, 1995a) policing (Manning, 1988); jailhouse lawyering (Milovanovic, 1988); rape (Arrigo, 1993a); feminist criminology (Smart, 1989, 1990); legal reasoning (Goodrich, 1987, 1990; Milovanovic, 1992); criminal justice eduction (Arrigo, 1995c); and mental illness (Arrigo, 1993b).

This paper furthers the topical trend to examine such implications but in the context of an integrative study on race, class, and gender in criminology. Accordingly, we will broadly explore three themes of significance germane to any postmodern analysis. Under consideration will be: 1) the role language plays in structuring (criminological) thought; 2) how such thought valorizes and legitimizes only certain expressions of subjectivity or desire in (criminological) discourse; and 3) how these dominantly codified meanings subsequently produce a circumscribed knowledge, invalidating alternative forms of sense-making resulting in the denial of different ways of knowing. Thus, underpinning our inquiry will be a singular question: namely, what form do discourse, subjectivity, and knowledge assume in the constitution of criminological theory? Along the way, speculative reference to race, class, and gender concerns or *"questions of diversity"* in criminal justice will be incorporated into the analysis. The aim of this excursion will be to contextualize the otherwise complex material and provide general exemplification.

One final thought relevant to our enterprise warrants some brief commentary. Although our analysis is informed by the critical ideology of postmodernism, we communicate our meaning by embracing a more logocentric (i.e., a conventionally shared) discourse. This is potentially problematic. If *"postmodern talk"* endeavors to distance itself from, or altogether repudiate, standard epistemologies, methods of inquiry, ontological metaphors, and forms of rhetoric, how can one utilize the tools of that very language code to, nevertheless, offer a postmodern critique of race, class, and gender in criminology? This is a philosophical dilemma which, for now, we concede. Notwithstanding, our aim is to *methodologically* assert how contributions in postmodern thought tell us something more or something other about race, class, and gender in criminology than other intellectual approaches. Accordingly, we adopt a more logocentric prose style to advance our thesis. Further, this pattern of communication is an effort to converse in a fashion familiar to the reader. Thus, while the form of our argumentation is situated within a conventional frame of reference, this activity does not diminish the soundness of the postmodern project; rather, it simply confirms one area where additional theoretical research beyond the confines of this article is required.

ON DISCOURSE CONSTRUCTION IN CRIMINOLOGY

Postmodern criminologists view language as value laden, non-neutral and politically charged. Discourse represents the interests and goals of oppressive power elites or other dominant collectives. This understanding of crimino-legal theory construction has roots in the sociology of labeling theory and early symbolic interactionism. Notwithstanding, both orientations fell short of the mark. As Henry and Milovanovic (1991: 296) explain:

> labeling separated meaning [in language] from the agents generating it...positi[ng] a *dualism* between agency and structure rather than a *duality* ...[Symbolic] interactionism said little about the way audiences—their imageries, symbolic repertoire [and language]—are constructed, constituted, and undermined by historically situated human agents in the context of a historically specific political economy (emphasis added).

Thus, both approaches failed to consider how discursive linguistic constructions communicate hidden meanings and represent embedded values, symbolizing the aspirations of certain definable groups. More recently, this emphasis on language as communicating embedded ideology has found some legitimacy through the Critical Legal Studies (CLS) Movement. The CLS agenda is infused with the more acerbic dynamics of postmodern discontent. CLS writers endeavor to unmask the layered dimensions of subjectivity and indeterminacy inherent in traditional understandings of law and crime, victimization and control, justice and punishment (Arrigo, 1993b: 51-55; Benson, 1989: 161-165; Kelman, 1987; Peller, 1985).

In criminological pursuits the CLS agenda and its emphasis on discourse construction has been supplanted by studies embracing Michel Foucault's work on *disciplinary institutions* and Jürgen Habermas's treatment of *steering mechanisms* (Arrigo, 1993b, 1992; see also, Lecercle, 1985 on the *violence of language*). In brief, these investigations point out how certain forms of technology or discoveries in science promote new modes of disciplining or de-pathologizing the non-conformist or deviant. Thus, only certain "scientific" discourses are privileged as knowledge/truth discursive formations. The normalizing mechanisms of (linguistic) surveillance exercise power by affirming only those knowledge assertions advancing the modern truth regime. Any resistance such as the invocation of alternative grammars (speech patterns or codes)—despite challenging the legitimacy of the prevailing discourse—is thwarted *through* socio-linguistic hegemony and reification.

The Los Angeles riots which immediately followed the first trial outcome for the officers implicated in the Rodney King beating illustrate the awesome effects of repudiating "desire-in-language." The courtroom drama, and the discourse which defines its system of communication (i.e., legalese), discredited an entire class and race of citizens as characterized by the behavior of many South Central Los Angeles (as well as other non-Californian) residents. Although the legal system maintains its own mantle of linguistic (and social) privilege in our lives, we turn to the court apparatus for the specter of equal treatment, fairness, protection, etc. We long for justice. We seek fulfillment in law. Supporters of King were in search of identity fulfillment.

Notwithstanding these pursuits, when embracing the (legal) system we reaffirm and re-legitimize the power of its (juridical) code to control our destiny. However, when our identity, as determined in speech, differs from the coordinates constituting the law, linguistic oppression follows. Depending upon the severity or intensity of the social problem at issue, the effects of such marginalizing discursive practices can produce alienation, rage, and even violence. Our contention is that this instrumental dynamic of language was as much at the center of the Los Angeles city riots as it is at the core of constructing criminological thought. In subsequent sections, we will explore the implications of discourse by specifically addressing that form desire assumes in criminological theory production and circulation.

The psychoanalytic formalizations of Jacques Lacan (1991, 1985, 1978, 1977, 1975) are also instructive for an appreciation of how postmodernists interpret the constitution of language. Several of his conceptualizations on discourse signal how much semiotic activity occurs prior to the coupling of the spoken word (paradigm) with the actual sequence(s) of speech (syntagm). As Lacan reminds us, desire in language begins at a more non-reflexive, unconscious level. What we say and how we say it (paradigm-syntagm semiotic axis) depends on the effects of other, pre-spoken forces, including the condensation-displacement axis and the metaphor-metonymic axis, constitutive of a semiotic grid.

In addition, Lacan (1991) has shown how various discourses represent certain forms of legitimated desire in intersubjective communication. His notion of the dominant discourse or the *discourse of the master* has been applied to various issues in law and criminology (e.g., Arrigo, 1996, 1995a, 1994a, 1994b; Milovanovic, 1994, 1993, 1992; Cornell, 1993, 1991; Caudill, 1993, 1992). The discursive structure of this discourse is represented as follows:

$$\frac{S1}{\$} \begin{array}{c} \text{------>} \\ \text{<------} \end{array} \frac{S2}{a}$$

Here S1 symbolizes master signifiers. These are key linguistic phenomena possessing the illusory potential for one to experience *"jouissance"* or that existential longing (excess), attainable in and through language. What makes them "illusory" will be demonstrated shortly. Elsewhere, we have explored selected criminal justice topics in the overlapping fields of law, psychiatry, and criminological theory (Arrigo, 1996, 1994a, 1994b). Of particular Lacanian relevance is how the machinery of the medico-legal apparatus enacts ideological domination and linguistic control viz., mentally disordered defendants.

Master signifiers in the forensic courtroom include such fundamental ideals as "care and treatment," "due process," "wellness," "the reasonable man/woman," etc. S2 signifies knowledge. Knowledge is *already* from a certain perspective, communicating meaning (and being) from within the coordinates of a particular "sign" or language system. In every instance of discourse the discordant voices of desire are brought under one accented linguistic reality and given preferred meaning(s), directly linked to the ideological state apparatus in question (here the clinicolegal system). Thus, knowledge, as self-referential, is always and already *mediated* by that specialized (medico-legal) code in use.

In addition to the systemic level of semiotic production in which primordial sense data are uniquely encoded with desire, is the intra-psychic (i.e., internal) and intersubjective (i.e., interpersonal) level of semiotic production which *re-presents* and further defines the circumscribed knowledge of the *discourse of the master.* In the S---> S2 dyadic relationship, master signifiers (e.g., "wellness," "reasonableness," "care and treatment") are in the position of *agent.* In the psychiatric courtroom, the agent (litigator) actively or consciously conveys the desiring message to the receiver (jurors/judge) of the coded discourse. The listener/receiver, in the position of the *other*, is both attentive to that which is communicated and is transformed by it. In other words, the other's knowledge must necessarily represent a perspectival awareness, articulated through a specialized code of speech. Again, master signifiers embody uniaccentuated desire consistent with system-supporting iterations advancing the interests of ideologically repressive state apparatuses (Althusser, 1971: 143).

In the process of situating oneself and being inserted within the parameters of a language system, the other produces a circumscribed knowledge. Jurors and judges deliberate upon the longing, despair, suffering of the disordered defendant *but only from within* the language of law and medicine. Behaviors which are reasonable, interactions which are explainable, desires that are predictable, discourse that is intelligible, awarenesses that are conventional, symbolize the argot of law and medicine (Arrigo, 1993b: 135-140; 1996). This is the dominant "scientific" code valorized in the clinicolegal system. Thus, there is a certain left-out knowledge (*pas-tout*). This not-all or *a* is the embodiment of the psychiatric citizen's *jouissance* denied, repressed, cleansed in forensic courtroom dialogue. The semiotic purification contained in juridical speech supports the presence of the slashed subject (the disordered defendant as $) awaiting the articulation of a battery of master signifiers which more authentically symbolize the divided subject's meaning and being. Thus, *jouissance is* illusory for these and other "different" citizens.

ON SUBJECTIVITY IN CRIMINOLOGY

For Lacan the unconscious is structured much like a language where the speaking being (*l'être parlant*) is more determined than determining; that is, more regulated by unconscious workings which are themselves situated in various discourses communicating multiple and, at times, contradictory meanings. Ultimately, however, the manifold voices (i.e., competitive grammars) stationed within the primary process region (i.e, the unconscious or *Autre*) are harnessed and brought under (anchored by) one language system, consistent with materialistically-based and system-maintaining discourse (Arrigo, 1996, 1995a, 1994a). Thus, one's activities are more appropriately *determined* and the subject is more accurately *de-centered* or divided. In other words, Lacan proposes a version of human agency determined by *both* conscious states and the effects of unconscious processes.

Intimately linked to the idea of subjectivity is the role of desire. In the Lacanian conception, desire represents that excess or that beyond existential fulfillment (i.e., *jouissance*), awaiting articulation. In criminological enterprises, the subject finds his/her need to convey personalized meaning (and being) in the act of speech denied (silenced) precisely because ideologically repressive state apparatuses (e.g., the criminal justice system) superimpose the coordinates of their discursive communicative structures (their linguistically "accented" reality) upon the discourse of others (e.g., persons of color, women, citizens with limited economic resources). Thus, the desiring subject, endeavoring to communicate his/her interiorized longing, seeking to articulate his/her intrinsic meaning and being, is imprisoned (determined) within the prevailing language system. Borrowing from Lacan (1991; see also Bracher, 1988; Melville, 1987; Arrigo, 1995b, 1994a), the de-centered subject is the unwitting participant in the *discourse of the master*. Put another way, subjects constitute and are constituted by that unique grammar, advancing only system-supporting declarations. Lost in the exchange is the possibility for establishing genuine, more authentic, forms of interaction and intersubjective communication.

Criminology provides many examples of how women and other minority collectives are subjected to the discipline's practice of linguistic hegemony and marginalization. One such illustration is criminal justice education (Arrigo, 1995c). Most (post-secondary) classrooms are conducted by middle class, white males. Women in justice-related disciplines have typically been educated by middle class, white males. Much of the legal and criminological theory, research, and policy available to us is written by middle class, white males. Clearly, at its very finest, these experiences *only* tell us something "about the very [middle class, white] male pursuits of crime and criminal justice" (McDermott, 1992: 237). The dilemma here is with language and thought. Speech and logic "shackle our way of being in unitary dimensions, effectively prohibiting...a genuinely feminine [i.e., a replacement] discourse" (Arrigo, 1992: 18). As a consequence, the (criminal justice) educational process is nothing more than the legitimation of phallogocentric desire.

Although hegemony—manifested in the presence of white malestream desire—may sustain itself in criminological endeavors, the postmodern critique offers several creative possibilities for the articulation of one's heretofore repressed desires. Lecercle's (1985) insistence on the disruptive language of the body (*delire*), Deleuze and Guattari's (1986, 1987) suggestion of *minor literatures* and Serres (1982: 65-70) notion of *noise,* are all de-centering activities which provide some transformative direction. Lacan's (1985: 145) excursion into alternative forms of fulfillment and his description of the *discourses of the hysteric* and analyst are additionally informative. The latter two concepts will be briefly explored in the next section where desire in language is more closely examined. Our fundamental point here, however, is the recognition that theoretical pursuits in postmodern criminology endeavor to emancipate marginalized subjects by legitimating their previously excluded voices and by re-validating those language systems which communicate the citizen's unencumbered meaning *and* essential being (Lacan, 1977: 275; Lee, 1990: 95-99, 168-170).

ON SENSE-MAKING IN CRIMINOLOGY

Much of the preceding discussion points to the question of knowledge and the conditions under which it is constituted in criminology. Postmodernists interpret sense-making in a unique way. Lacan's formalizations are instructive, particularly his assessment of both the *discourse of the master and the discourse of university*. Conventional criminology privileges "scientific" knowledge and, thus, its linguistic coordinates (i.e., positivism, objectivism, absolutism) represent the dominant discourse in justice-based investigations. Postmodern criminology seeks the discovery of "narrative" knowledge (Sarup, 1989: 120-121; see also, Arrigo, 1992: 24-27; 1993a: 33-37 on *imaginative discourse*; Lacan, 1985: 143-147 on *mythic knowledge*; Cornell, 1991: 168-196 on the *imagination and utopian possibility*). Truth, justice, reason, progress, and other similar abstractions are based on myths, symbols, and metaphors, representing the historicity of a given culture as an incomplete and unfolding life story. Postmodernists endeavor to articulate, know, and validate the stories of excluded groups, as well as the codes of speech which constitute their logos. In this regard, then, knowledge is provisional, positional, and relational. In other words, logic is local not global (Dews, 1987), meaning is contingent not certain (Sarup, 1989), understanding is fragmented not complete (Lyotard, 1984), truth is a departure not an arrival (Barthes, 1988).

In further support of the postmodern agenda are contributions from feminist ideology. In part, the maxim: "the personal is empirical" (McDermott, 1992: 237-245) signals how liberal feminists interpret knowledge. However, that which is personal may also be the site of power and, therefore, may also advance the subordination of those who experience differently. Postmodern feminist thought, however, is equipped with the insights of Foucault, Irigaray, Marx, Kristeva, Habermas, and Lacan. Selected works in law and criminology have been especially careful to point out that any systematic constitution as a doctrinal approach possesses the capacity to function as an oppressive methodology (Arrigo, 1993a: 32, 38-43). Thus, there must be a flexible debunking to that which is offered as knowledge. "What is posited must also be reversed, only to loop around again as a supplement to the reversal" (Arrigo, 1992: 20-21).

The application of postmodern principles of sense-making to law and criminology challenges and disrupts the sedimented icons of modernist justice. Embedded in the language of such signs as "social control," "burdens of *proof,*" "a demand for *factual evidence,*" "punishment," "*actual* legal intent," "*expert* testimony," "*causes* of crime," "the *reasonable* wo/man standard," are notions of power, communicating only certain truths, representing the knowledge claims of the logocentric/misogynous *master discourse.*

Reconstituting (criminological) knowledge, then, in ways more fully affirming of individual and/or collective difference is the project which postmodern theorists and practitioners consider. Further analysis of Lacan's discursive formulations signal how dissimilar forms of *jouissance* can find embodiment in the structure of alternative grammars. The *discourse of the hysteric* and *analyst* developed by Lacan are particularly important. In what follows, we provide only the barest of essentials for both schematizations.

The hysteric represents the oppositional subject. For our purposes, the use of the term hysteric is compatible with the rebel advocate assisting the poor and disenfranchised, the social/community activist addressing political or economic injustices, the criminal justician attempting to be more inclusive of race, class, and gender dynamics in research and practitioner pursuits, or minority collectives experiencing the brutality of the system. The discursive structure for this discourse is symbolized as follows:

$$\frac{\$}{a} \xrightarrow{} \frac{S1}{S2}$$

$$\begin{array}{ccc} \$ & \text{-------}> & \underline{S1} \\ a & <\text{-------} & S2 \end{array}$$

The marginalized and despairing subject as slashed or divided endeavors to convey his/her suffering to the other (i.e., police, court, correctional officials). This other, in the position of agent, interpellates the repressed subject in customary ways or offers only conventional (criminal justice) master signifers to the divided individual's longing. Thus, that which is left out (*pous tout*) in the exchange, represents both the source and product of the subject's unfulfilled and disembodied desire.

For Lacan, the potential for overcoming the dictatorial hold of language experienced by the hysteric exists within the *discourse of the analyst*:

$$\underline{a} \text{ --------> } \underline{\$}$$
$$S2 \text{ <-------- } S1$$

The analyst as a "cultural revolutionary" (Milovanovic, 1993: 327-330) or as a "newsmaking criminologist" (Barak, 1988: 565; 1994) legitimates the discourse of the divided subject. S/he *de-constitutes* traditional categories of understanding (Henry and Milovanovic, 1991: 308) and seeks to articulate new or "virgin" master signifiers embodying the subject's desire, producing *mythic knowledge* (Lacan, 1985: 143-147; Lee, 1990: 191-195; Bracher, 1988: 47). This product symbolizes the hysteric's truth (i.e., race, class, and gender "truths" in criminology) which in turn supports what is left out and the process sustains itself in a cyclical fashion. Thus, following the Lacanian postmodern prescription, desire in language can foster multiple discourses, can embody multi-accentuated desire and can be reflective of different expressions of knowing.

When exploring the intersections of race, class, and gender—especially in the context of our postmodern analysis—a necessary and foundational component to understanding the prevailing construction of criminological discourse, subjectivity, and knowledge includes Lacan's psychoanalytic semiotics. In other words, the pre-thematized locus of power, agency, identity, meaning, desire, truth, and so forth in the academy's conception of criminology resides *in the language of its unconscious*! Fortunately, these organizing principles can be interpreted through the application of Lacan's insights, especially his four discourses.

What our provisional treatment of Lacan's discursive schematizations suggests is how *any* composition of difference—whether on the basis of skin color, sex, or economic status—confronts the *logic of identity* (Young, 1990: 98-99; Adorno, 1973), the *politics of sameness* (Arrigo, 1993b: 28-29; Irigaray, 1985) or the *metaphysics of presence* (Derrida, 1976; 1981). In the domain of criminological theory, the manifestation of these disciplinary phenomena represent the hegemonic reduction of individual and collective heterogeneity and multiplicity to normalizing homogeneity and unity. Thus, we have the silencing of a pluralistic criminology.

Conventional theory-building in criminology begins by invoking the *uniquely encoded discourse of the master (and/or university)*. *This specialized grammar produces a circumscribed knowledge, embodying that desire compatible with the coordinates defining the traditional criminological sphere.* It is this very discourse, subjectivity, and sense-making which exposes all replacement articulations and their corresponding logics (diverse logics in search of affirmation and fulfillment) to semiotic purification or marginalization. It is this very process which silences alternative vistas by and through which to advance criminology. It is upon this very process that the categories of race, gender, and class intersect, succumbing as they often do to the *discourse of the master.* Lost in this covert enterprise of de-legitimacy is the opportunity to forge more participatory, inclusive, and humanistic understandings of criminology and criminological theory.

CONCLUSIONS

This essay was a modest effort to broadly outline some of the more theoretically interesting, though speculative, matters of import pertinent to any postmodern study examining the intersecting categories of race, class, and gender in criminology. The task which lies ahead is to further this ideological foray into critical criminological thought. Notions of discourse, subjectivity, and knowledge are only three key constituents of theory construction. Additional themes, such as: identity; sexuality; time/space consciousness; causality; embodiment; etc., also require further elucidation.

The postmodern challenge that awaits is to identify and assess those values, those assumptions, embedded in sociological and ontological themes of criminological concern fostering the oppression of disparate groups. Further, the invitation of postmodern criminology is to seek avenues by and through which repressed or silenced voices may find fuller, more complete expression and legitimacy—particularly in their encoded articulations of crime, law, justice, and community. Clearly, much work lies ahead. If critical or radical criminology is to be adequately poised to address the problematic of race, class, and gender in criminology then not only must the postmodern critique, and its transformative possibilities, receive greater attention in the academy, but so, too, must its innovative agenda find greater receptivity in criminal justice practice. Although both concerns remain in their infancy stage, the time *is* ripe for change!

REFERENCES

Adorno, T. 1973. *Negative Dialectics.* New York: Continuum.

Althusser, L. 1971. *Lenin and Philosophy and Other Essays.* New York: New Left Books.

Arrigo, B. 1996. *The Contours of Psychiatric Justice: A Postmodern Critique of Mental Illness, Criminal Insanity and the Law.* New York: Garland.

_____. 1995a (pp. 69-92).   Subjectivity in Law, Medicine, and Science: A Semiotic Perspective on Punishment, in C. Sistare (Ed.), *Punishment, Social Control, Coercion.*

_____. 1995b (pp. 447-472). The Peripheral Core of Law and Criminology: On Postmodern Social Theory and Conceptual Integration. *Justice Quaterly.*

_____. 1995c 1(2):115-148.   [De]constructing Classroom Instruction: Contributions of the Postmodern Science for Crimino-legal Education: *Social Pathology.*

_____. 1994a. Legal Discourse and the Disordered Criminal Defendant: Contributions from Psychoanalytic Semiotics and Chaos Theory. *Legal Studies Forum,* 18(1): 93-112.

_____. 1994b. The Insanity Defense: A Study in Psychoanalytic Semiotics and Chaos Theory. In R. Kevelson (Ed.), *The Eyes of Justice,* (pp.7-83). New York: P. Lang.

_____. 1993a. An Experientially-Informed Feminist Jurisprudence: Rape and the Move Toward Praxis.   *Humanity and Society* 17(1): 28-47.

_____. 1993b. *Madness, Language, and the Law.* Albany, NY: Harrow and Heston.

_____. 1992.   Deconstructing Jurisprudence: An Experiential Feminist Critique. *Journal of Human Justice,* 4(1): 13-30.

Bakhtin, M. 1981. *The Dialogical Imagination.* Austin: University of Texas Press.

Barak, G. 1988. Newsmaking Criminology: Reflections of the Media, Intellectuals, and Crime. *Justice Quarterly,* 5: 565-587.

Barthes, R. 1988. *The Semiotic Challenge.* New York: Hill and Wang.

Baudrillard, J. 1988. M Poster (ed.). *Selected Writings.*   Stanford: Stanford University Press.

_____. 1981. *For a Critique of the Political Economy of the Sign.* St. Louis: Telos Press.

Benson, R. W. 1989. Semiotics, modernism and the law. *Semiotica*, 73-1/2: 157-175.

Benveniste, E. 1971. *Problems in General Linguistics.* Coral Gables, Fla.: University of Miami Press.

Bracher, M. 1988. "Lacan's Theory in the Four Discourses." *Prose Studies*, 11: 32-49.

Caudill, D. 1993. "'Name-of-the-Father' and the Logic of Psychosis: Lacan's Law and Ours," in R. Kevelson (Ed.), *Flux, Complexity, Illusion*, (pp. 124-143), New York: Peter Lang.

_____. 1992. Lacan and Law: Networking with the Big O[ther]. *Studies in Psychoanalytic Theory* 1(1): 25-55.

Cornell, D. 1993. *Transformations: Recollective Imagination and Sexual Difference.* New York: Routledge.

_____. 1991. *Beyond Accommodation: Ethical Feminism, Deconstruction and the Law.* New York: Routledge.

Deleuze, G., and Guattari, F. 1987. *A Thousand Plateaus.* Minneapolis: University of Minnesota Press.

_____. (1986). *Kafka: Toward a Minor Literature.* Minneapolis: University of Minneapolis Press.

_____. 1977. R. Hurley, M. Seem, and P.R. Lane (trans.). *Capitalism and Schizophrenia: The Anti-Oedipus.* New York: Viking.

Derrida, J. 1981. *Positions.* Chicago: The University of Chicago Press.

_____. 1976. *Of Grammatology.* Baltimore: The Johns Hopkins University Press.

Dews, P. 1987. *Logics of Disintegration: Post-structuralist Thought and the Claims of Critical Theory.* London, NY: Verso.

Foucault, M. 1980. *Power/knowledge: Selected Interviews and Other Writings 1972-1977.* London: Harvester.

Goodrich, P. 1990. *Languages of Law.* London: Weidenfeld and Nicolson.

_____. 1987. *Legal Discourse.* New York: St. Martin's Press.

Habermas, J. 1975. *Legitimation Crisis.* Boston: Beacon Press.

Henry, S., and Milovanovic, D. 1995. *Constitutive Criminology.* London, UK: Sage.

_____. 1991. Constitutive Criminology: The Maturation of Critical Theory. *Criminology*, 29(2): 293-315.

Hunt, A. 1993. *A Constitutive Theory of Law.* London: Routledge.

Irigaray, L. 1985. *This Sex Which Is Not One*. Translated by C. Porter and C.Burke. Ithaca, New York: Cornell University Press.

Kelman, M. 1987. *A Guide to Critical Legal Studies*. Cambridge and London: Harvard University Press.

Lacan, J. 1991. *L'envers de la Psychanalyse*. Paris, France: Editions du Seuil.

_____. 1985. *Feminine Sexuality*. New York: W.W. Norton.

_____. 1978. *The Four Fundamental Concepts of Psychoanalysis*. Translated by A. Sheridan. New York: W.W. Norton.

_____. 1977. *Ecrits: A Selection*. Translated by A. Sheridan. New York: Norton.

_____. 1975. *Encore*. Paris, France: Edition du Seuil.

Lecercle, J.J. 1985. *Philosophy Through the Looking Glass: Language, Nonsense, Desire*. London: Hutchinson.

Lee, J.S. 1990. *Jacques Lacan*. Amherst: University of Massachusetts Press.

Lyotard, J-F. 1984. *The Postmodern Condition: A Report on Knowledge*. Minneapolis, Minn.: University of Minnesota Press.

Manning, P. 1988. *Symbolic Communication: Signifying Call and the Police Response*. Cambridge, MA: The MIT Press.

McDermott, M.J. 1992. The Personal Is Empirical: Research Methods and Criminal Justice Education. *Journal of Criminal Justice Education*, 3(2): 237-249.

Melville, S. 1987. Psychoanalysis and the Place of Jouissance. *Critical Inquiry*, 13: 349-70.

Milovanovic, D. 1994. The Decentered Subject in Law: Contributions of Topology, Psychoanalytic Semiotics and Chaology. *Studies in Psychoanalytic Theory*, 3(1): 93-127.

_____. 1993. Lacan, Chaos, and Practical Discourse in Law, in R. Kevelson (Ed.). *Flux, Complexity, Illusion*, (pp. 311-337). New York: P. Lang.

_____. 1992. *Postmodern Law and Disorder: Psychoanalytic Semiotics and Juridic Exegesis*. Liverpool: Deborah Charles.

_____. 1988. Jailhouse lawyers and Jailhouse Lawyering. *International Journal of the Sociology of Law*, 16: 455-475.

Peller, G. 1985. The Metaphysics of American Law. *California Law Review*. 73(4): 1151-1290.

Sarup, M. 1989. *Post-Structuralism and Postmodernism*. Athens, University of Georgia Press.

Schwartz, M. and Friedrichs, D. 1994. Postmodern Thought and Criminological Discontent: New Metaphors for Understanding Violence. *Criminology,* 32(2): 221-246.

Serres, M. 1982. *Hermes: Literature, Science and Philosophy.* Baltimore: Johns Hopkins.

Smart, C. 1990. Feminist Approaches to Criminology or Postmodern Woman Meets Atavistic Man, in L. Gelsthorpe and A. Morris (Eds.). *Feminist Perspectives in Criminology,* (pp. 97-108). Milton Keynes: Open University Press.

_____. 1989. *Feminism and the Power of the Law.* London and New York: Routledge.

Sarup, M. 1989. *Poststructuralism and Postmodernism.* Athens, GA: The University of Georgia Press.

Voloshinov, C. 1986. *Marxism and the Philosophy of Language.* Cambridge, Mass: Harvard University Press.

Young, I.M. 1990. *Justice and the Politics of Difference.* Princeton: Princeton University Press.

Young, T. R. 1992. Chaos Theory and Human Agency: Humanist Sociology in a Postmodern Age. *Humanity and Society,* 16(4): 441-460.

CHAPTER 5

Peacemaking Criminology: Introduction and Implications for the Intersection of Race, Class, and Gender

Susan L. Caulfield

REFLEXIVE STATEMENT

To begin with, writing a chapter with the hope of defining the area of peacemaking criminology proved to be a real struggle. Part of this writer's perspective, as a self-defined peacemaking criminologist, involves the appreciation of diverse voices and approaches. Being a peacemaker, it is important to view any situation from another's perspective. For this peacemaker, all persons matter, as all are part of something larger and difficult to define. To write a defining piece has the potential for an authoritarian approach, which is in direct contrast to the core values of the overarching perspective of peacemaking. How to approach this task, then, became a struggle of immense proportions for this writer. At the same time, sharing the overarching perspective of peacemaking, and its possible implications for the study of race, class, and gender, was viewed as very important and necessary. This reflexive statement is also important and necessary. I want the reader to know where I am coming from and what I hope to accomplish with this chapter.

I am coming from a perspective that I recognize as limited. What I offer to the reader is the image I have of peacemaking criminology. I am sure this image differs from that of other peacemaking criminologists. I hope, however, that this image is reflective of some of the basic tenets of peacemaking, so that the reader will get a sense of what the core of peacemaking may look like. I choose not to get distracted by the various works that peacemaking criminologists may pursue, as any one of them could lead the reader to suspect that peacemaking criminology looks a lot like some other form of criminology. Instead, I choose to focus on what a friend helped me understand to be the overarching umbrella of a perspective, or what I refer to throughout as the core of a perspective. I believe that if I get too specific in defining this perspective, such specificity might deny peacemaking the richness which it deserves. After defining the overarching perspective of peacemaking, I offer some thoughts on how it might be integrated into studies of race, class, and gender. It is my hope that the reader will see the utility of peacemaking perspectives and how they might enrich the discipline of criminology.

INTRODUCTION TO PEACEMAKING CRIMINOLOGY

Peacemaking is one of the more recent perspectives to be developed within critical criminology. It is a perspective which brings a multidisciplinary approach to the study of crime and harm. Like the rest of critical criminology approaches, peacemaking criminologists seek to identify harmful acts, theorize causation, and implement policy. Importantly, as Quinney (1989: 5) noted, it is a criminology "that seeks to alleviate suffering and thereby reduce crime. This is a criminology that is based necessarily on human transformation in the achievement of peace and justice." The purpose of this chapter is, first, to provide a basic overview of peacemaking criminology and, second, to demonstrate ways in which peacemaking criminology can contribute to a study of the intersection of race, class, and gender. In addressing both purposes, it is instructive to first describe the overarching umbrella of peacemaking criminology. Often times, we get too distracted by the finer points of a perspective, or by the desire to understand distinct details of something. Peacemaking criminology does not easily lend itself to a scrutiny of minute details. Instead, this writer sees peacemaking criminology as having a specific core set of values, from which a multitude of work has developed and continues to develop. With the help of a colleague, this writer came to understand peacemaking criminology (or any perspective, for that matter) as resembling something akin to a web. There is a core set of values or beliefs, followed by concentric rings of work. However, these rings of work are not separate from the core or from each other; instead, there are strands that connect the different works, to each other, and back to the core. Importantly, the work of peacemaking criminologists cannot be subsumed under a specific paradigm or discipline. Indeed, the work of peacemaking criminologists varies from the straightforward discussion of peace (Quinney, 1991), to analysis of specific harms, such as sexual assault, homelessness, and battering (Barak, 1991; Caringella-MacDonald and Humphries, 1991; DeKeseredy and Schwartz, 1991; Tifft and Markham, 1991), to critique of theory (Caulfield, 1991), to the development of alternatives to the criminal justice process, such as mediation and reconciliation (Cordella, 1991; Immarigeon, 1991; Volpe, 1991), to suggestions for the implementation of peacemaking within the criminal justice process itself (Pepinsky, 1991).

Peacemaking criminology is not, in practice, that new to criminology; however, the label is new, and not, it seems, an entirely comfortable label to wear. Any search for works in peacemaking criminology will produce few citations. However, this does not mean that the work is not out there. As we know from feminist criminology, the work may be feminist in orientation, yet not labeled as such (see, e.g., Caulfield and Wonders, 1994). Peacemaking clearly has roots in humanism. As Hartjen (1985: 461) noted in 1985, there is a need for "criminologists to get out of the crime control business and into the business of human understanding." Tifft (1979) wrote of the need for criminologists to move beyond a rights-based prospective approach to the resolution of harm and look, instead, to a needs-based retrospective approach, as this latter approach would more likely fit the different needs of persons caught up in the harmful effects of crime. Crime control models have not worked at reducing harm. Instead, the practices of crime control models perpetuate harm, through practices such as incarceration, isolation, execution, and systemic biases throughout the criminal justice process. Clearly, traditional approaches to the study of crime and the reduction of harm are not functioning so as to really reduce harm and meet the needs of various individuals or groups. Peacemaking criminology is an attempt to better understand the human condition and create practices with the goals of peace and social justice. Overall, peacemaking criminology defines work that is true to the core values of peace.

THEMES OF A PEACEMAKING CORE

This core, for peacemaking criminology, is concerned with the way of peace. As with any critical approach, it is important to begin by stepping outside of traditional paradigms, and to seek alternative perspectives to both understanding and explaining a phenomenon. If criminologists really want to reduce harm and promote peace, then they need to find ways that transcend the traditional approaches. In doing this, it is instructive to examine the central ideas identified by Richard Quinney (1991) in *Criminology as Peacemaking*. In writing "The Way of Peace," Quinney identified four key themes: (1) an awareness of human suffering; (2) right understanding; (3) compassion and service; and (4) the way of peace and social justice. These themes may appear, at first glance, to be supplemental to the focus of criminology. To some, they may appear as beyond the scope of criminology. However, for peacemaking criminologists, these themes are an important beginning to the reduction of harm. As Quinney nicely outlines, these themes take us from an awareness of what we wish to accomplish, a critique of traditional approaches and thinking, and a direction of what to focus on, to an overall goal that includes peace and social justice. These themes transcend traditional approaches to criminology, and force us to address our transcendental selves, such as the dialectic between our rational, pragmatic side and our humanist side. What follows is a discussion of the four themes identified by Quinney.

Peacemakers are, first of all, concerned with human suffering, and the alleviation of it. After all, to live peacefully, and to pursue peace, involves the reduction of suffering. "The forms of suffering, including crime, especially, are symptoms of the sufferings within each of us" (Quinney, 1989: 5). In addressing the notion of human suffering, Quinney locates the problem in the mind, in the rational thought that permeates modern life. In discussing this, Quinney notes that "Peace and harmony come with the awareness of the oneness of all things and the transcendence of this small self to the wholeness of reality. All of this is to be found outside of the abstracting interpretations of the rational mind" (1991: 5). "To continue solely in the rational mode of thought is retrogressive for the maturing person, and for a discipline as well" (Quinney, 1991: 6). Our suffering begins and ends in the human mind. Ending human suffering is part of the objective of peacemaking; recognizing the link of suffering to rational thought suggests that we must find another approach to understanding phenomenon. Importantly, we also need to recognize the connections of all; this has implications for the studying of the intersection of race, class, and gender. Most notably, if we are all connected, then it may do us a disservice, at some point, to focus on our differences. At the same time, only by understanding our differences can we have a thorough perspective on what is included in our suffering. Indeed, it is possible that the differences must be understood separately before they can be brought back to the core and integrated into any study. I will return to this point in the section on the intersection of race, class, and gender.

Quinney next writes about the importance of right understanding, an understanding of the true nature of reality. If on the path of right understanding, according to Quinney, we will create thoughts, words, and deeds that will end our suffering. "It is the presumed objectivity and rationality of modern science that we hope to avoid in a new criminology" (Quinney, 1991: 7). To leave behind the tenets of science or positivism, and recognize the transcendent dimension of human existence is an important step in ending suffering. As Schwartz (1989: 2) interprets Quinney, for peacemaking, the way to avoid the warfare model of criminology is "to realize that political and economic solutions are bound to fail without a simultaneous transformation of the human being." Careful attention needs to be paid to the inner life of each and every person, from criminologist to practitioner to harm-producer. The importance of all is addressed in the next theme, that of compassion and service.

According to Quinney, we are all interrelated, with "we" referring to humans, animals, plant life, all of it. Suffering arises from separation. One can see this when harmed groups are pitted against each other in their search for relief. Instead of recognizing the commonalities of suffering, lines are drawn in the sand, separations are delineated, and suffering is given more life, rather than put to rest. Rather than anger, jealousy, or pride, what we need to embrace is compassion, the ability to respond to another's pain without resentment or aversion. In order to do this, we have to struggle with alienation and how alienation is perpetuated by current structural arrangements. As Anderson (1991) writes, critical criminology needs to be integrated with the approaches of Gandhian and Marxist humanism, both of which reject Western capitalist societies and envision a society free of alienation. Goodman (1956) long ago wrote of the effects of alienation.

Addressing the absurd situations in which youths find themselves, Goodman noted that to be "cut off" from one's work is to lose interest in one's work, to find little reason to invest in one's work. U.S. society does much to alienate individuals, which has adverse consequences; yet, little is done to decrease alienation. Quite the contrary, criminal justice practices do much to further the alienation of individuals and groups. As Caulfield (1991) noted, criminology can fall prey to the same process when it perpetuates subcultural methodology, a methodology designed to separate and, hence, alienate. After all, when we can focus on the "other," we will not see ourselves.

Lastly, as Quinney notes, only by understanding our own suffering and the interconnections of all can we be prepared to act in a way of peace. Peace and social justice are intertwined. Quoting Muste, Quinney writes, "There is no way to peace, peace is the way." To end suffering and harm, an oft-stated goal of criminology, we need to be engaged in peacemaking, to strive for a life of harmony. Peace cannot be achieved at the societal level if there is no peace at the individual level. Using harmful techniques as a way to bring about peace is not possible; the actors themselves must live peace if they are to bring peace to the larger social setting. To end suffering in the social world is to create a just outcome and this cannot occur without peaceful means. Work that is aimed toward peace and justice has often occurred in criminology. It is work that has sought non-harm-producing alternative practices to the ways of criminal justice. However, criminal justice, as a system in the United States, is based in violence. So based, it cannot achieve non-harmful outcomes. Peaceful outcomes and social justice, to be achieved, require a process that stresses them, not a process that is antithetical to them.

THE WAY OF PEACEMAKING

Pepinsky and Quinney's (1991) book on peacemaking is an important starting point in understanding this perspective of criminology. As Quinney notes in "The Way of Peace," the criminal justice system was founded on violence and is the "moral equivalent" of a "war machine." This latter point, often manifested in the various *wars* on crime or drugs, is indicative of a crime control model, a model which can be seen as problematic in addressing the problems of crime. Peacemaking criminologists, to borrow from Hartjen (1985), seem to support a move away from crime control and towards human understanding.

Peacemaking criminology often focuses on the social and structural arrangements of society, particularly U.S. society, and the implications of such arrangements for harmful behavior. Notably, Tifft and Markham's (1991) work outlines the belief structure that allows for battering against both women and other countries, notably the countries of Central America. If the process is similar, and the beliefs are similar, then the idea is that we can learn how to reduce violence by learning what processes, arrangements, and beliefs need to be changed. Tifft (1993) details how if we wish to reduce violence in our society, be it battering or war, we need to address the structural arrangements that foster harmful practices.

Peacemaking can also strive for change at the institutional level, through the development of alternative methods of conflict resolution, such as mediation and reconciliation. Zehr (1990) details how, by using a different lens, we can create less harmful outcomes, such as through victim-offender reconciliation programs. There are clear implications here for how we approach conflict in criminal justice, in the classroom, and in the home. By allowing voices to be heard, and alternatives to be addressed, we may reduce, rather than increase harm.

Caulfield and Wonders (1994), in discussing change, note that it begins within our own interpersonal relationships. "Reducing conflict, fostering communication, and eliminating corporal punishment from our homes and violence from our relationships are all part of making the personal political, and are also part of creating a better and more just world for us all" (Caulfield and Wonders, 1994: 228). "The *radical* nature of peacemaking is clear: no less is involved that the transformation of our human being" (Quinney, 1989: 5). The way of peacemaking, then, begins at the intrapersonal level and must be integrated interpersonally, within institutions, within the society, and within the global context.

Peacemaking and the Intersection of Race, Class, and Gender

Peacemaking has clear implications for studying the intersection of race, class, and gender. It will be useful to relate these implications to the four themes identified by Quinney and suggested by this author as representing the core of peacemaking criminology. "An awareness of human suffering" is linked to this intersection inasmuch as it requires us to understand the effects of race, class, and gender on human suffering. Much has been documented of the effects of hierarchy on the human condition. We know, as critical criminologists, that those placed differentially in the social structure have varying degrees of harm imposed on them by that very same structure. It is established that to be at the lower end of all three hierarchies is to be ill-situated to compete in the U.S.; to be a person of color, lower-class, and a woman is to have three strikes against one before even contemplating entrance into any competition. Importantly, to remove oneself from the path of rational thought is important here. There are those who wish to suggest that racism and sexism are in the past and that criminal justice and criminology have made great strides in the elimination of discrimination. They may even point to statistics which suggest that incidents of discrimination are occurring less and less. However, those who make such claims often fall prey to one of two mistakes. First of all, by denying the importance of history, they fail to see that an understanding of our condition is a historical process. To know the present, we need to know the past and, therefore, cannot dismiss it. Second, those who make such claims would be well served to honor the perspective of others. As Collins (1993: 25) notes: "While many of us have little difficulty assessing our own victimization within some major system of oppression...we typically fail to see how our thoughts and actions uphold someone else's subordination." In addition, to move outside the rational mind is an important step in recognizing suffering. Those who develop feminist methodologies are well aware of this. If one *feels* harmed, then they are harmed. This connects with the second theme of the peacemaking core, right understanding.

Right understanding instructs us that we need to leave behind the tenets of science or positivism and pay careful attention to the inner life of each and every person. This has what appear to be diametrically-opposed implications for studying the intersection of race, class, and gender. Far too much of positivist approaches have been concerned with the "counting of deviant heads." To analyze race, class, and gender, without concomitant attention to context would belie a peacemaking perspective. People of color are not just people of color, income does not define a person, and women are not just women. The intersection of race, class, and gender has the potential to recognize the complexity of the human condition and do more service to the people who may be helped by such analysis.

The third theme of peacemaking, compassion and service, can also be related to the desire to intersect race, class, and gender. In writing of compassion and service, Quinney (1991) notes how suffering arises from separation. All too often in U.S. culture, groups are pitted against each other and seemingly forced to compete—for resources, services, attention, even for theories. When groups are separated in this manner, no attention is paid to the commonalities of suffering, to the fact that much of what is harmful to these groups can be located within similar structural arrangements. This is an important implication for those who seek peace. If commonalities would be addressed, it is possible for the fourth theme to be realized, that is both a process and outcome of peace and social justice.

To have peace and social justice in criminology as a practice, one would have to avoid harmful practices. In studying the intersection of race, class, and gender, one would have to be careful not to perpetuate harmful practices, such as by assuming the voice of the persons one wishes to study. This would mean that subjects not be harmed by methodology, by covert research practices, by assumptions made by "others."

We need to recognize that the intersection of race, class, and gender is not limited to studying those who fall at the bottom of the respective hierarchies. Instead, a more peaceful and just approach would be to examine the context of individuals, to locate them where they find themselves. For example, while the patriarchal structure of U.S. society may reward males more than females, it does not reward all males equally. This may be obvious to some but is not always recognized in our practices, theories, or policies. Instead, males may not receive a peaceful acceptance due to the fact that some males are privileged. Similar points could be made in reference to whites and those of higher social classes. No one characteristic can be seen as defining any person. A peaceful approach would suggest that we need to understand individual context. Granted, this may seem problematic for those approaching a research design, but it has roots in the notion of individualized justice. There is something in U.S. history which suggests that the effort to secure individualized justice outweighs the presumed necessity of efficiency.

Perhaps it would be useful to view race, class, and gender as rings on a web, as coming back to the core, much as the different works of peacemaking criminologists are interrelated to the core. As Collins (1993: 26) writes:

> To focus on the particular arrangements that race or class or gender take in our time and place without seeing these structures as sometimes parallel and sometimes interlocking dimensions of the more fundamental relationship of domination and subordination may temporarily ease our consciences. But while such thinking may lead to short term social reforms, it is simply inadequate for the task of bringing about long term social transformation.

Each is separate and important, and crucial in its own right. However, as we know of the human condition, none of the three stands alone as an indicator of any person. Understanding the connectedness of all, and the inner connectedness of each, is an important peacemaking contribution to any study of race, class, and gender within criminology.

CONCLUDING THOUGHTS

Overall, the perspective of peacemaking criminology suggests that we step outside of traditional paradigms and perspectives, and place ourselves, as human beings, within the process itself. We need to recognize the commonality of suffering, how it is linked to the human condition, how traditional approaches have exacerbated suffering, how compassion and service are necessary if we are to live and work toward peace and social justice.

The implications for the intersection of race, class, and gender in criminology are not as precise as they might be from another perspective. Instead, what we learn here is that a core value of peace means that attention to humanness is essential. Attention to the individual context of lives is important, for if we wish to alleviate harm in our society, we must first recognize the myriad forms it takes. True, we are differentially affected by structural arrangements. Members of some groups suffer in more overt ways than do members of other groups. What is suggested in this writing is not that such suffering should be ignored or dismissed. Quite the contrary, all suffering should be attended to. However, a key tenet of peacemaking is that the suffering of all has a very basic and common root, it is a part of the human condition, and it is exacerbated by current structural and discipline-oriented conditions. Therefore, if we are to alleviate suffering, we need to go to the root of it. We need to live lives which are peace- and justice-oriented. Only in this way can we begin to address the more structurally-imposed hierarchical nature of suffering.

Indeed, studying the differential effects of racism, classism, and sexism is key to any peacemaking perspective. If we go beyond the mere appearance of something, such as a demographic, and unmask the essence of something, that is the context, we have much to learn. While it is important to recognize the individual ways in which people suffer, we must be careful of being too distinct. We must ask ourselves how effective we can be with distinct approaches if there is no web to connect them. Exposing the essence of the suffering people face because of race, class, and gender brings the sufferings of inequality right to the fore. In doing so, it brings us back to the core: that in order to end suffering and harm, we must eliminate the structural conditions that give rise to such suffering and harm. As those conditions are violent and, hence, perpetuate violent situations, we must seek an alternative, peaceful path if we hope to reduce suffering and, ultimately, reduce crime.

REFERENCES

Anderson, Kevin. 1991. Radical Criminology and the Overcoming of Alienation: Perspectives from Marxian and Gandhian Humanism. Pp. 14-29 in Harold E. Pepinsky & Richard Quinney (Eds.), *Criminology as Peacemaking*. Bloomington, IN: Indiana University Press.

Barak, Gregg. 1991. Homelessness and the Case for Community-Based Initiatives: The Emergence of a Model Shelter as a Short-term Response to the Deepening Crisis in Housing. Pp. 47-68 in Harold E. Pepinsky & Richard Quinney (Eds.), *Criminology as Peacemaking*. Bloomington, IN: Indiana University Press.

Caringella-MacDonald, Susan, & Humphries, Drew. 1991. Sexual Assault, Women, and the Community: Organizing to Prevent Sexual Violence. Pp. 98-113 in Harold E. Pepinsky & Richard Quinney (Eds.), *Criminology as Peacemaking*. Bloomington, IN: Indiana University Press.

Caulfield, Susan L. 1991. The Perpetuation of Violence Through Criminological Theory: The Ideological Role of Subculture Theory. Pp. 228-238 in Harold E. Pepinsky & Richard Quinney (Eds.), *Criminology as Peacemaking*. Bloomington, IN: Indiana University Press.

Caulfield, Susan L. & Wonders, Nancy A. 1994. Gender and Justice: Feminist Contributions to Criminology. Pp. 213-229 in Gregg Barak (Ed.), *Varieties of Criminology: Readings from a Dynamic Discipline*. Westport, CT: Praeger Publishers.

Collins, Patricia Hill. 1993. Toward a New Vision: Race, Class, and Gender as Categories of Analysis and Connection. *Race, Sex & Class*, 1(1):25-45.

Cordella, J. Peter. 1991. Reconciliation and the Mutualist Model of Community. Pp. 30-46 in Harold E. Pepinsky & Richard Quinney (Eds.), *Criminology as Peacemaking*. Bloomington, IN: Indiana University Press.

DeKeseredy, Walter S. & Schwartz, Martin D. 1991. British Left Realism on the Abuse of Women: A Critical Appraisal. Pp. 154-171 in Harold E. Pepinsky & Richard Quinney (Eds.), *Criminology as Peacemaking*. Bloomington, IN: Indiana University Press.

Goodman, Paul (1956). *Growing Up Absurd*. New York: Vintage Books.

Hartjen, Clayton. 1985. Humanist Criminology: Is It Possible? *Journal of Sociology and Social Welfare*, 13(3):444-468.

Immarigeon, Russ. 1991. Beyond the Fear of Crime: Reconciliation as the Basis for Criminal Justice Policy. Pp. 69-80 in Harold E. Pepinsky & Richard Quinney (Eds.), *Criminology as Peacemaking*. Bloomington, IN: Indiana University Press.

Pepinsky, Harold E. 1991. Peacemaking in Criminology and Criminal Justice. Pp. 299-327 in Harold E. Pepinsky & Richard Quinney Richard (Eds.), *Criminology as Peacemaking*. Bloomington, IN: Indiana University Press.

Pepinsky, Harold E. & Richard Quinney. 1991. (Eds.) *Criminology as Peacemaking*. Bloomington, IN: Indiana University Press.

Quinney, Richard. 1989. The Theory and Practice of Peacemaking in the Development of Radical Criminology. *The Critical Criminologist*, 1(1):5.

Quinney, Richard. 1991. The Way of Peace: On Crime, Suffering, and Service. Pp. 3-13 in Harold E. Pepinsky & Richard Quinney (Eds.), *Criminology as Peacemaking*. Bloomington, IN: Indiana University Press.

Schwartz, Martin D. 1989. The Undercutting Edge of Criminology. *The Critical Criminologist*, 1(2):1,2,5.

Tifft, Larry L. 1993. *Battering of Women: The Failure of Intervention and the Case for Prevention*. Boulder, CO: Westview Press.

Tifft, Larry L. 1979. The Coming Redefinition of Crime: An Anarchist Perspective. *Social Problems*, 26(4):392-402.

Tifft, Larry L., & Markham, Lyn. 1991. Battering Women and Battering Central Americans: A Peacemaking Synthesis. Pp. 114-153 in Harold E. Pepinsky & Richard Quinney (Eds.), *Criminology as Peacemaking*. Bloomington, IN: Indiana University Press.

Volpe, Maria R. 1991. Mediation in the Criminal Justice System: Process, Promises, Problems. Pp. 194-206 in Harold E. Pepinsky & Richard Quinney (Eds.), *Criminology as Peacemaking*. Bloomington, IN: Indiana University Press.

Zehr, Howard. 1990. *Changing Lenses*. Scottdale, PA: Herald Press.

CHAPTER 6

Mass-Mediated Regimes of Truth: Race, Gender, and Class in Crime "News" Thematics[1]

Gregg Barak

INTRODUCTION

In order to help clarify the relationship between media and social control—between how the mass media, law enforcement bureaucracies, and popular culture interact—and in order to appreciate how the news media in particular construct and reconstruct criminal events *between the crime waves and moral panics* (Cohen, 1972; Cohen and Young, 1973; Hall et al., 1978; Best, 1990; Jenkins, 1992; 1994), I will focus on three themes of the crime news business that have evolved in the USA during the 20th century: the predator criminal as a media icon; the depiction of sexually violent crimes against women; and the portrayals of high profile police-citizen encounters.

It is suggested that "criminal predators," "sexual victims," and "police-citizen" conflicts have become staples of news reporting. These staples of crime and justice reporting have become commonplace representations, "framing," "signifying," "mapping," and "converging" ordinary news images that have come to mean crime and punishment in everyday life and popular culture. When there are no contemporary "crime waves" or "moral panics" (i.e., drug wars, wars on crime, cultism, serial killers, etc.) to be established and contextualized, or while the news media finds itself in between "claimsmaking-newsmaking" stories about the emergence and development of a "new" trend or twist on crime and violence, then the mass media is able to fill this constructual void by providing a steady diet of a growing and omnipotent danger of crime. Between the waves, at least, not only does this constant bombardment by the mass media today require almost no explanation or contextualization of crime and criminals per se, but it also performs in an essentializing way to reduce the primary responses of "crime control" to those activities carried out by the legal order and the formal agencies of law enforcement and criminal justice.

In short, the "mass reality of crime" has evolved to the point where certain domains or assumptions about crime and justice are no longer questionable. Instead, they are simply regarded as crime and crime-fighting truths such as the "crime problem" is getting worse or the courts have created too many legal obstacles in the "war on crime." As Stuart Hall, Philip Jenkins, and others have shown, crime news construction "is a cumulative or incremental process, in which each issue is to some extent built upon its predecessors, in the context of a steadily developing fund of socially available knowledge" (Jenkins, 1994: 220). In effect, the staples of crime and justice news no longer have to compete for attention with other claims makers whose topics must remain fresh and interesting (Best, 1989). In a sense, these staples have reached the mass-mediated level of perpetual legitimacy or relevancy because of the persuasiveness of "in your face" crime and justice images expressed daily in popular fiction, tabloid journalism, and prime time news.

MASS-MEDIATED THEMES OF CRIME AND JUSTICE

Identities, individual and collective, have always been constructed at three articulated sites: the biological, the social, and the cultural. Whether we are discussing premodern, modern, or postmodern societies, this has been true for "non-criminal" and "criminal" identities alike. While I am not subordinating the biological and social to the cultural sites per se, I am arguing that "class" based representations today are largely constructed by mass-mediated culture, especially since the workingclass community, itself a creation of the urban-based mass-production industries, has passed into history. In television, for example, with the primary exceptions of beer commercials and police stories, the working-class has all but disappeared. As a result there are basically three kinds of "classes" constructed by the mass media: the "rich" classes, the "middle" classes, and the "criminal" classes.

Mass-mediated visual culture occupies the "objective" space of dreamwork and imagination, having usurped the school's role of providing symbolic coherence. The media is that "place where kids situate themselves in their emotional life, where the future appears as a narration of possibilities as well as limits" (Aronowitz, 1992: 195). Of course, mass visual culture provides the "objective" space of dreamwork and imagination for adults as well. This pertains, again, to images of criminals, victims, and crime-fighters alike. In the postmodern world, mass "media are *unique* sites precisely because of the specific place of technology in the production of culture" (ibid.). Similarly, what constitutes popular or mass culture has also become technologically mediated so that television is not merely a manipulator of popular culture, but it is also the decisive element in the construction of imaginary life and is appropriated as popular culture.

In particular, the culturally mediated visions of crime projected by the mass media, or the selections and presentations by the news media on criminal justice, are viewed as the principal representations by which the average person comes to know or make sense out of crime and justice in America. In actuality, crime and justice information (or knowledge) constructs some of the most potent imagery the media can present. Knowledge about crime and crime control is "spun" with the effect that it has historically reinforced specific forms of social control and order maintenance. Recognizing the tremendous influence that the mass media has on the development of beliefs and attitudes about crime and criminals, and on the subsequent development of policies of criminal justice reaction, one cannot separate either mass media or popular culture from crime control.

Moreover, research on the media effects of crime and criminal justice reveals an association between television viewing and what has been called a "mean world view" and a "retributive justice perspective." The former is characterized by mistrust, cynicism, alienation, and perceptions of higher than average levels of threat and crime in society; the latter is characterized by support for the political, legal, and punitive status quo. Furthermore, evidence exists that exposure to television increases fear of crime and perceived vulnerability and that it increases the adoption of self-protective anti-crime behaviors. Finally, it must be appreciated that all of this translates into attitudes regarding who can employ violence against whom, who are likely to be criminal, and who are appropriate victims of crime (Surette, 1992).

The point is that through imaging, the conscious and unconscious are stimulated so that identities, "good" and "bad," are formed through identification with the gendered, racialized, and class-based characters and persons that appear in the media. The concern here is not with the role that the mass media plays in the formation of individual identities, but rather, with the formation of popular images/themes of crime and justice that shape our collective personalities when it comes to issues of "law and order." It is to three of these popular themes that we now turn.

I. The Predator Criminal as a Media Icon

Despite the infrequency of predatory criminal events past and present, predator criminality dominates our image of crime and predator criminals underscore our criminal justice policies. Stated differently, the crimes that dominate public consciousness and policy debates are not common crimes but the rarest ones. Whether we are discussing entertainment or news, the crimes that commonly define "criminality" are the acts of predator criminals.

"Our desire to understand and control these seemingly incomprehensible and uncontrollable criminals is long standing and is reflected in much of our classic literature" (Surette, 1994: 132). But the contemporary mass media have raised the phantom of the predator criminal from a minor character to a customary, ever-present image or media icon. As with other icons, they represent a largely unquestioned set of beliefs about the world; a reconstructed reality where perceptions are often more important than reality itself, and where the mass media has the means to shape the actual world to fit the media image. In the world of crime and justice, the media icon of the predator criminal pushes life to imitate art.

Historically, the image of the predator criminal has long dominated the news and entertainment media. By 1850 the dominant image of the criminal in the popular print media had shifted from earlier romantic, heroic portraits to more mundane, negative images. During most of the 19th century, the two most popular media genres— detective stories and crime thrillers—described crime as originating in individual personality or moral weakness. This theme still prevails in the late 1990s, check out the True Crime sections of your local book dealers. What is common to these portrayals of crime and crime fighting during both the 19th and 20th centuries is that the images presented: (1) serve to reinforce the status quo, as the prevailing social, political, and economic conditions are rarely, if ever accounted for, in explanations addressing crime and its control; (2) maintain that competent, often heroic individuals are pursuing and capturing criminals; and (3) encourage the belief that criminals can be readily recognized and crime ultimately solved through the efforts of law enforcement and the administration of criminal justice (Surette, 1992).

Detective and crime thrillers from the turn of the last century mark the beginning of a more violent entertainment crime media that is less critical of social conditions. These genres laid the foundation for the construction of a social reality of crime which is predatory and rooted in individual failures rather than social ills. The first film criminals of the 1930s were descendants of violent western outlaws, but unlike the western bandits, the early 20th century film criminal was usually portrayed as an urban predator. Typically, these urbanized criminals were depicted as ruthless and corrupt and after wealth at any cost. As gangsters and undercover policemen and detectives appear more regularly in the films of the 1930s and 1940s, the portraits of violence become more graphic. The image of the predator criminal was quickly adopted by television in the 1950s. From then to the present time, television's portrayals of crime have greatly exaggerated individual acts of violence.

In fact, representative content studies of television reveal that 87% of televised crime consists of murder, robbery, kidnapping, and aggravated assault. The two most dominant media crimes are murder and robbery with the former constituting nearly one-fourth of all crimes portrayed (Surette, 1992). Yet, even using the FBI's official crime statistics on "crimes against the person" versus "crimes against property," we know that the former accounts for only about 10% of the total transgressions.

In the entertainment media, the repeated message is that crime is perpetrated by predatory individuals who are basically different from the rest of us, and that criminality is rooted in individual problems. Contradictorily, in the mass media, crime is behavior criminals choose freely, and media criminals are not bound or restrained in any way by normal social rules and values. During the course of the 20th century an evolution in the portrayal of the predator criminal can be observed: Media criminals have become less human, less rational, and less Eurocentric; they have become more animalistic, vengeful, and ethnic/racial. At the same time, the crimes of these media criminals have become more violent, senseless, and sensational. And, their victims have become more random, helpless, and innocent. The public comes to "see" or conclude that violence and predation between strangers is a normal way of life.

The news media like the entertainment media has always chased crime and the pursuit of predator criminality has always been its favorite story. From the late nineties to about WWI, with the introduction of focused news journalism or what came to be called "yellow journalism," the news media has had a strong interest in predator criminality. Represented by the Hearst and Pulitzer newspapers in New York, this new style of journalism devoted space to disasters, scandals, gossip, and crime—especially violent personal street crimes such as murder, rape, and assault. Today, of course, we have the tabloid TV crime shows pretty much carrying on the tradition of "yellow journalism." While both of these forms of crime news construction emphasize the bizarre and the violent, they similarly ignore or underplay the much more common offenses such as burglary, theft, and fraud.

More importantly, it is argued that these tabloid news entertainment programs are driving the emergence and development of prime time TV news and news magazine shows. Today, we have approximately "nine or 10 times as much news and news-feature programming as in earlier decades" (Alter, 1994: 66). Even a decade ago, there was less than three hours of news magazine programming per week. Today that figure is more than ten hours and growing, and that does not count cable or syndicated shows. Hence, the "good news" is that TV is more informative than ever before; the "bad news" is that TV coverage of crime and justice in general has not improved on the inadequacies of tabloid news-entertainment coverage, both tending to focus on the predatory criminal.

No discussion of the contemporary criminal predator would be complete without some reference to gender, race, and class. For the most part, the criminal predator as a media icon has been employed to describe lower-class and working-class men. But, as Karlene Faith has demonstrated in *Unruly Women: Essays on Confinement and Resistance*, bad-girl stereotypes have increasingly been used by the mass media, especially in films, to portray female criminals as "masculinated monsters." In "Gendered Imaginations," Faith (1993: 56-66) identifies four themes that characterize this genre of filmmaking: (1) Devil Women; (2) The Lesbian as Villain; (3) Teenage Predators; and (4) The Super-Bitch Killer Beauties.

Of course, today's prevailing criminal predator has become a euphemism for young black male America underpinned with the all-American fear of black hate, as these relate to a racist and racial America. As Thulani Davis recently wrote (*Time*, Feb. 28, 1994: 29), black hate:

> is only a new wrinkle in the increasingly negative portrayals of blacks as a whole. Since the Reagan Administration's rollback of civil rights, African Americans have consistently been brought to the American public as predators—street thugs and welfare hustlers, inveterate whiners, cynical, pathological.

Davis (1994: 29) continues: "each of us who is the dark Other constantly has to prove we are not its realization...." In other words, African Americans are put on the defensive to demonstrate that they are not the demonized Others who are supposedly responsible for all that is wrong with this society.

In sum, the media in all its varied forms projects the predator criminal or horrendous crime as the norm, when nothing could be further from the truth. At the same time, it is implied that some kind of inter-narrative discourse between the criminal predator as a media icon and the more sensationalistic "crime wave" portrayals of, for example, serial killers or homicidal pedophiles, exists. In other words, as "serial killers" or "homicidal pedophiles" displaced criminal predators as the more threatening or ominous criminal types, the predators, once relegated to newsworthy stories about the exceptional or the new, were subsequently transformed into common or ordinary everyday news stories.

II. The Coverage of Sex Crimes Against Women

With all the coverage of sex crimes in the media, one would hope that its reportage was improving. According to Benedict, author of the 1992 critically acclaimed *Virgin or Vamp: How the Press Covers Sex Crime,* coverage of sex crimes has been steadily declining since the early eighties:

> All in all, rape as a societal problem has lost interest for
> the public and the press, and the press is reverting to its
> pre-1970 focus on sex crimes as individual, bizarre, or
> sensational case histories—witness the furor over the
> celebrity rape case against William Kennedy Smith. Along
> with the loss of interest has come a loss of understanding
> (Benedict, 1992: 251).

Benedict's book is based on a detailed examination of four very specific
and prominent sex-crime cases: the 1979 Greta and John Rideout
marital rape case in Oregon; the 1983 pool table gang rape of a woman
in a New Bedford, Massachusetts bar; the 1986 sex-related killing of
Jennifer Levin by Robert Chambers in New York; and the 1989 gang
rape and beating of the Central Park jogger in New York.   The
interesting point is that while each of these cases, in chronological
order, raised questions about marriage, ethnicity, class, and race, none
of them raised questions of gender.   After all, each of these crimes
involved male perpetrators and female victims.   Accordingly, it seems
only reasonable to assume that issues or questions of masculinity,
femininity, sexuality, sexual orientation, etc. would have been explored
by the mass media in the coverage of these stories.   But, in fact, the
media was silent on these gender related topics.   These news media
omissions reveal the extent to which power/gender relations and
cultural attitudes surrounding sex, women, and violence are still taboo
topics.

According to Benedict and others, the news media portrayals of
these sex crimes generally reflected: journalism's predominantly male
and white constituency, especially in relationship to crime coverage; the
still prevalent stereotypes associated with both rape and sex; the
absence of any recognition or reference to misogyny in American
society; and the tendency of the press to prefer individual to societal or
cultural explanations of crime.   Coverage also revealed the extent to
which these reporters and editors seemed more able to admit to their
racism than their sexism.   In short, these news people were more able
to recognize the sick socialization of blacks in urban ghettos than the
sick socialization everyone gets at schools, fraternities, and in society
at large.   As a result, issues of patriarchy and gender privilege in
relation to crime and control are essentially neglected.

To put it directly, the press would not research and explain gang
rape or cover the rape of the jogger as a gender-based crime.   Benedict

argues further that this reveals both the racism of coverage and the backlash against feminism in the media of the United States during the 1980s. Even those news stories that bothered to examine "the mind of the rapist," were grounded in a familiar combination of individual pathology and such myths as rape is sex or rape is motivated by lust. More fundamentally, the press' lack of understanding of the crime of rape was revealed by their inability to describe even the gruesome, bloody, comatose, near death, jogger's rape in nonsexual terms.

Rather than talking in terms of the boys *grabbing* or even *touching* the jogger's breasts and legs, news accounts used such terms as *fondling* and sexually *exploring*. Instead of substituting such terms as *having sex with* for rape, implying consent on the part of the victim, why not use the term penetrate or why not the more realistic terms used by defendant Kharey Wise in his description of his "running" buddies' acts that night which appeared in the New York *City Sun*: "Steve and Kevin both fucked her. Ramon was holding her too and he was grabbing her tits and Antron was laughing and playing with her leg." The point being: that the latter phraseology used by the boys refers to the acts as rapacious behavior, the former phraseology of the journalists by contrast refers to the acts of making love. In other words, it seems to be the case, at least based on mass media representation, that the news media still does not know the difference between rape and sex.

The common "spin" that kept these sex crime news stories alive was the press' ability to once again revert to one of its favorite formulaic presentations of the "good" and "bad" morality play. Found in this familiar drama are the images of two Western puritanical classics portrayed in the story of Eve as temptress and corruptor (the 'vamp'), and in the later Victorian ideal of woman as pure and uninterested in sex (the 'virgin'). Combined with these antiquated and unrealistic thematic representations of women as either whores or Madonnas, are the postmodern habits of media journalism. Whatever the gauge, women fare badly at the hands of the mass media. Taken in its totality, the representations of sex, crime, and rape both in myth and in news media construction, serve to reinforce negative images of women and of social justice.

Sex crime victims tend to be squeezed into one of two images: either a wanton female who provoked the assailant with her sexuality or pure and innocent, a true victim attacked by monsters. Either way, these narratives are destructive to the victims of rape and to public understanding of the subject. The vamp version is destructive because it blames the victim of the crime instead of the perpetrator. The virgin version is destructive because it perpetuates the idea that woman can only be "good girls" or "bad girls," paints women dishonestly, and relies on portraying the perpetrators of rape as inhuman monsters.

Benedict correctly underscores the fact that the stigmatization of women by the coverage of sex crime victims in general and of victims of rape in particular, will only be eliminated when these victims are taken seriously without having to hide behind the narratives of innocence and virginity, and when the mainstream news media assert in their representations "the role of women and the way men are trained to see them as objects of prey," as was demonstrated in the jogger case. Until such time as adequate attention is given by the media to the much more common and persuasive forms of violence and abuse of women, the media acts in a way to help reproduce the relations of gender inequality.

This point was recently underscored by bell hooks in *Z Magazine* (Feb. 1994), when she analyzed misogyny, gangsta rap, and the movie *The Piano*, all in relation to the treatment given these topics by the mass media. As hooks (1994: 26) wrote, to the white-dominated media "the controversy over gansta rap makes great spectacle. Besides the exploitation of these issues to attract audiences, a central motivation for highlighting gangsta rap continues to be the sensationalist drama of demonizing black youth culture in general and the contributions of young black men in particular." She continues: "It is a contemporary remake of *Birth of a Nation* only this time we are encouraged to believe it is not just vulnerable white womanhood that risks destruction by black hands but everyone" (ibid.). In other words, the outcome is that gangsta rap rather than being viewed as a reflection of the dominant culture is, instead, viewed as an aberrant pathology. In the process, rape, male violence against women, girls, etc. which is a part and parcel of patriarchy becomes deflected from its source; in its place, stand young black males who are forced to accept the blame for all the violence. As hooks points out, gangsta rap is part of the contemporary anti-feminist backlash and its expression by young black males has far less to do with their "manhood" than it does with their "subjugation and humiliation by more powerful, less visible forces of patriarchal gangsterism" (p. 27). In short, hooks wants us to locate "gangsta rap" in the center of, rather than at the margins of, what this nation is all about.

She also wants us to face up to the unasked questions such as: Why are huge audiences, especially young white consumers, so turned on by the music, by the misogyny and sexism, by the brutality? Where is the anger and rage at females expressed in this music coming from? Why the glorification of violence, death, and destruction? Without getting into an examination of the larger structures of domination, exploitation, and oppression necessary to answer hooks' questions, suffice it to say, it is much easier to attack gangsta rap than to confront the culture that produces the need for such trash.

III. The Portrayals of High Profile Police-Citizen Encounters

Turning from crime portrayals to crime-fighting portrayals provides an opportunity to explore an important dimension in the social construction of crime control. I refer to the complex organizational relations involving the police and the news media, and to the role they play in the mass-mediated consumption of crime and justice information. For example, whatever the differences in the organizational demands of the media and the police, both of these institutions of social control have, for the most part, with some notable exceptions, developed a symbiotic relationship where the media has become part of the policing apparatus of our society. At the same time, it turns out that police interests operate in conjunction with those of the media. The police have recognized the reality that they will grow and be nurtured if they are perceived as crime-fighters, but not if the public recognized their inability to protect people against crime.

Together, the media co-dependent on the police as a source for presenting "newsworthy" or "authentic" images of crime and justice, and the police co-dependent on the media for their "positive" public images, cooperate with one another in the presentation of framed images that reinforce the prevailing sociopolitical orthodoxies. Contextual analyses that would, for example, raise questions about the existing arrangements of wealth and power are, with rare exceptions, excluded from public discourse. The broader, systematic relations of social problems are also ignored, although the symptoms may be bemoaned. Problems are always depicted as being resolved by individual efforts within the system, rather than collective efforts against the system. For example, in the two cases about to be discussed, the murder of Carol Stuart by her husband in Boston and the beating of Rodney King by the Los Angeles police, media coverage identified the problems of racism and police brutality, but the systemic underlying "causes" for them were never examined (Kasinsky, 1994).

Police and media interactions in both the Stuart and King cases reveal potentially very different approaches that the media can take in covering crime and crime control. In the Stuart case the media's reactive approach led to their collusion with the official police version of what transpired. In this role, the media exercised little or no independence in their investigative efforts. By contrast, in the King case, an independent videotaped account enabled the media to take a proactive role. In the King beating, all the texts of discussion were not subsumed into the official police versions of reality. The outcomes, as we will see, were very different too. In the Stuart case the media contributed actively to not only condemning an innocent person but also to exercising stereotyped judgement against an entire community of persons of color. In the King case the media's proactive stance educated and pressured authorities in Los Angeles and Washington to take a more active role in investigating and acting against institutional racism, even if nothing ever came of these investigations.

The Stuart murder was a typical story of violent homicide, but some atypical aspects helped it become the focus of national media attention. The changing media frames portraying police as heroes, fools, and villains over a two-year period, gives us some insight into how the media creates public textual discourse. What we want to specifically ask is, how did the police and media collaborate in filtering out information that led them to the wrong suspect?

When the story first appeared in the Boston dailies on October 23, 1989, the news reported that the Stuarts, driving home from a hospital in downtown Boston after a child-birthing class, had been shot in their car by an unknown African American gunman who fled the scene. With his seven-month-pregnant wife slouched beside him, Charles Stuart dialed an emergency number on his cellular car phone, reaching state police headquarters. The state police dispatcher, who directed police units to the couple's car, became known as a hero. The police detectives on the case were also portrayed in the media as heroes.

With hundreds of police searching the site of the crime, the Mission Hill area, it was only a short time later that a "prime suspect" was identified who fit the initial description given by Charles Stuart to the police. The suspect, William Bennett, was thirty-nine and was portrayed as an unemployed African American man, an ex-con who had spent the past thirteen years in prison for crimes that included shooting a police officer. The media not only reiterated these stereotypes in its stories of the Stuart murder, it emphasized repeatedly the black face of urban violence. And, at an inconclusive point in the investigation, the media prematurely publicized the details of evidence of only the main police suspect to the exclusion of contradictory evidence as told by other key witnesses.

Less than three months later, on January 5, 1990, Charles Stuart became the number one suspect as the police were told he killed his wife. Within a few hours, Stuart took his life by jumping off the Tobin Bridge. Throughout January, the media speculated on Stuart's motives and recast its formerly heroic detectives into bungling fools. The police and prosecutors' sense of urgency to find a black suspect had led them to the wrong man. With this dramatic turnabout, the media now represented the police in a shrill tone, as villains with racist motives. William Bennett was released, and the African American community now expressed its indignation with the police vis-á-vis the media.

A few days later Mayor Flynn devoted a portion of his State of the City address to the black community's reaction to the police handling of the Stuart murder in the context of its threat to race relations. In December, 1990, the Massachusetts Attorney General released its report that concluded that the Boston police department had "engaged in improper and unconstitutional conduct in the 1989-90 period with respect to stops and searches of minority individuals in the Roxbury, Dorchester, and Mattapan communities" (Kasinsky, 1994: 219). Subsequently, there was more negative press about the Stuart case when the Grand Jury was investigated as well. Finally, in September 1991, there was further media coverage of police incompetency as a brother-in-law and friend of Stuart's appeared before the criminal courts.

What this case reveals upon closer scrutiny is the extent to which the media cooperated with the police. Both pursued William Bennett as the main suspect and both did not seriously consider alternative avenues of investigation. For example, none of the press interviewed police informants who claimed that the police coerced statements from at least three young witnesses, who were coached to point the finger at Bennett. More interesting than the police railroading of Bennett was the fact that a young woman reporter, Michelle Caruso, from the

Boston Herald, had an alternative theory that Charles Stuart was the main suspect.

She even attempted to convince the prosecutor to pursue this avenue of investigation. On November 11, 1989, Caruso sounded the only cautionary note among all the major dailies which had named Bennett as the only suspect, even though he had not yet been charged with a crime. Caruso, a trained police reporter, ended up not going with her story that would have spelled out all the doubts that she had about the indictment of Bennett. The reason: Caruso did not consider her female police informant to be a sufficiently legitimate source. The end result was that Caruso did not pursue an alternative investigative line that challenged the police account. Instead, she went with the media pack that was being led by the police homicide unit. As is typical of most news-reported crime, the media simply relied on the organizational representation of official police texts as the authoritative source for what is happening.

The collaboration in this instance, of course, accused an innocent African American who had been set up by the police. In the newsmaking process, the media had helped the police implicate the predominantly black community of Mission Hill. A serious travesty of justice was committed against the above individuals as well as against the public who had a right to full knowledge of all the evidence when the investigation had been properly concluded.

Let us now turn to the Rodney King story and what became a highly unusual media representation of police behavior. As already implied, in the American media it is not common for police officers to be portrayed as villains. The King case was an exception. That is, the police were presented as major perpetrators of violence and as racial harassers and bigots. In the Stuart case, we saw how the police and the media following the police lead collaborated. In the King case, we will see what happens when the police "spin" and the media "spin" clash.

In short, the King beating produced two competing images and texts presented by the police and the media. The dominant police interpretation was that the overzealous beating of King was an "isolated event." The media's interpretation was that the beating reflected "widespread police brutality" against minority communities. Unfortunately, most of the talk and discussion of police violence in the mass media was lightweight in nature, failing to analyze police-community relations in any depth or meaning.

As the Christopher Commission Report stated:

> Our Commission owes its existence to the George Holliday videotape of the Rodney King incident. Whether there even would have been a Los Angeles Police Department investigation without the video is doubtful, since the efforts of King's brother, Paul, to file a complaint were frustrated, and the report of the involved officers was falsified. Even if there had been an investigation, our case-by-case review of the handling of 700 complaints indicates that without the Holliday videotape the complaint might have been adjudged to be "not sustained," because the officers' version conflicted with the account by King and his two passengers, who typically would have been viewed as not "independent" (Quoted in Kasinsky, 1994: 222-23).

In other words, without the repeated showings of Holliday's videotape capturing the actual beating of King by the L.A.P.D. on CNN and all the major TV networks, there would not have been competing images and discussions of what transpired on the night of March 3, 1991. Chief of the Los Angeles Police, Darryl Gates, long-time enemy of progressive thinking police, tried to put a "spin" on this as an aberrant, isolated event and that the officers involved would be punished. Chief Gates, who was eventually forced to resign, was not a credible spokesperson based on his past record of being a supporter of "curbside justice" and based on the view that many thought him to be a "racist."

Most of the African American and Hispanic communities were putting forth a "spin" that this was a common experience shared by families and friends alike. Other images and versions of "what happened," focused on the question of "excessive force" and whether or not King was cooperating with or resisting the efforts of the officers who were trying to arrest him. Other texts at variance with the official police "spin" revolved around the tape-recorded conversations of officers reporting the incident to their supervising officer, Sergeant Koon. These officers acted with little concern for censure of their comments or behavior by the police. They expected the chief to back them up, as he had done in the past. Of course, that was before they knew that George Holliday had captured their beating of King on videotape.

In this highly unusual media case, the public showing of a citizen's videotape precluded the "business as usual" course of action. The result of an independent source allowed, even encouraged, if you will, a mass-mediated public opinion that gave credibility to the view that police brutality was not an isolated event. The Congressional Black Caucus called for a wider inquiry on police brutality and harassment of minorities in general. Attorney General Thornburgh ordered a national inquiry on police violence. At least for a while, police brutality was the major news theme, coupled with sub-themes of racial discrimination and harassment. In a short time, however, the larger themes of racism and police brutality began to fade, giving way eventually to the personality conflicts between Chief Gates and his political adversaries. A "quick-fix" solution emerged, the African American community and the Los Angeles Mayor got rid of Gates who, in turn, became the easy political scapegoat in the whole messy affair.

In sum, the Rodney King case was framed by the media as being more than an isolated case of police brutality. In fact, the use of brutality by the L.A.P.D. was presented by the media as representative of a widespread phenomenon in the United States. The use of an initial independent source permitted the media to be more critical than usual of excessive police force. Unfortunately, the critical capacity of the mainstream media did not extend to a serious exploration of the underlying causes of police brutality and racism. More specifically, the media did not print the full texts of the police reports, including the verbatim accounts of police radio conversations and the complete texts of witnesses not the least of which were other law enforcement officers who contradicted the official police account of the incident. These other perspectives or narratives would have provided readers and viewers with additional information to make more informed judgements as to whether or not excessive force was used by police on Rodney King.

CONCLUSIONS

With respect to the three crime and justice themes explored above—criminal predators, sexual victims, and police-citizen encounters—it has been argued that each has evolved to the point where they have become "givens" in the social construction of crime and crime control. Contextualization of these ordinary crimes and their control no longer seems necessary as these images of crime and justice have become firmly entrenched in the mass consciousness as typifying everyday criminality. Unlike the episodic or periodic "crime waves" or "moral panics" that require contextualization, these staples of crime and justice news production provide a constant input for inflaming the public fear and anxiety about crime and its control.

Nevertheless, the implications of this essay call upon criminologists to provide contextualization and re-contextualization for all kinds of crime news representation, whether in the mass media or in scholarly journals. By engaging the mass media, criminologists and others can interact in the social production of crime and justice representations that are publicly consumed as the prevailing crime truths or ideologies. In doing so, "newsmaking criminologists" (Barak, 1988; 1994) can attempt to consciously alter the public's perceptions and understandings of crime and justice. In confronting the prevailing myths, stereotypes, and biases concerning crime and justice in America, criminologists can interrupt "the smooth passage of 'regimes of truth,' disrupt those forms of knowledge about crime which have assumed a self-evident quality, and engender a state of uncertainty in those responsible for servicing the network of power-knowledge relations" (Smart, 1983: 135).

In short, the development of a newsmaking criminology directed at the dual processes of breaking down the prevailing structures of meaning and of displacing these with alternative conceptions, distinctions, words and phrases, which convey new meanings and new possibilities, is consistent with the postmodernist agenda of deconstruction and reconstruction (Henry, 1994). In the area of criminology, perhaps the classic example of a criminologist successfully interjecting "replacement discourse" into the popular culture was when Edwin Sutherland, in the 1940s, introduced the concept of "white collar crime." By bringing attention to a large area of criminal behavior that had been neglected by criminologists, the media, and the public alike, Sutherland was able to create a new kind of public consciousness regarding crime and punishment.

Finally, in the spirit of a newsmaking criminology there must be in the place of "control talk," "organizational talk," and "law talk," a talk that brings back into focus or context the political, economic, and social relations that envelop crime and crime control. In doing so, this talk will have to accommodate the changing inter- and intra-narrative relations found both within and between the socially constructed "crime

waves" and "moral panics." In the future, mapping out these narrative
relations becomes a necessary prerequisite for fully understanding the
mediation of crime and justice themes.

NOTE

1.   Another version of this chapter appears in *Social Justice*, 21:3
(Fall, 1994).

REFERENCES

Alter, Jonathan. 1994. It Isn't All Junk Food. *Newsweek* (April 11):
    66.
Aronowitz, Stanley. 1992. *The Politics of Identity: Class, Culture,
    Social Movements*. New York: Routledge.
Barak, Gregg (ed.). 1994. *Media, Process, and the Social
    Construction of Crime: Studies in Newsmaking Criminology*. New
    York: Garland Publishing.
Barak, Gregg. 1988. Newsmaking Criminology: Reflections on the
    Media, Intellectuals, and Crime. *Justice Quarterly*, 5(4): 565-
    587.
Benedict, Helen. 1992. *Virgin or Vamp: How the Press Covers Sex
    Crimes*. New York: Oxford.
Best, Joel. 1990. *Threatened Children: Rhetoric and Concern about
    Child Victims*. Chicago: University of Chicago Press.
Best, Joel (ed.). 1989. *Images of Issues*. New York: Aldine de
    Gruyter.
Cohen, Stan. 1972. *Folk Devils and Moral Panics: The Creation of
    the Mods and Rockers*. Oxford: Blackwell.
Cohen, Stan, and Jock Young (eds.). 1973. *The Manufacture of
    News: Social Problems, Deviance and the Mass Media*. London:
    Constable.
Davis, Thulani. 1994. We Need to Do Some Work. *Time* (February
    28): 29-30.
Faith, Karlene. 1993. Gendered Imaginations: Female Crime and
    Prison Movies. *The Justice Professional*, 8(1): 53-70.

Hall, Stuart, with Chas Critcher, Tony Jefferson, John Clarke, and Brian Roberts. 1978. *Policing the Crisis: Mugging, the State, and Law and Order.* London: Macmillan.

Henry, Stuart. 1994. Replacement Discourse as Newsmaking Criminology, in Barak's *Media, Process, and the Social Construction of Crime.*

hooks, bell. 1994. Sexism and Misogyny: Who Takes the Rap? *Z Magazine.* (February): 26-28.

Jenkins, Philip. 1992. *Intimate Enemies: Moral Panics in Contemporary Great Britain.* New York: Aldine de Gruyter.

Jenkins, Philip. 1994. *Using Murder: The Social Construction of Serial Homicide.* New York: Aldine de Gruyter.

Kasinsky, Renee. 1994. Patrolling the Facts: Cops, Media, and Crime, in Barak's *Media, Process, and the Social Construction of Crime.*

Smart, Barry. 1983. *Foucault, Marxism and Critique.* London: Routledge and Kegan Paul.

Surette, Ray. 1994. The Criminal Predator as a Media Icon, in Barak's *Media, Process, and the Social Construction of Crime.*

Surette, Ray. 1992. *Media, Crime and Criminal Justice: Images and Realities.* Pacific Grove, CA: Brooks/Cole Publishing Company.

SECTION II

APPLICATIONS

CHAPTER 7

Sentencing Women to Prison: Equality Without Justice[1]

Meda Chesney-Lind

As the number of people imprisoned in the U.S. continues to climb, we have achieved the dubious honor of having the second highest incarceration rate in the world—following the newly formed Russian nation (Mauer, 1994). Along the way, America's love affair with prisons claimed some hidden victims—economically marginalized women of color and their children.

During the nineteen eighties, the number of women imprisoned in the U.S. tripled. Now, on any given day, well over 90,000[2] women are locked up in American jails and prisons. Increases in the number of women incarcerated surpassed male rates of increase for every year except one during the last decade, and the first few years of this decade saw the numbers of women in prison continue to climb (though their rates of increase now roughly parallel those seen in the male populations). Between 1990 and 1992, for example, the number of women in prison increased by 14.6% and the number of women in jail jumped by 9.3%. The starkest increases were seen at the federal level, where the number of women in prison jumped by 28% in just two years (Bureau of Justice Statistics, 1993a:2; Bureau of Justice Statistics, 1993b:4).

BUILDING MORE WOMEN'S PRISONS

As a result of this surge in women's imprisonment, our country has gone on a building binge where women's prisons are concerned. Prison historian Nicole Hahn Rafter observes that between 1930 and 1950 roughly two or three prisons were built or created for women each decade. In the nineteen sixties, the pace of prison construction picked up slightly with seven units opening, largely in southern and western states.   During the nineteen seventies, seventeen prisons opened, including units in states such as Rhode Island and Vermont which once relied on transferring women prisoners out of state. In the nineteen eighties, thirty-four women's units or prisons were established; this figure is ten times larger the figures for earlier decades (Rafter, 1990:181-2).

TRENDS IN WOMEN'S CRIME

Was this the only response possible? Are we confronting a women's crime wave so serious that building new women's prisons is our only alternative? A look at the pattern of women's arrests provides little evidence of this. In 1983, there were 17,429 women in our nation's prisons. By 1992, that number had grown to 50,409, an increase of 189 percent (Bureau of Justice Statistics 1991b:1). By contrast, total arrests of women (which might be seen as a measure of women's criminal activity) increased by only 41 percent during the period. Indeed, during the last two years of that period (1990 and 1992), years that saw women's jail and prison populations soar to new heights, the number of adult women arrested showed little change: the number of women arrested *declined* between 1990-1991 and increased by less than one percent between 1991-1992 (Federal Bureau of Investigation 1992: 222; Federal Bureau of Investigation 1993: 226).

Turning specifically to trends in the arrests of women for Part One offenses (including murder, rape, aggravated assault, robbery, burglary, larceny-theft, motor vehicle theft and arson)—these increased by 34 percent during the years between 1983 and 1992 (Federal Bureau of Investigation 1993: 224). Looking at these offenses differently, however, reveals a picture of stability rather than change over the past decade. Women's share of these arrests (as a proportion of all those arrested for this offense) rose from 21 percent to 22 percent between 1983 and 1992—hardly anything to get excited about. Women's share of arrests for serious violent offenses moved from 10.8% to 12.3% during the same period displaying, if anything, the non-violence of women's offending (Federal Bureau of Investigation, 1993: 222). Clearly, dramatic increases in women's imprisonment cannot be laid at the door of radical changes in the volume and character of women's crime.

In fact, most of the increase in women's arrests is accounted for by more arrests of women for non-violent property offenses such as shoplifting, check forgery, welfare fraud, as well as for substance abuse offenses such as driving under the influence of alcohol and, as we shall see later, drug offenses.

CHARACTERISTICS OF WOMEN IN PRISON

The characteristics of women in U.S. prisons also suggest that changes in policy rather than women's crime explain what has happened. The American Correctional Association (ACA) recently conducted a national survey of imprisoned women in the U.S. and found that overwhelmingly they were young, economically marginalized, women of color (57 percent), and mothers of children (75 percent), although only a third were married at the time of the survey (American Correction Association 1990; see also Bureau of Justice Statistics, 1994). About half of them ran away from home as youths, about a quarter of them had attempted suicide, and a sizable number had serious drug problems.

Over half of the women surveyed were victims of physical abuse and 36 percent had been sexually abused, and about one-third of the women in the ACA study never completed high school and a similar number quit because they were pregnant. Twenty-two percent had been unemployed in the three years before they went to prison. Just 29 percent had only one employer in that period.

Most of these women were first imprisoned for larceny-theft or drug offenses. At the time of the survey, they were serving time for drug offenses, murder, larceny-theft, and robbery. While some of these offenses sound serious they, like all behavior, are heavily gendered. Research indicates, for example, that of women convicted of murder or manslaughter, many had killed husbands or boyfriends who repeatedly and violently abused them. In New York, for example, of the women committed to the state's prisons for homicide in 1986, 49 percent had been the victims of abuse at some point in their lives and 59 percent of the women who killed someone close to them were being abused at the time of the offense. For half of the women committed for homicide, it was their first and only offense (Huling, 1991).

WOMEN, VIOLENT CRIMES, AND THE WAR ON DRUGS

Another indication of that fact that women are not more serious offenders comes from statistics on the proportion of women in state prisons for violent offenses declined from 48.9 percent in 1979 to 32.2 percent in 1991 (Bureau of Justice Statistics, 1988; Bureau of Justice Statistics, 1994). In states like California, which have seen large increases in women's imprisonment, the decline is even sharper. In 1992, only 16 percent of the women admitted to California prison were being incarcerated for violent crimes, compared to 37.2 percent in 1982 (Bloom, Chesney-Lind, and Owen, 1994).

Other recent figures suggest that without any fanfare, the "war on drugs" has become a war on women, and it has clearly contributed to the explosion in women's prison populations. One out of three women in U.S. prisons in 1991 were doing time for drug offenses (up from one in 10 in 1979) (Bureau of Justice Statistics, 1988: 3; Bureau of Justice Statistics, 1991; U.S. Department of Justice, 1994: 3). While the intent of get tough policies was to rid society of drug dealers and so-called king-pins, over a third (35.9%) percent of the women serving time for drug offenses in the nation's prisons are serving time solely for "possession"(Bureau of Justice Statistics, 1988:3).[3] The war on drugs, coupled with the development of new technologies for determining drug use (e.g. urinalysis), plays another less obvious role in increasing women's imprisonment. Many women parolees are being returning to prison for technical parole violations, because they fail to pass random drug tests; of the six thousand women incarcerated in California in 1993, approximately one-third (32%) were imprisoned due to parole violations. In Hawaii, 55 percent of the new admissions to the Women's Prison during a two-month period in 1991 were being returned to prison for parole violations (largely drug violations).[4]

Nowhere has the drug war taken a larger toll than on women sentenced in federal courts. In the federal system, the passage of harsh mandatory minimums for federal crimes coupled with new sentencing guidelines intended to "reduce race, class and other unwarranted disparities in sentencing males" (Raeder, 1993) have operated in ways that distinctly disadvantage women.[5] They have also dramatically increased the number of women sentenced to federal institutions. In 1989, 44.5% of the women incarcerated in federal institutions were being held for drug offenses, only two years later, this was up to 68%.[6] Twenty years ago, nearly two-thirds of the women convicted of federal felonies were granted probation, but in 1991 only 28% of women were given straight probation (Raeder, 1993: 31-32). Mean time to be served by drug offenders increased from 27 months in July 1984 to a startling 67 months in June 1990 (Raeder, 1993: 34). Taken together, these data explain why the number of women in federal institutions has skyrocketed since the late 1980s. In 1988, before full implementation of sentencing guidelines, women comprised 6.5% of those in federal institutions in 1988; by 1992, this figure had jumped to 8%. The number of women in federal institutions climbed by 97.4% in the space of three years (Bureau of Justice Statistics, 1989: 4; Bureau of Justice Statistics, 1993b: 4).

What about property offenses? Nearly 30 percent of the women in state prisons are doing time for these offenses. California, again, gives us a closer look: over a third (34.1%) of women in California state prisons were incarcerated for property offenses of which "petty theft with a prior offense" is the most common offense. This generally includes shoplifting and other minor theft. One woman in ten in California prisons is doing time for petty theft. Taken together, this means that one woman in four is incarcerated in California for either simple drug possession and petty theft with a prior.

GETTING TOUGH ON WOMEN'S CRIME

Data on the characteristics of women in prison as well as an examination of trends in women's arrests suggest that factors other than a shift in the nature of women's crime are involved in the dramatic increases in women's imprisonment. Simply put, it appears that the criminal justice system now seems more willing to incarcerate women.

What exactly has happened in the last decade? While explanations are necessarily speculative, some reasonable suggestions can be advanced. First, it appears that mandatory sentencing for particular offenses at both state and federal levels has affected women's incarceration, particularly in the area of drug offenses. Sentencing "reform," especially the development of sentencing guidelines, also has been a problem for women As noted earlier, in California this has resulted in increasing the number of prison sentences for women (Blumstein et al., 1983). Sentencing reform has created problems in part because these reforms address issues that have developed in the handling of male offenders and are now being applied to women offenders.[7] Daly's (1991) review of this problem notes, for example, that federal sentencing guidelines ordinarily do not permit a defendant's employment or family ties/familial responsibilities to be used as a factor in sentencing. She notes that these guidelines probably were intended to reduce class and race disparities in sentencing, but their impact on women's sentencing was not considered.

Finally, the criminal justice system has simply become tougher at every level of decision-making. Langan notes that the chances of a prison sentence following arrest have risen for all types of offenses (not simply those typically targeted by mandatory sentencing programs) (Langan, 1991: 1569). Such a pattern is specifically relevant to women, since mandatory sentencing laws (with the exception of those regarding prostitution and drug offenses), typically have targeted predominantly male offenses such as sexual assault, murder, and weapons offenses. In essence, Langan's research confirms that the whole system is now "tougher" on all offenses, including those that women traditionally have committed.

A careful review of the evidence on the current surge in women's incarceration suggests that this explosion may have little to do with a major change in women's behavior. This stands in stark contrast to the earlier growth in women's imprisonment, particularly to the other great growth of women's incarceration at the turn of the twentieth century.

Perhaps the best way to place the current wave of women's imprisonment in perspective is to recall earlier approaches to women's incarceration. Historically, women prisoners were few in number and were, seemingly, an afterthought in a system devoted to the imprisonment of men. In fact, early women's facilities were often an outgrowth of men's prisons. In those early days, women inmates were seen as "more depraved" than their male counterparts because they are acting in contradiction to their whole "moral organization" (Rafter, 1990: 13).

The first large-scale and organized imprisonment of women occurred in the U.S. when many women's reformatories were established between 1870 and 1900. Women's imprisonment then was justified not because the women posed a public safety risk, but rather because women were seen to be in need of moral revision and protection. It is important to note, however, that the reformatory movement that resulted in the incarceration of large numbers of white working-class girls and women for largely non-criminal or deportment offenses did not extend to women of color. Instead, as Rafter has carefully documented, African American women, particularly in the southern states, continued to be incarcerated in prisons where they were treated much like the male inmates. They not infrequently ended up on chain gangs and were not shielded from beatings if they did not keep up with the work (Rafter, 1990: 150-1). This racist legacy, the exclusion of black women from the "chivalry" accorded white women, should be kept in mind when the current explosion of women's prison populations is considered.

Indeed, the current trend in adult women's imprisonment seems to signal a return to the older approaches to women offenders: women are once again an afterthought in a correctional process that is punitive rather than corrective. Women also are no longer being accorded the benefits, however dubious, of the chivalry that characterized earlier periods. Rather, they are increasingly likely to be incarcerated, not because the society has decided to crack down on women's crime specifically, but because women are being swept up in a societal move to "get tough on crime" that is driven by images of violent criminals (almost always male and often members of minority groups) "getting away with murder."

This public mood, coupled with a legal system that now espouses "equality" for women with a vengeance when it comes to the punishment of crime and rationality in sentencing, has resulted in a much greater use of imprisonment in response to women's crime. In this meanspirited time, there also seems to be a return to the imagery of woman's depravity from earlier periods—women whose crimes (and their race) put them outside of the ranks of "true womanhood." As evidence of this, consider the new hostility signaled by the bringing of child abuse charges against women who use drugs, even before the birth of their children (Noble, 1988; Chavkin, 1990: 483-7).

The fact that many of the women currently doing time in U.S. prisons are women of color, doing time for drug offenses, further distances them from images of womanhood that require protection from prison life. For this reason, when policy makers are confronted with the unanticipated consequences of the new "get tough" mood, their response is all too frequently to assail the character of the women they are jailing rather than to question the practice.

REDUCING WOMEN'S IMPRISONMENT[8]

The profiles of women under lock and key, at both national and local levels, suggest that women's crime has not gotten more serious. Instead, the whole system is now "tougher" on all offenses, including those that women have traditionally committed. Basically, we are now imprisoning women who, in past years, would have received non-incarceratory sentences.

Is this our only choice? Definitely not. Every dollar spent locking up women could be better spent on services that would prevent women from becoming so desperate that they resort to crime and violence to survive. These are not simply hypothetical tradeoffs. New York state, for example, has just spent $180,000 per bed to add 1,394 new prison spaces for women. Yet, 12,433 women and children in that state were denied needed shelter in 1990 and nearly three-quarters of these denials were because of lack of space (Huling, 1991: 6).

Most of these female offenders are poor, undereducated, unskilled, victims of past physical and/or sexual abuse, and single mothers of at least two children. They enter the criminal justice system with a host of unique medical, psychological and financial problems. This profile suggests that women may be better served in the community, due to the decreased seriousness of their crimes and the treatable antecedents to their criminality.

A growing number of states are beginning to explore non-incarcerative strategies for women offenders. Commissions and task forces charged with examining the impact of criminal justice policies on women are recommending sentencing alternatives and expansion of community-based programs that address the diverse needs of women who come into conflict with the law.

In California, the Senate Concurrent Resolution (SCR) 33 Commission on Female Inmate and Parolee Issues examined the needs of women offenders. The Commission's upcoming report is based on three central concepts: 1) Women inmates differ significantly from males in terms of their needs, and these gender-specific needs should be considered in planning for successful reintegration into the community; 2) Women are less violent in the community and in prison, and this fact provides opportunities to develop non-prison based programs and intermediate sanctions without compromising public safety; and 3) Communities need to share the responsibility of assisting in this reintegration by providing supervision, care, and treatment of women offenders.

Overcrowding and overuse of women's prisons can be avoided by planning creatively for reduced reliance on imprisonment for women (see Immarigeon and Chesney-Lind, 1992). Many advocate a moratorium on the construction of women's prisons and a serious commitment to the decarceration of women. They believe that every dollar spent locking up women could be better spent on services that would prevent women from resorting to crime. As one prisoner at the Central California Women's Facility commented:

> You can talk to them about community programs. I had asked my P.O. for help—but his supervisor turned him down. I told him that I was getting into a drinking problem, asked if he could place me in a place for alcoholics but he couldn't get permission. I was violated with a DUI—gave me eight months. I think people with psychological problems and with drug problems need to be in community programs.

There are a range of effective residential and non-residential community-based programs serving women offenders throughout the U.S. Bloom and Austin (1990) reviewed limited program evaluation data and found the following common characteristics that appeared to influence successful program outcomes: Continuum of care design, clearly stated program expectations, rules and sanctions, consistent supervision, diverse and representative staffing, coordination of community resources and access to ongoing social and emotional support. They also suggested that promising approaches are multi-dimensional and deal with women's issues specifically (see also Austin, Bloom and Donahue, 1992).

Institutional issues for men and women also differ, and because of this equality is not necessarily justice. When dealing with the situation of women in jail and prison, employing the "male model of inmate" can have inappropriate and disastrous results. Many women enter these institutions from a street life that is heavily gendered and where their methods of survival have made them a special population with special and unique needs. The most obvious difference between female and male inmates is that women are generally both mothers and major caregivers to their children; jail and prison procedures fail to take this into account throwing the woman's whole family into chaos. Visitation rules that fail to be sensitive to this problem are one major reason that one national study found that over half (54.3 percent) of women in prison have *no visits* from their children during their incarceration (Bloom and Steinhart, 1993: 26).

Other obvious differences between women and men includes health status, differing attitudes about physical appearance, privacy, and clothing; these areas of life have been successfully sidestepped by approaches to gender discrimination that focus on the public sector, but jails and prisons are actually lodged in the private world where gendered habits are far more salient. In short, the challenge in the next century is to move to notions of equality and justice that are more nuanced than the naive, cookie cutter approaches of the nineteen seventies.

CONCLUSION

Women's share of the nation's prison population, measured in either absolute or relative terms, has never been higher. Women were four percent of the nation's imprisoned population shortly after the turn of the century. By 1970 the figure had dropped to three percent. By 1992, however, more than 5.7 percent of those persons incarcerated in the country were women. In California in 1993, women were 6.3 percent of those in prison.

This paper has shown that women's imprisonment, rather than being fueled by a similarly dramatic increase in serious crimes committed by women, is instead a product of changes in law enforcement practices, judicial decision making, and legislative mandatory sentencing guidelines.

As a nation, we face a choice. We can continue to spend our shrinking tax dollars on the pointless and costly incarceration of women guilty of petty drug and property crimes, or we can seek other more sensible and cost effective solutions to the problems of drug-dependent women.

The question is: Do we as a society have the courage to admit that the war on drugs (and women) has been lost and at a great price? The hidden victims of that war have seen their petty offenses criminalized and their personal lives destroyed. Is this our only choice?

Definitely not. By focusing on strategies that directly address the problems of women on the economic and political margins and away from expensive and counterproductive penal policies, we could stop the pointless waste of scarce tax dollars. To do this, we must begin now to demand changes in public policy so that the response to women's offending is one that addresses human needs rather than the short-sighted objectives of politicians who cannot see beyond the next sound bite or election. We must also be prepared to challenge the greed of the "correctional industrial complex" which seeks to replace the mindless spending of the cold war with the equally mindless, but profitable, incarceration of the nation's poor and dispossessed.

The decarceratation of virtually all women in prison would not jeopardize public safety, and the re-investment of money saved in programs designed to meet women's needs will enrich not only their lives but the lives of many other women who are at risk for criminal involvement. Finally, by moving dollars from women's prisons to women's services we will not only help women—we also help their children. In the process, we are also breaking the cycle of poverty, desperation, crime, and imprisonment rather than perpetuating it.

NOTES

1. The number of women in prison in the United States has reached an unprecedented level. The paper considers possible explanations for this increase, including a careful review of available evidence on the character of women's offending. These data do not indicate a significant shift in the character of women's crime. Instead, they suggest than an increased willingness to incarcerate women for offenses, such as property and drug offenses. Such a willingness is, in part, explained by an increased willingness to punish economically marginalized women in increasingly harsh ways for theirs attempts to cope with the burdens of poverty and racism. Since these women previously received nonincarceratory sentences for these offenses, equally dramatic reductions in women's prison populations ought to be within reach. The paper concludes with a call to consider a moratorium on women prison construction and the development of strategies to decarcerate of women currently in prison. An earlier version of this paper was presented at the National

Institute of Corrections Seminar on "Critical Issues in Managing the Women Offender," July 10-15, 1994.

2.   According to federal statistics, during 1992, 50,409 women were held in state and federal correctional facilities and, the "average daily population" of U.S. jails included 40,874 adult women.

3.   In 1979, 26 percent of women doing time in state prisons for drug offenses were incarcerated solely for possession.

4.   Personal communication with the author, September 1992.

5.   Raeder notes, for example, the judges are constrained by these guidelines from considering family responsibilities, particularly pregnancy and motherhood, that in the past may have kept women out of prison.   Yet the impact of these "neutral" guideline is to eliminate from consideration the unique situation of mothers, especially single mothers, unless their situation can be established to be "extraordinary."   Nearly 90% of male inmates report that their wives are taking care of their children; by contrast only 22% of mothers in prison could count on the fathers of their children to care for them during   their imprisonment (Raeder, 1993:69); which means that many women in prison, the majority of whom are mothers, face the potential if not actual loss of their children. This is not a penalty that men in prison experience.

6.   The comparable male figure was 58% 1993, up from 39.6% in 1989 (Raeder, 1993:26).

7.   Blumstein and his associates note that California's Uniform Determinate Sentencing Law "used the averaging approach, one consequence of which was to markedly increase the sentences of women—especially for violent offenses" (Blumstein et al., 1983: 114).

8.   This and the next section of the paper rely heavily on similar sections in *Women in California Prisons*.

REFERENCES

American Correctional Association. 1990. *The Female Offender: What Does the Future Hold?* Washington, D.C.: St. Mary's Press.

Austin, James, Barbara Bloom, and Trish Donahue. 1992. *Female Offenders in the Community: An Analysis of Innovative Strategies and Programs*. National Council on Crime and Delinquency. Washington D.C.: National Institute of Corrections.

Bloom, Barbara, Meda Chesney-Lind, and Barbara Owen. 1994. *Women in Prison in California: Hidden Victims of the War on Drugs*. San Francisco: Center on Juvenile and Criminal Justice.

Bloom, Barbara, and David Steinhart. 1993. *Why Punish the Children*. San Francisco: National Council on Crime and Delinquency.

Blumstein, Alfred, Jacqueline Cohen, Susan E. Martin, and Michael H. Tonry eds. 1983. *Research on Sentencing: the Search for Reform*. Vols 1 and 2. Washington: National Academy Press.

Bureau of Justice Statistics. 1988. *Profile of State Prison Inmates*. 1986. U.S. Department of Justice.

Bureau of Justice Statistics. 1989. *Prisoners in 1988*. Washington: U.S. Department of Justice.

Bureau of Justice Statistics. 1992. *Prisoners in 1991*. Washington: U.S. Department of Justice.

Bureau of Justice Statistics. 1993a. *Jail Inmates 1992*. Washington: U.S. Department of Justice.

Bureau of Justice Statistics. 1993b. *Prisoners in 1992*. Washington: U.S. Department of Justice.

Bureau of Justice Statistics. 1994. *Women in Prison*. U.S. Department of Justice.

California Prisoners and Parolees. 1990. Sacramento, California.

Chavkin, Wendy. 1990. Drug Addiction and Pregnancy: Policy Crossroads. *American Journal of Public Health*, Vol. 80: 4 (April): pp. 483-487.

Daly, Kathleen. 1991. Gender and Race in the Penal Process: Statistical Research, Interpretive Gaps, and the Multiple Meanings of Justice. mimeo, April.

Federal Bureau of Investigation. 1991. *Uniform Crime Reports* 1990. Washington D.C. : U. S. Department of Justice.

Federal Bureau of Investigation. 1992. *Uniform Crime Reports* 1990. Washington D.C. : U.S. Department of Justice.

Federal Bureau of Investigation. 1993. *Uniform Crime Reports* 1992. Washington D.C. : U. S. Department of Justice.

Huling, Tracy. 1991. Breaking the Silence. Correctional Association of New York, March 4, mimeo.

Immarigeon, Russ, and Meda Chesney-Lind. 1992. *Women's Prisons: Overcrowded and Overused.* San Francisco: NCCD.

Langan, Patrick A. 1991. America's Soaring Prison Population. *Science,* Vol. 251 (March 29): 1569.

Mauer, Marc. 1994. *Americans Behind Bars: The International Use of Incarceration, 1992-1993.* Washington, D.C.: The Sentencing Project.

Noble, Amanda. 1988. *Criminalize or Medicalize: Social and Political Definitions of the Problem of Substance Use During Pregnancy.* Report Prepared for the Maternal and Child Health Branch of the Department of Health Services.

Raeder, Myrna. 1993. Gender and Sentencing: Single Moms, Battered Women and Other Sex-based Anomalies in the Gender Free World of the Federal Sentencing Guidelines. Unpublished manuscript.

Rafter, Nicole Hahn. 1990. *Partial Justice: Women, Prisons and Social Control.* New Brunswick, NJ: Transaction Books.

CHAPTER 8

White Collar Crime and the Class-Race-Gender Construct

David O. Friedrichs

Surely one of the central elements of the image of white collar crime is this: it is not the crime of the lower class. For that matter, it is not the crime of racial minorities and women. The white collar offender, in any meaningful conception of the term, is more likely to be a wealthy white male than a poor black female. The traditional preoccupation of students of crime with lower class crime was in fact an important source of inspiration for the promotion and development of the concept of white collar crime by E. H. Sutherland (1940). But beyond this historical association the white collar crime literature—which has expanded exponentially since the 1970s—has paid rather little attention to class in relation to this type of crime, and even less to race and gender. What has been said about the interconnections has not infrequently been somewhat confusing and contradictory. The objective of the present chapter is to sort through some of the issues which arise in the intersection of white collar crime with class, race and gender. A basic premise of this chapter is that the correct posing of questions on these issues is more important than adopting the pretense that we can provide meaningful, definitive answers.

CLASS, RACE, AND GENDER

A very large literature has been devoted to the challenge of defining class, race and gender. Conceptions of these terms have tended to range from those which treat them as objectively real entities in the world, to those which treat them as social constructs only. Since it is impossible within the space constraints of this brief chapter to grapple with the complex definitional debates surrounding these concepts, the following will have to suffice: class, race and gender are essentially somewhat fluid social constructs linked with differences of material circumstance, physical features, and anatomical attributes, respectively. Up to a point they reflect differences which are real and objectively identifiable; beyond a certain point they reify and amplify differences and become arbitrary and oppressive categories. The ultimate arbitrariness of these social constructs renders any comparisons —especially those involving class and race—provisional, and prone to distortions. Postmodernists who regard class, race and gender as outdated modernist concepts are probably correct in the sense that some of their traditional associations are eroding or evaporating, but they are surely incorrect if they suggest that they are wholly meaningless and irrelevant in the contemporary world (Dickens and Fontana, 1994: 11; Hollinger, 1994: 162). The variables of class, race, and gender have traditionally been applied quite autonomously, and each is a source of particular forms of oppression (Rothenberg, 1995). The position taken here also acknowledges that these variables have interrelationships and points of intersection which must be considered. In choosing to focus on certain variables—such as class, race and gender—we by default exclude consideration of other variables. Such choices may at least imply a privileging—which can be contested—of certain variables over others. Even the choice of ordering the variables we focus on—e.g., class, race, and gender as opposed to race, gender and class—may be suggestive of assigning a higher priority to one variable over another. It should be acknowledged at the outset, then, that any choices made in this connection are open to interpretations of a hidden agenda.

CRIMINAL CONDUCT: ACCOUNTING FOR CLASS-RACE-GENDER DIFFERENCES

Differences in patterns of criminal conduct relative to class, race and gender can be accounted for in quite different ways. First, any such differences can be attributed to alleged inherent differences which divide humans: e.g., that lower class individuals are members of the lower class precisely because they are more likely to have pathological tendencies than are middle and upper class individuals; that people of color are more likely to have innate attributes associated with predatory crime than so-called white people; and that females are naturally less likely to be aggressive than males. While the more blatantly elitist, racist and sexist dimensions of such accounts are widely treated as disreputable in contemporary criminology, the reality of certain inherent intergroup differences is certainly assumed by a not insignificant number of criminologists. James Q. Wilson and Richard Herrnstein's (1985) *Crime and Human Nature* can be cited as one prominent work which adopts—at least up to a point—such a view. Although the earlier attempts to identify such factors as sex as fundamental determinants of involvement with crime were largely rejected during the mid-20th century period—and replaced with an emphasis on gender—at least some feminist criminologists call for a reconsideration of inherent differences between the sexes (Allen, 1989). Accordingly, attention to biological or innate differences is not necessarily an exclusively conservative preoccupation, despite a common tendency to regard it in this way.

In a second account different levels of involvement in criminal conduct between classes, races and the sexes are linked with different patterns of socialization. Here, of course, we have a long-standing tradition within criminology which emphasizes subcultural influences and involvement with criminal conduct as a function of a learning process. In the case of white collar crime E. H. Sutherland's (1949) book *White Collar Crime* is the classic statement of at least one important strand of this position. For Sutherland it was a given that white, middle and upper class males were wholly dominant among those who committed white collar crimes, that this dominance was fundamentally linked with patterns of learning and association, and that there was no need to systematically explore class, gender, and race correlations.

In a third account, intergroup differences have to be attributed to differences in the structure of opportunity. It is so manifestly obvious that class, race, and gender have traditionally structured opportunities—and, in particular, have imposed constraints on the entry of lower class individuals, racial minorities and women into white collar occupations—that specific documentation is hardly required here. As John Hagan (1994: 103) suggests, on the matter of class, it is linked with power, and those in the higher class are likely to have power through ownership and authority positions that facilitates the commission of white collar crimes. The specific circumstances necessary to carry out white collar crime, and in many cases certain attendant skills, are very obviously closely interrelated with the structure of opportunity.

In a fourth account, the different apparent patterns of involvement in crime between classes, races, and the sexes reflects biases in the operation of the legal system and the criminal justice system. Traditionally, the operation of justice system biases pertaining to all of these variables has been indicated by a large body of scholarly work, although various conceptual and methodological issues render it difficult to achieve a full consensus on the reading of the relevant evidence (e.g., see Daly, 1994; MacLean and Milovanovic, 1990). There does seem to be some basis for avoiding broad, one-dimensional generalizations on any such relationships. Much of the scholarship on the operation of bias in the justice system has focused on conventional offenders, or such issues as the death penalty, and has not been concerned with white collar crime.

CLASS AND WHITE COLLAR CRIME

E. H. Sutherland (1940: 1), in his original characterization of white collar crime, referred to it as "crime in the upper or white-collar class, composed of respectable or at least respected business and professional men...." One strain of white collar crime scholarship has stressed, in particular, the elite character of white collar crime, and has specifically referred to it as "crimes of capital," "crimes of the powerful," or "elite crime and deviance" (e.g., Coleman, 1994; Michalowski, 1985; Pearce and Snider, 1992; Simon and Eitzen, 1993). The most prolific and versatile contemporary white collar crime scholar, John Braithwaite (1985), and the senior active scholar in the field with a long record of contributions, Gilbert Geis (1992), have both identified with the position that Sutherland's original stress on crimes of the rich and powerful should be retained. And these scholars are surely correct in their view that ideally, when the concept of white collar crime is restricted to crimes of those with privilege and power, our attention is focused on especially consequential (and often neglected) dimensions of crime.

The introduction of the concept of occupational crime has led to a way of thinking about white collar crime which substantially de-emphasizes the association with social elites and the upper class and stresses in its place the occupational context of the illegality. Insofar as this conception includes chambermaids who steal from the luggage of hotel guests and day care workers who molest their charges it suggests an essentially classless conception of such crime (e.g., Green,

1990). The term "occupational crime"—although it is often used quite interchangeably with white collar crime—is by definition not linked specifically with class membership.

A third approach to the relationship between white collar crime and class is essentially empirical. It adopts a practical, operational definition of white collar crime (typically based upon formal categories of state law) and then examines the class membership of those processed as white collar offenders in accordance with this definition. On this basis the Yale University project on white collar crime could declare that white collar crimes were "crimes of the middle class" (Weisburd, Wheeler, Waring, and Bode, 1991). The more important thesis of the Weisburd et al. (1991: 60-61) study is the claim that social status and class are much less of a factor in determining the seriousness of white collar crime than is control over organizational structures and resources. On this basis managers are often more directly implicated in the most serious white collar crime than are owners. But the promotion of a view of white collar crime as essentially middle class also calls for an evaluation. First, on one level, this finding would be hardly surprising simply on the basis that there are far more middle class individuals than upper class individuals. One question is: what is their representation relative to a larger population? Second, is such a finding principally one about those who commit what can meaningfully be called white collar crime, or about how the criminal justice system chooses to define and process white collar offenders?

The influence of class position on the disposition of white collar crime cases has been much disputed, with part of the difficulty being a lack on consensus on the appropriate meaning of "class" (Benson, 1989). Studies carried out by Wheeler et al. (1982) and Weisburd et al. (1991) came up with the surprising finding that higher-status white collar crime offenders received more severe sentences than lower-status white collar crime offenders. How might such a counter-intuitive finding be explained? It may well be that the very small number of high-status offenders who get to the formal sentencing process in a criminal justice proceeding are vulnerable to tough sentences because their offenses are quite substantial and their visibility is quite high. Hagan and Parker (1985) found that higher level corporate executives were less likely than were subordinate managers to be indicted and tried—and ultimately sentenced—for white collar crimes because the law in our system makes it more difficult to establish criminal culpability on that level. Tough sentences for high-level offenders who are actually indicted, tried and convicted, with attendant high levels of publicity, allow the judge to send a very direct message to the offenders' community of peers. But in spite of occasional cases of a high-level offender receiving a stiff sentence it is far from clear that they are uniformly at a disadvantage. A study by Benson and Walker (1988) did not lend support to the finding that higher-status offenders get tougher sentences. Rather, the finding of the 1982 study cited above is hypothetically attributed to the fact that it was carried out in urban Federal districts with an especially high volume of white collar crime cases, and with many liberal judges.

What, in sum, can be said about the connection between white collar crime and class? Although some students of white collar crime (especially those in the progressive camp) wish to see the term restricted to the economically or power-driven crimes of elites committed within the context of their legitimate occupation or on behalf of an organizational entity it is probably rather futile to imagine that this objective can be realized (the equivalent of getting the genie back into the bottle). However valid this argument for a restrictive use of the term white collar crime is, it does seem to have become a losing battle in the sense that the term has been much more broadly applied for some time now. It has been coopted by government bureaucrats, among others, and applied to offenses which most typically are carried out by middle (or lower middle) class individuals, not upper middle class and certainly not upper class individuals. Rather, it is probably more realistic and practical to concede at the outset that the term "white collar crime" is used in diverse ways, and to then explore the specific links between different meanings of the term and social class membership. What is needed most, then, is an appropriate emphasis on the different scope and consequences of white collar crime associated with different levels of privilege and power.

RACE AND WHITE COLLAR CRIME

Disadvantaged minorities (e.g., blacks, or African Americans) are highly unlikely to be charged with such white collar crimes as antitrust or corporate wrong-doing, although they are well-represented among low-level white collar crime offenders involving embezzlements and fraud (Weisburd, Wheeler, Waring, and Bode, 1991: 71; 83). According to Uniform Crime Report data, blacks are as proportionately overrepresented for white collar crime arrests (33%, in 1986) as for conventional offenses (Harris, 1991: 117). But the claim of Gottfredson and Hirschi (1990: 193) that blacks have a higher overall rate of involvement in white collar crime than do whites is highly misleading. Rather, they commit the types of low-level white collar crimes that are especially likely to be reported to the police and processed and are recorded in the FBI's Uniform Crime Report. The kinds of fraud for which black arrest rates are significantly higher than those of whites are often not occupation related, including welfare fraud (Steffensmeier, 1989).

Altogether we have little truly reliable demographic data on the whole class of white collar offenders, but such data as we have strongly suggest that if blacks are overrepresented for lower-level offenses, whites are overrepresented for middle and high-level offenses (Harris, 1991: 118; Weisburd et al., 1991: 83). When blacks are accused of any such middle or high-level offenses either they, or others on their behalf, may invoke a claim of racist scape-goating (Nasar and Frantz, 1994). Such claims are neither likely to be easily proven nor disproven.

At this writing much attention is being directed at Richard Herrnstein and Charles Murray's (1994) *The Bell Curve*. Principal themes of this book include the following: American society is increasingly stratified by intellectual ability; such ability is predominantly a product of genetic inheritance; black Americans as a group are intellectually inferior to whites (and especially to Asians). Lower levels of intellectual aptitude are linked with various social pathologies, including involvement with conventional crime. The significance of this argument is that it provides the appearance of lending scientific support to certain fairly widespread public sentiments and attendant conservative policy initiatives. Suppose one accepted the authors' claims about the validity of IQ tests as valid measures of intelligence, that average differences (of approximately 15 points) in white/black scores have to be attributed principally to genetic as opposed to environmental factors, and that lower average intelligence in turn could be linked with involvement in such social pathologies as conventional crime. Of course, there are many grounds to challenge these claims on the basis of the meaning of the IQ test itself, problems with operationally defining race, and confounding evidence of the environmental effects on test performance, among other factors. But for our purposes here, there is an entirely separate objection in the implication that people of lower-than-average intelligence do more harm to society than do those of higher-than-average intelligence, and it is far from self-evident that this is the case.

Those who have in this century been responsible for the most horrendous crimes, or those of the broadest scope—e.g., Hitler and Stalin—have been accused of many things, but not of low intelligence. It is a recurring theme of much of the white collar crime literature that the overall harm of white collar crime considerably exceeds that of conventional crime. The harms associated with conventional crime may indeed be especially direct and traumatic, but it does not follow that they are more harmful overall than white collar forms of crime. Is the more intense public concern with conventional street offenders than with white collar offenders a reflection of interracial hostility, or a fundamentally rational response to a more directly threatening form of crime?

I am not aware of any studies that indicate that white collar offenders as a group are of lower-than-average intelligence. Indeed, at least a certain proportion of white collar offenses absolutely require above-average intelligence. As an example, Michael Milken is widely known as one of the most notorious white collar criminals of the 1980s, but far from being regarded as of lower-than-average intelligence Milken was quite widely described as a genius of sorts (Stewart, 1991). Whether or not this label was appropriate even his worst detractors would concede that Milken—a graduate of the University of California-Berkeley and the Wharton School of Finance—was highly intelligent, with a special aptitude for quantitative analysis. If the formidable conceptual and operational problems in making valid comparisons of intellectual aptitude between different groups could be overcome it would be interesting to investigate how the IQs of white collar offenders compare with those of non-offending peers. Hypothetically, they might have higher average IQ scores than either the population at large or non-offending peers. On the first point, a higher than average IQ might be a prerequisite for obtaining a white collar position necessary to carry out the more significant white collar offenses. On the second point, at least certain forms of white collar crime might require higher than average intelligence to plan and carry out. But one must then confront the following difficulty: those who can be officially identified as white collar offenders (and are processed accordingly) may well not be representative of the whole class of those who commit white collar offenses; indeed, the very fact that they have been caught may signify that they are less intelligent than offending peers who have not been caught!

Racial Minorities as Victims of White Collar Crime

Given the diffuse and often latent character of much white collar crime it is especially difficult to measure victimization. To the extent that blacks are overrepresented among the socially and economically disadvantaged they are also likely to be overrepresented among victims of certain forms of white collar crime which disproportionately affect the vulnerable. They are more likely, in this reading, to consume lower quality, unsafe products; they are more likely to have jobs characterized by unsafe working conditions; they are more likely to live in neighborhoods prone to environmental hazards. In a landmark study in the 1960s it was demonstrated that "the poor pay more," and to the extent that blacks are disproportionately concentrated in lower class neighborhoods they are victims of retailers (Caplowitz, 1963). In this context it is the interconnection between class and race which is crucial. Race alone becomes a significant factor when racism is operating in addition to structural class bias, although of course it is not especially easy to separate out these effects.

In some cases the claim is made that minority group members are being specifically targeted for a form of victimization at the hands of corporations. In 1990, Reverend Calvin O. Butts and some of his followers began white-washing billboards featuring tobacco and liquor advertisements directed at residents of Harlem (Strom, 1990). According to Reverend Butts, "The prevalence of alcohol and cigarette advertisements in Soweto and America's inner cities manifests the elastic ruthlessness of companies' greed and proclivity to exploit the poor and disenfranchised people." Technically, Reverend Butts could be considered to be engaged in a criminal misdemeanor of vandalism. Conversely, he might be regarded as waging battle against willful exploitation of vulnerable people by private, profit-oriented corporations. At the same time the R. J. Reynolds Company developed a cigarette brand, Uptown, directed at inner-city blacks (Quinn, 1990). This also met with some protest, and led to a halt to the test-marketing of the brand. There is some evidence that a significantly higher percentage (39%) of black males smoke, compared with 30.5% of white males, and that blacks suffer a lung-cancer rate 58% higher than that of whites (Quinn, 1990). Obviously a dissenting view may hold that the sale and promotion of a perfectly legal product (however harmful its effects) cannot meaningfully be characterized as a form of white collar crime, and further that it is patronizing to suggest that lower class blacks are unable to make informed, discriminating choices about their practices. Whether this is crime disproportionately directed at racial minorities, or something else, is very much a matter of interpretation.

GENDER AND WHITE COLLAR CRIME

Males greatly outnumber females among white collar crime offenders. The exact dimensions of the proportional imbalance is not presently available to us, and any claims to the contrary are likely to be artifacts of a particular reading of the data. For example, in one account, 26% of those arrested for Federal white collar offenses in 1984-1985 were female, and 74% were male (this sex ratio discrepancy was less than that for conventional, or nonwhite collar offenses, which were 13% female to 87% male) (Manson, 1986). On the other hand, another study using somewhat different Federal data finds that less than 20% of the white collar offenders were female, and over 80% were male, while the common crime sample yielded a smaller discrepancy of over 30% female and less than 70% male (Weisburd, Wheeling, Waring, and Bode, 1991: 70). In part, the kinds of crimes selected for comparison will skew results in one direction or the other, especially as women are quite clearly better represented among those engaging in low-level frauds, and underrepresented among those engaged in crimes of violence. The male dominance of the corporations and outside-the-home occupations, especially the more powerful positions—or "the gendered structure of opportunity" (Braithwaite, 1993: 225)—would seem to clearly be the single most important factor explaining the overall discrepancy, or underrepresentation of female offenders. Crime generally has been a male domain, and male criminals have overwhelmingly been the principal concern of both the criminal justice system and criminology itself. To the extent that a certain amount of female criminality was recognized in earlier times, it was attributed to inherent biogenic and psychological factors.

A substantial amount of attention to female criminality has only developed since the 1970s, mainly as one response to the women's movement. Some of the first wave of criminologists to attend to female criminality (mainly women themselves) suggested that any increasing involvement of women in crime could be attributed to the liberating impact of the women's movement, or more generally the release of women from some of the traditional constraints of gender roles (Simon, 1975; Adler, 1975). Such an interpretation has been strongly challenged, however, especially on the grounds that there does not appear to be any logical relationship between the types of offenses where female involvement has risen, and any meaningful conception of women's liberation.

Not all students of female criminality agree that it has increased measurably in recent years, or that male and female rates of involvement in crime are converging (Weisheit, 1992). Simon (1990), on the basis of Uniform Crime Report data from 1963 to 1987 finds that the overall pattern of women's participation in criminal activities did not change dramatically from the early 1970s on, although there have been measurable increases in property and white collar offenses. Indeed, she concludes that for women "it is property offenses, especially white collar offenses involving small to medium amounts of money, that they seemed to have carved out as their specialty" (Simon, 1990: 11). More specifically, official data from the FBI's Uniform Crime Report and Bureau of Justice Statistics reports indicate significant increases in female arrests for fraud and embezzlement in the late 1980s (Walsh and Licatovich, 1992: 1). But such conclusions and statistics have been criticized because it is far from clear that all of the embezzlements, forgeries, and frauds upon which it is based have anything to do with white collar crime, or are occupationally related (Daly, 1989: 769; Walsh and Licatovich, 1992). If, for example, a significant percentage of welfare frauds are included in the data, it may be stretching the concept too far to see it as a form of white collar crime.

Daly (1989), in her survey of gender and white collar crime, has drawn the following conclusions: 1) the female share of corporate, or organizational, crime is very low, with only 1% of the women's white collar crime cases (compared to 14% of the men's) falling into this category; 2) the female share of most forms of occupational crime is low, although for bank embezzlement it was 50%; 3) females were much less likely than males to work in crime groups, and more likely to commit their white collar crimes alone; 4) the average gain from white collar crimes committed by females was much lower than that for males; and 5) females were much more likely to claim financial need of their families than males as a motivation for their involvement with white collar crime. First, it should be noted that women continue to be dramatically underrepresented in the higher echelons of the corporate world. Even where they have high level executive positions with large corporations it is far from clear that women are as likely as men to participate in the critically important policy decisions. But we do not presently have reliable information on whether women who are in a position to actively promote or implement corporate crime activities are less motivated to do so than are men, and are less likely to be caught or prosecuted if they do so than are men (Walsh and Licatovich, 1992). For the present, corporate white collar crime is overwhelmingly dominated by men.

Second, the relatively high rate of involvement of women in bank embezzlement cases does suggest that at least for more conventional forms of white collar crime women are quite capable of becoming involved when given the opportunity to do so. A recent survey of corporate security directors found that women in positions of authority and trust were in fact engaged in a substantial number of significant crimes against their employer, although these crimes were underreported to public authorities (Walsh and Licatovich, 1992: 18). The crimes are underreported because the corporations often fear embarrassing disclosures and publicity if the matter is pursued, or the accused woman may threaten a sex discrimination or sexual harassment lawsuit.

Daly's third finding, that women white collar offenders are more likely to work alone, may reflect either the types of crimes they commit, or a female disinclination toward patterns of male bonding. Women are much less likely to have the opportunity to commit crimes on behalf of corporations or other organizations (Braithwaite, 1993). The involvement of women in white collar crime is more a reflection of their powerlessness rather than their power.

The fourth finding of Daly, that the amounts involved in the white collar crimes of women are on the average considerably smaller than the amounts involved in the white collar crimes of men surely also reflects the differences of opportunity.

Finally, if there is some evidence that the motivating factors for female white collar crime tend to be somewhat different from those for male crime, it is also clear that women are motivated by diverse factors. In the recent study cited above of women corporate executives who commit crimes such as fraud, embezzlement, and computer crimes against their employers, it was found that contributing factors included addiction (33.8%), financial need (36.7%), and the sense that their work was undervalued by their employer (41.1%)(Walsh and Licatovich, 1992: 19). Of course, it is never easy to establish clearly which factors are rationalizations after the fact, and which actually inspired the criminal activity.

If the socialization of females and the job opportunity structure for women increasingly comes to resemble that for males one would ordinarily expect that patterns of involvement in all forms of white collar crime will become more similar. We do not yet have studies which can reliably establish whether women simply by virtue of their sex are less predisposed toward white collar criminality, although there are at least indications that this may be so.

Women as Victims of White Collar Crime

The other dimension of the connection between gender and white collar crime is the claim that in certain respects women are especially vulnerable to being victims of such crime, particularly in its corporate form (DeKeseredy and Hinch, 1991; Hinch and DeKeseredy, 1992; Gerber and Weeks, 1992). First, over the past several decades there has been a dramatic movement of women into the outside-the-home workplace. As noted earlier, however, women are overrepresented in the lower level jobs, such as clerical and assembly line positions. They are, accordingly, more vulnerable to harm in the form of repetitive strain injuries, exposure to video displays and toxic substances, brown lung disease, and so forth. Women are also more vulnerable than men to sexual harassment and assault in low-level clerical and store clerk positions. As consumers, women have disproportionately consumed harmful pharmaceutical products, and are uniquely harmed by products such as intra-uterine devices (as in the Dalkon Shield Case, which seriously injured thousands of women). Since women also disproportionately assume the burdens of housekeeping, they are more fully exposed to harmful household appliances, cleaning products, and pesticides. Some students of this issue view the alleged greater vulnerability of women to corporate crime as a reflection of both capitalism and patriarchy, or male dominance (Gerber and Weeks, 1992; Hinch and DeKeseredy, 1992). Women are underrepresented in the corporate decision-making process, in this account, and their concerns for health and safety issues are not accorded a high priority.

The preceding argument can be overstated, and it goes without saying that many men are victimized in the same way as women, and are also overrepresented in some vulnerable positions (e.g., miners). But it is important to be attentive to various possible connections between white collar crime and gender.

THE CLASS-RACE-GENDER CONSTRUCT AND WHITE COLLAR CRIME

Any serious survey of the evidence on white collar crime offenders, as long as it looks beyond the profound limitations of statistics generated by state agencies, lends strong support to the proposition that the class-race-gender construct structures criminal opportunities and shapes criminal behavior. Class-advantaged white males in particular are almost uniquely situated to take advantage of an extraordinary range of opportunities to commit the most substantial forms of corporate and occupational crime. Conversely, class-disadvantaged non-white females are highly unlikely to be so situated. White collar crime reminds us in a forceful way that the enduring stereotypical links between "criminality" and class, gender, and race are confounded by a more inclusive consideration of crime. Some criminologists, including Hagan (1989) and Thio (1988), have developed "structural" or "power" theories of crime which claim that criminality is more pronounced among the powerful and privileged than among the powerless and underprivileged. The advantaged, in this interpretation, have stronger deviant motivations, enjoy greater deviant opportunities, and are subject to weaker social controls. The claim about stronger deviant motivations is based on the contention that the powerful are potently conditioned to aspire toward material success, and accordingly experience relative deprivation much more strongly than do the underprivileged, or powerless. In another vein, John Braithwaite (1989) has developed an integrative theory of crime that proposes that nations with high levels of inequality of wealth and power will have high rates of both white collar and conventional crime, because they will produce a broad range of illegitimate opportunities that are more rewarding than legitimate opportunities. Anthony Harris (1991: 119) has suggested that upper class whites and underclass blacks may well have in common a pronounced (and arguably quite rational) lack of fear about committing crime, in the one case due to a sense of immunity and in the other a relative indifference to the consequences. "Economic wilding"—or "the morally uninhibited pursuit of money by individuals or businesses at the expense of others" (Derber, 1992: 17)—may be said to have consequences more broadly devastating than the "wilding" of inner city, black youths, and in a parallel vein, the "real looters" of the recent era were not the urban, minority youths participating in a riot but the high-level corporate executives who reaped enormous rewards for themselves while causing much economic devastation for workers, consumers and taxpayers (Rothstein, 1992).

CONCLUSION

Altogether, a consideration of white collar crime in relation to class, race, and gender continues to bring into especially sharp relief the structural inequalities and biases of a contemporary capitalist society. Exposing such relationships has been one element of the modernist project. In an evolving, postmodern era, such categories are called into question, and the boundaries between them seem to erode. If the meaning of these categories is increasingly transformed, the character of white collar crime is also affected.

REFERENCES

Adler, F. 1992. *Sisters in Crime*. Prospect Heights, IL: Waveland Press.

Allen, J. 1989. Men, Crime and Criminology: Recasting the Questions. *International Journal of the Sociology of Law*, 17:19-39.

Benson, M. L. 1989. The Influence of Class Position on the Formal and Informal Sanctioning of White-Collar Offenders. *The Sociological Quarterly*, 30: 465-479.

_____ and E. Walker. 1988. Sentencing the White-Collar Offender. *American Sociological Review*. 53: 294-302.

Braithwaite, J. 1985. White Collar Crime. Pp. 1-25 in *Annual Review of Sociology*, Volume 11, edited by R. H. Turner and J. F. Short. Palo Alto, CA: Annual Reviews.

_____. 1989. *Crime, Shame and Reintegration*. Cambridge: Cambridge University Press.

_____. 1993. Shame and Modernity. *The British Journal of Criminology*, 33: 1-18.

Caplowitz, D. 1963. *The Poor Pay More*. New York: The Free Press.

Coleman, J. W. 1994. *The Criminal Elite — The Sociology of White-Collar Crime*. New York: St. Martin's.

Daly, K. 1989. Gender and Varieties of White-Collar Crime. *Criminology*, 27: 769-793.

_____. 1994. *Gender, Crime and Punishment*. New Haven: Yale University Press.

DeKeseredy, W., and R. Hinch. 1991. *Women Abuse: Sociological Perspectives*. Toronto: Thompson Educational Publishing.

Derber, C. 1992. *Money, Murder, and the American Dream*. Boston: Faber & Faber.

Dickens, D. R., and A. Fontana, editors. 1994. *Postmodernism and Social Inquiry*. New York: The Guilford Press.

Friedrichs, D. O. 1992. White Collar Crime and the Definitional Quagmire: A Provisional Solution. *The Journal of Human Justice*, 3: 5-21.

_____. 1996. *Trusted Criminals: White Collar Crime in Contemporary Society*. Belmont, CA: Wadsworth Publishing Co.

Geis, G. 1992. White-Collar Crime: What Is It? Pp. 31-52 in *White-Collar Crime Reconsidered*, edited by K. Schlegel and D. Weisburd. Boston: Northeastern University Press.

Gerber, J., and S. L. Weeks. 1992. Women as Victims of Corporate Crime: A Call for Research on a Neglected Topic. *Deviant Behavior*, 13: 325-347.

Gottfredson, M. R., and T. Hirschi. *A General Theory of Crime*. Stanford, CA: Stanford University Press.

Green, G. 1990. *Occupational Crime*. Chicago: Nelson Hall.

Hagan, J. 1989. *Structural Criminology*. New Brunswick, NJ: Rutgers University Press.

_____. 1995. The Poverty of a Classless Criminology. *Criminology*, 30: 1-18.

_____. 1994. *Crime and Disrepute*. Thousand Oaks, CA: Pine Forge Press.

_____, and P. Parker. 1985. White Collar Crime and Punishment. *American Sociological Review*. 50: 302-316.

Harris, A. R. 1991. Race, Class, and Crime. Pp. 95-120, in *Criminology: A Contemporary Handbook*. Belmont, CA: Wadsworth Publishing Co.

Herrnstein, R. J., and C. Murray. 1994. *The Bell Curve — Intelligence and Class Structure in American Life*. New York: The Free Press.

Hinch, R., and W. DeKeseredy. 1992. Corporate Violence and Women's Health at Home and in the Workplace. In *The Sociology of Health Care in Canada*, 2nd edition, edited by B. Bolaria and H. Dickinson. Toronto: Harcourt Brace Jovanovich.

Hollinger, R. 1994. *Postmodernism and the Social Sciences: A Thematic Approach*. Thousand Oaks, CA: Sage.

MacLean, B. D., and D. Milovanovic. 1990. *Racism, Empiricism and Criminal Justice*. Vancouver, BC: Collective Press.

Manson, D. 1986. *Tracking Offenders: White-Collar Crime*. Washington, D. C.: U. S. Bureau of Statistics.

Michalowski, R. 1985. *Order, Law and Crime — An Invitation to Criminology*. New York: Random House.

Nasar, S., and D. Frantz. 1994. Fallen Bond Trader Sees Himself as an Outsider and a Scapegoat. *New York Times* (June 5): A1.

Pearce, F., and L. Snider, editors. 1992. Crimes of the Powerful. A Special Issue of *The Journal of Human Justice*, 3 (Spring).

Quinn, M. 1990. Don't Aim That Pack at Us. *Time* (January 29): 60.

Rothenberg, P. S. 1995. *Race, Class and Gender in the United States — An Integrated Study*. 3rd edition. New York: St. Martin's Press.

Rothstein, R. 1992. Who are the Real Looters? *Dissent* (Fall): 429-430.

Simon, D., and D. S. Eitzen. 1993. *Elite Deviance*. 4th edition. Boston: Allyn & Bacon.

Simon, R. 1975. *Women and Crime*. Lexington, MA: Lexington Books.

_____. 1990. Women and Crime Revisited. *Criminal Justice Research Bulletin*, 5: 1-11.

Simpson, S. S. 1989. Feminist Theory, Crime, and Justice. *Criminology*, 27: 605-630.

Steffensmeier, D. 1989. On the Causes of 'White-Collar' Crime: An Assessment of Hirschi & Gottfredson's Claims. *Criminology*, 27: 345-358.

Stewart, J. 1991. *Den of Thieves*. New York: Simon & Schuster.

Strom, S. 1990. Billboard Owners Switching, Not Fighting. *New York Times*, (April 4): B1.

Sutherland, E. H. 1940. White-collar Criminality. *American Sociological Review*, 5: 1-12.

_____. 1949. *White Collar Crime*. New York: Holt, Rinehart & Winston.

Thio, A. 1988. *Deviant Behavior*. Third edition. New York: Harper & Row.

Walsh, W. F. and B. Licatovich. 1992. Analysis of Female Corporate Criminality. A Paper Presented at the Academy of Criminal Justice Sciences, Pittsburgh, PA (March).

Weisburd, D., S. Wheeler, E. Waring, and N. Bode. 1991. *Crimes of the Middle Classes — White-Collar Offenders in the Federal Courts*. New Haven: Yale University Press.

Weisheit, R. (1992) Patterns of Female Criminality. Pp. 39-72 in *Order under Law: Readings in Criminal Justice*, edited by R. Culbertson and R. Weisheit. Prospect Heights, IL: Waveland Press.

Wheeler, S., D. Weisburd, and N. Bode. 1982. Sentencing the White-Collar Offender: Rhetoric and Reality. *American Sociological Review*, 47: 641-659.

Wilson, J. Q., and R. Herrnstein. 1985. *Crime and Human Nature*. New York: Touchstone.

CHAPTER 9

Victimization of Homeless Youth: Public and Private Regimes of Control[1]

Suzanne E. Hatty
Nanette J. Davis
Stuart Burke

*Living on the street is like living on the edge...
There's no place for you.*

Homeless young person, Sydney, 1994.

*To the rest of the country, we are the dregs of
society. Life on the streets is very hard. The
authorities beat us whenever they like.*

Homeless man, living on the streets of Bogotá,
Colombia, since the age of seven, 1994.

INTRODUCTION

Homelessness in the United States has been described as a "national tragedy" (Goodman, Saxe, and Harvey, 1991). Now perceived as a social problem of significant proportions (Barak, 1991; Toro, and McDonell, 1992) and a major policy issue (Honig and Filler, 1993), homelessness occupies a great deal of national and international attention. Indeed, advocates for the homeless in the U.S. claim that the problem of homelessness must be kept on the public agenda. One such advocate, Maria Foscarinis (1991: 1232) has said:

> Renewed and increased public pressure is now necessary to press for long-term—not merely emergency—solutions to homelessness. Generalized public concern must be channelled into focused demands for solutions....Now is the time for action.

Yet, the issue of homelessness has been captured by political interests; it cannot be separated from the processes and practices of power. As Barak (1994: 898) notes, "the plight of the homeless is a permanent and fixed expression of contemporary U.S. public policy that has yet to address seriously the problems of a postindustrial society in a changing global economy." This applies equally to adult and youth homelessness; indeed, the latter emerged in the 1970s and 1980s as a critical social issue requiring ameliorative action (Zide and Cherry, 1992), and now commands national attention.

This chapter will examine the intersectionality of gender, race, and class as they impact upon homelessness. This approach is premised on a recognition of the ways in which the varied subject positions occupied by homeless individuals are organized around axes of difference. It also recognizes the interconnection between gender, class, and race within the "politics of domination" (hooks, 1990) which pervade the hegemonic social structures characteristic of modern industrialized nations. Further, it acknowledges that the social practices which determine the multiple social realities upon which gender, race, and class are inscribed are those which colonize, silence, and oppress. These practices relegate the homeless subject to the margins, the space inhabited also by the gendered and racialized subject. Consequently, the status, and the experience, of homelessness increases the calculus of difference. The homeless woman or the homeless person of color is radically divested of an authorial voice, or even a language in which to communicate their experience. However, according to bell hooks (1990), the margin is both a site of repression and a site of resistance. It is on the margin that counterhegemonic cultural practices are developed; it is here that there may be a celebration of the "polyphonic nature of critical discourse" (1990: 133).

In this chapter, we place the "politics of domination" at the core of our analysis. In particular, we examine the centrality of power to the understanding of homelessness by applying the theory of structured violence to the production and reproduction of populations of homeless youth. We also examine the regimes of social control which operate to propel young people onto the streets of the world's cities and which continue to shape and constrain their lives once on the streets. We contrast this against the various forms of resistance adopted by young people who are routinely subjected to an array of violent acts. We argue that young people are subjected to regimes of social control once on the streets, and that criminalization of homeless youth is one outcome of the dialectic processes of control and resistance, and that killing (or execution) of "surplus populations" of homeless youth can be understood as the culmination of these processes. We argue that such executions represent the triumph of individual and State agencies of social control over the resistant strategies of youth.

THE DEFINITION AND SCOPE OF HOMELESSNESS

How do we define homelessness? A review of the literature relating to homelessness shows a lack of consensus amongst researchers as to the definition of homelessness (Robertson and Greenblatt, 1992). In earlier research, homelessness appeared to relate mainly to the experience of men. In the United States, the "hobos" of the 1920s were defined as "homeless" although most had addresses and places in which to sleep. They were referred to as "homeless" because they were adult males living outside a normative family structure. As Shlay and Rossi (1992: 131) observe: Having a place to live with family made a house into a home. Without a place and family to live with, a man was homeless.

In much of the contemporary research, homelessness is defined as a condition or situation. Definitions of the "homeless" include "those who sleep in shelters, or on the street, in vehicles, or abandoned buildings" (Shinn, 1992: 1). "Homelessness" is defined as "a state of living in which [young people] do not rent or own or have customary and regular access to a conventional dwelling" (McCarthy and Hagan, 1992b: 413). Rotherum-Borus, Koopman and Ehrhardt (1991: 1188) assert that: Homeless youth includes those who left their homes without consent (runaways), those thrown out of home (throwaways), those who leave problematic social service placements (system kids), and those lacking basic shelter (street kids).   Other researchers define runaway and homeless youth as those "who live without the support of traditional societal structures, such as family, school, church, and community institutions" (Farrow, Deisher, Brown, Kulig and Kipke, 1992: 717).   There is also reference to the "literal homeless" who sleep in shelters, or on the street, in cars or abandoned buildings (Rossi, 1989).

An increasing trend in contemporary research is to portray homelessness as an experience rather than a personal attribute, condition, or situation.   Robertson and Greenblatt (1992) note that development of the concept of homelessness as "experience" has emphasized the longitudinal aspect of homelessness rather than as simply an individual's status at any one point in time.

In line with this trend, distinctions have been drawn between different stages of homelessness.   Belcher, Scholler-Jaquish, and Drummond (1991) identify three stages of homelessness: marginal, recent, and chronic.   Chamberlain and MacKenzie (1993) also identify three separate temporal concepts associated with youth homelessness. In their schema, the experience of homelessness is not seen as a static condition, but one that shifts and changes under the influence of time spent out of "home."   In viewing homelessness as "experience" rather than "condition," Chamberlain and MacKenzie (1993) identify the following three temporal concepts: first, the permanent break from home and family; second, short-term homelessness involving at least one night away from home, but not involving a period of time sufficient to change self-identity; and, third, chronic homelessness involving the adaptation of the young person to homelessness as a "way of life" leading to significant changes in self-identity.

The recent National Inquiry into Homeless Children in Australia (1989), convened by the Human Rights and Equal Opportunity Commission, defined homelessness as "a lifestyle which includes insecurity and transiency of shelter."   Further, the Commission declared that homelessness "is not confined to a lack of shelter...[but] signifies a state of detachment from family and a vulnerability to dangers including exploitation and abuse broadly defined, from which the family normally protects a child. "

For the purposes of this chapter, we adopt the following definition of homelessness. Homelessness is an experience based on *exclusion* (voluntary or involuntary) from traditional societal institutions, including family, education, employment, Church, and State and community services. This experience of exclusion is accompanied by the loss or abandonment of accommodation in the private domain. The experience of homelessness is characterized by significant risk to physical and psychological well-being. Indeed, victimization is integral to the experience of homelessness (Burke and Hatty, 1994; Davis, Hatty and Burke, 1995; Hatty and Davis, 1994). This is similar to the definition of homelessness proposed by Barak (1994: 897), who states, "Homelessness refers to a marginalized condition of detachment from society and to the lack of bonds that connect settled persons to a network of institutions and social orders. "

COUNTING THE HOMELESS

It is difficult to assess accurately the number of homeless people in the United States due to the high level of politicization within social science research on homelessness (Shlay and Rossi, 1992). Counting the homeless is a political exercise, with advocates believing that there is a need to show startlingly high numbers of homeless, particularly of those considered to be the "worthy homeless" deserving of intervention and support (Wright, 1988; Rossi, 1987).

Consequently, precise numbers of homeless are impossible to gauge. The World Health Organization (1993) claims that, worldwide, there are approximately 100 million children who live on city streets without care or shelter. Within the United States, it is claimed that, each year, there are approximately 2 million homeless and runaway youth (Podschun, 1993). It has been estimated in a national study in the United States that, "in 31 medium and large-sized cities, an average of more than 7,000 people are homeless ... this includes 60,000 in New York City alone" (Morse, 1992: 3). Other large metropolitan areas in the United States also show high figures, including Los Angeles with approximately 40,000 homeless (Leavitt, 1992). It is claimed that Canadian cities have approximately 150,000 homeless youth (Radford, King, and Warren, 1990).

In Australia, the Human Rights and Equal Opportunity Commission (1989) estimated that between 50,000 and 70,000 youth were homeless, or in danger of becoming homeless. The Youth Refuge Association estimated in 1991 that in New South Wales there were between 20,000 to 25,000 young people, aged 12-18 years seeking accommodation because of homelessness (Coffey and Wadelton, 1991). This number does not include those living in squats, sleeping outdoors, living in temporary accommodation, and the like.

Irrespective of the controversy surrounding the definition of homelessness and the size of the homeless population, the presence of adults and children on the streets of the world's cities remains a critical social problem.

HOMELESSNESS: THE INTERNATIONAL CONTEXT

In the United States, changes in the structure of the labor market, the effects of recession, reduced social welfare programs, deinstitutionalization of the mentally ill, and contraction of the available low-cost housing stock have all contributed to the burgeoning of the "new homeless" population (Elliott and Krivo, 1991; Robertson and Greenblatt, 1992), comprised of a heterogeneous collection of women, young people, children, and individuals with social and psychological difficulties (Simons and Whitbeck, 1991). The conditions of inequality which laid the foundation for the escalation of this social problem have continued to multiply (Barak, 1994). During the 1990s, the United States has embraced a "new conservativism." Speaking of this "new conservative hegemony," Lawrence Grossberg (1992: 313,316) observes that:

> Enormous changes, many with devastating consequences, have taken place in the political, economic, cultural and social life of the United States during the past decade. The leading definition of the agenda of U.S. politics and the trajectory of U.S. society have been transformed. Relations of inequality, domination and oppression, many of which were beginning to be dismantled, have become the taken-for-granted structure of social organization.

These structures of inequality and oppression receive their expression in new-found levels of disadvantage. Child poverty has continued to rise during the 1980s, reaching a peak in 1995. Poverty now reportedly affects nine million U.S. children, and it has been estimated that nearly one in four U.S. children now live in poverty. The latest data from the US Census Bureau indicates that approximately half the population of African American children is living below the poverty line. Moreover, over fifty percent of African American children living in rural and urban areas are classified as poor, and about thirty-five percent of these children living in suburban areas are regarded as poor. Over two-thirds of impoverished African American children live in female-headed households, and over a quarter of African American children spend between eleven and seventeen years in poverty (see Davis and Hatty, in press). Income inequality between minority groups, and the predominantly white economic elites, and between men and women, have significantly increased the problem of homelessness in U.S. society. High levels of unemployment, family breakdown, and reduced welfare benefits provide the social and economic context for the marginalization and exclusion associated with homelessness.

In Australia, contributants to the homelessness problem include economic recessions, loss of manufacturing jobs, changes in welfare policy and provision, trends toward deinstitutionalization, and the widening gap between the wealthy and the poor. In both the U.S. and Australia, *youth* homelessness is embroiled in debates about children's rights, parental and State responsibilities, and rational choice models of crime and deviance. In Australia, at present, a Commonwealth Parliamentary Committee is inquiring into the problem of youth homelessness. This follows on the heels of a national inquiry conducted in 1989 by the Human Rights and Equal Opportunity Commission.

In Britain, homeless people have proliferated on the streets of London and other large cities. The deregulation of the labor market and the erosion of the legislative and industrial frameworks which protected the rights of workers have been associated with marked rises in unemployment and big decreases in wage rates for the manual and unskilled labor force. The welfare state, systematically dismantled in Thatcher's Britain, no longer provides a safety net for the poor and the disadvantaged. There are now more children living in poverty in Britain than in any other European country, with the exception of Portugal and Ireland. Phillip Knightley (1994: 10) asserts that "Britain is the first industrialized nation to go into decline;" "the homeless have reappeared on the streets of London like ghosts from a Dickensian past," and that "crime is rife," with the return of the "highwayman and the footpad [mugger]."

In France, the social response to the growing number on homeless people living on the streets of Paris has been the formation of a special police squad. This police squad, nicknamed Les Bleus because of their blue uniforms, patrols the streets of Paris at night and identifies individuals who are deemed to be homeless ("sans domicile fixe"). The police then place these individuals on a bus and take them beyond the limits of the city to a hospital in the suburbs. One homeless man, watching the police activity in the Metro, commented, "It's repression. It's like something from last century" (cited in Keane, 1993: 10).

In other countries, the poor, the disenfranchised, and the homeless are not so fortunate. In places such as Colombia and Brazil, those living on the street including young, unaccompanied children, are systematically killed by death squads drawn from the ranks of police, private security firms, or the community. In these countries, the State is instrumental in creating a climate in which the solution to the social problem of homelessness is murder (Huggins, 1993; Buchanan, 1994).

VIOLENCE, VICTIMIZATION AND THE STREETS

Most street children describe major losses in their lives.
Many have lost family members through.... murder, and
even death squads.

World Health Organization,
Geneva, 1993.

The fact is that there are homeless children and young people dying
in Australia... This is not something our nation can ignore.

Brian Burdekin,
Chair of the National Inquiry into Homeless Children,
Human Rights and Equal Opportunity Commission, 1989.

Why are so many children living on the streets of the world's cities? In order to answer this question, we need to address issues of power, violence and social control. We argue in this chapter that a theory of structured violence which underscores the institutionalized and routine nature of the abuse of those who lack social power is relevant to our understanding of homelessness.

A theory of structured violence is premised on the idea that those who are devoid of certain forms of *social* power (for example, economic power) are subjected to social and individual control. This control often assumes the form of violence (physical, sexual and psychological). These regimes of control are typical of societies saturated with anxiety about distinctions between self and Other. Those who are deemed to differ from the dominant social group in important respects (and this might include women, racial minorities, the poor and children) acquire the label of Other. The category of Other becomes the repository of qualities and characteristics that the dominant group wishes to disown or reject. These qualities or characteristics are those defined as negative in society. Consequently, the Other is often described as irrational, lazy, emotional, unreliable, wicked, feminine, and, often, not fully human. The defining characteristic of the Other is lack—an absence of those qualities that are valued in society. Those groups (and individuals) perceived as Other are generally viewed as homogeneous, and yet lesser and mysterious. Cornel West (1993: 210) refers to the "homogenizing impulse" which underlies dominant discourse about groups defined as Other—in this instance, African-Americans. The tendency to collapse differences obscures the effects of class, gender and sexual orientation; according to West (p. 211), it also "overlooks how racist treatment vastly differs owing to class, gender, sexual orientation, nation, region, hue, and age."

For those defined as Other, specific regimes of discipline and control are invoked to ensure the perpetuation of existing social structures and relations, and to dissipate the anxiety associated with the presence of the Other in the midst of the dominant social group. The pervasive imbalance of power between the dominant social group and those viewed as outside or beyond this social group permits and legitimizes the application of violent forms of control, and perpetuates and exacerbates both inequality and suffering amongst the powerless. The benefits accrued by the dominant social group include enhanced status, coercive authority, obedience, and the gaining of approval or material resources. Such violence is instrumental—rather than expressive—in character (see Campbell, 1993: Campbell and Muncer, 1987, 1994).

Structured violence functions at the corporate and the individual level. The State may utilize various forms of violence to control the activities of its citizens. This may range from acts of physical abuse to full-scale terror (see Barak, 1990). State terror, which flourished in the age of imperialism (Perdue, 1989), assumes many forms. The State may become an instrument designed to intimidate its citizens through fear, or it may become an instrument of torture. Speaking of Colombia, Taussig (1984) refers to the regime of terror which operates in this country. Here, terrorization occurs through physical violence meted out by police and military forces. This violence is often dispensed in public, and instills great apprehension and fear in the population. Within this "space of death" (Taussig, 1984), "there is no civilization, power can be made manifest as unfettered, undisguised force" (Marcus, 1991: 129).

Structured violence also operates at the level of the family unit. Women and children may be subjected to various types of abuse and violence within the family, with this violence being both private and hidden (Graycar and Morgan, 1989; Hatty, 1992a, 1992b, 1993). The interpretation of this violence as a form of social control has been accepted for some time (see Hanmer and Maynard, 1987; Hanmer, Radford, and Stanko, 1989).

The regimes of control involving corporate and individual violence should be regarded as both interrelated and interdependent. The distinction often drawn between public and private violence and violence exercised by State agencies or individuals should not obscure the connections and similarities between these violent behaviors. Control of the threatening and feared Other is the rationale underlying these interlocking strategies of violent imposition.

We argue that the sheer frequency and volume of violence directed at children in the family, and their perceived need to escape in order to survive, is a critical factor in producing youth homelessness. However, as we will show, the attempt to escape the culture of violence—its very embeddedness in the lives of young people—is thwarted by the hazards of street life. For homeless youth, whether living without security or shelter, the search for a safe haven is often futile. Further, in some locations, homeless youth are exposed to an array of harms and injuries which may undermine their physical survival. In some countries, young people are viewed as not only paradigmatic victims (see Davis and Hatty, 1990) but are viewed as less than human—as "social junk."

HOMELESS YOUTH: AN AUSTRALIAN STUDY

This paper draws on three data sets and interprets this data within a qualitative framework. The first data set entails intensive interviews with 105 homeless girls in inner-Sydney (1992), most of whom were living in a refuge (or had previously lived in such settings). Fifty percent of these young women were living in a shelter at the time of the interview; the average number of shelters utilized by this group was eleven. Excluding nine young women who had stayed in 50 or more shelters, there was an average of 5.6 different shelters used by the remaining 71 girls. The age range for the shelter sample was 13-21 years. A typical respondent was between 14 to 18 years. Additional interviews were undertaken with chronically homeless women over the age of 21 years, and young women living in juvenile detention centers in Sydney.

Fourteen young women were living in such centers at the time of the interview. Most of the respondents in the total sample were Anglo-Celtic in origin, and the majority were from metropolitan centers (Sydney or Melbourne). Twenty-two young women were born overseas and had migrated with their parents as children to Australia. Only 9 of the young women were Aboriginal.

The average age for first living on the streets was between 12-15 years, but some young women were homeless at much younger ages, for instance, one was 6 and the other 9 when first on the streets. Almost 60 percent of the young women had been on the street for six months or more. Over 40 percent reported they have been on the streets for over one year, usually moving from one location to another.

The second data set consists of detailed individual profiles of homeless youth (males and females), all of whom were located in a Sydney youth refuge sponsored by the Salvation Army (1993). These profiles were obtained through in-depth interviews. The third data set is comprised of interview data obtained from youth who had moved from Sydney to the far North Coast of New South Wales (1994). These youth were voluntary relocatees and were not living in a shelter of other community agency or institution. These three data sets permit us to compare and contrast the experiences of street life in Australia across different locations (urban and regional centers) and across gender, race, and class. This allows for a more sensitive analysis of the mobile and changeable lifestyle of homeless youth.

Few studies have examined youth homelessness from the perspective of the intersection of gender, race, and class. Also, few studies have utilized a variety of methodological strategies. The focus in this chapter is on the severe dislocation experienced by youth who become homeless, typically through family conflict or violence. We highlight the vulnerability of young people, whose age status often precludes them from adult standards of equity and justice. The experiences of young women, and of Aboriginal youth, highlight the disproportionate hardship and victimization of young people who are marginalized and excluded from the social order.

This analysis is contextualized within an international perspective which takes account of the fact that children and youth in some countries are marked out for death. Hence, we interpret the victimization experiences of homeless youth as located along a continuum of violence, ranging from sporadic and mildly injurious assault to systematic killing.

VIOLENT BEGINNINGS

Violence is endemic to the lives of runaway and homeless youth. Frequently, the violence has been a staple feature of the family experiences of these youth. The homeless young women interviewed in the inner-Sydney study reported extraordinarily high levels of violence in their families of origin. Approximately 65 percent of the young women stated that they had been physically abused within the family, about 43 percent by their father. Half of the girls interviewed said that they had been sexually abused, the majority by fathers or stepfathers. Over 80 percent of the young women claimed that they had been emotionally abused by family members. The comments of the young women illustrate the severity of the violence and the impact it had upon them: "I'd get bashed or locked in my room if I did something wrong. I was always afraid to talk to my parents in case I got flogged." Another young woman said: "I'd hide under the bed 'cause I was afraid Dad would bash me. He's dead now. When he died, it was as if the whole world lifted. He can't hurt me any more." Other young women were aware of the negative consequences of sexual abuse. One young woman in inner-Sydney commented on the role that this abuse had played in shaping her life: "I had no privacy. I didn't belong to me. My uncle would come on to me all the time. I had to get out." Young men, too, report that experiences of violence in the family are a catalyst to fleeing the home. Research indicates that boys are also terrorized within the family and that boys are deeply affected by this victimization. Interviews with homeless young men uncover the extensive histories of abuse and violence within this group; clearly, these experiences prove to be so intolerable that life on the streets is preferable. Two homeless young men living on the far North Coast of New South Wales reflect on their experiences of abuse at the hands of family members: "I lived with my mum and stepfather until he walked out on us when I was fourteen. He was an arsehole. He used to bash me and my older sister when he has drunk, although he left the other kids in the family alone. He also used to bash my mum and she had to go to hospital a couple of times. He put me in hospital twice as well as my older sister." "When my parents split up, I moved in with dad. He was drinking pretty heavily, getting pissed most nights. He started belting into me just like he used to belt into my mum and sister, and I shot through. I just couldn't cop it any longer."

Individuals subjected to child abuse may respond to this experience in a variety of ways, for example, children and adolescents may engage in behaviors which have the effect of removing them from the abusive situation, either psychologically or physically. International research studies show that girls, victimized in the home, will often respond to this abuse by running away. Chesney-Lind and Shelden (1993) reviewed several studies which found that between two-thirds and three-quarters of runaway girls in shelters or juvenile detention facilities had been sexually abused. In addition, the percentage of girls who had been physically abused was high. The authors concluded that there was a strong positive correlation between the girls' victimization and their runaway behaviors. Hence, it should not surprise us that homeless girls and young women frequently report physical and sexual abuse in their families of origin. Nor should it surprise us that these young women believe that fleeing from the abusive situation is the only viable option available to them. Consequently, due to the lack of resources to assist young women running from violent homes, these young people often find themselves living on the street.

The Street Children Project coordinated in ten countries by the World Health Organization (1993: 3) reported that, "Most street children describe major losses in their lives....Although poverty and rapid urbanization are major contributing factors to the problem of street children, many children claim that physical and sexual abuse were the reasons for their leaving home."

The presence of abuse and maltreatment in the backgrounds of runaway youth has been documented by many researchers. The experience of physical or sexual abuse has often been cited as the reason why young people leave home (Burgess, Janus, McCormick, and Wood, 1986; Kurtz, Kurtz, and Jarvis, 1991). In a recent study, it was noted that there is "clear evidence that the families of homeless youth tend to be characterized by parent-child conflict, discipline problems, physical and sexual abuse, lack of affection and caring, and substance abuse" (Dadds, Braddock, Cuers, Elliott and Kelly, 1993: 414). It has been suggested that a substantial proportion of the homeless youth population are victims of parental abuse: "evidence demonstrates that more than half the current runaway and homeless youth population are victims of physical abuse, neglect, or sexual abuse... For most of these young people, running is a means of survival" (Powers, 1990: 9). In the United States, running away is a serious offense for young people, punishable by arrest and incarceration (Jones, 1988). Young women make up sixty-three percent of young people appearing in juvenile court charged with running away from home (Chesney-Lind and Shelden, 1993). In similar circumstances in Australia, young women may be declared wards of the State. Where this occurs, young women may be held in an institution. Other young women may be referred to overburdened accommodation services (Quixley, 1990). However, many Australian states are pursuing a policy of deinstitutionalization, with the removal of State wards from "care" at age 16 years, or thereabouts. New South Wales is currently closing many of its juvenile institutions, and "relocating" the young inmates to community-based placements. Many young wards of the State are lost to the system. Their whereabouts are unknown. The vulnerability of these young women cannot be overestimated. As Howe notes (1990: 49): "[Young women] are policed in everyday life...they are sanctioned in their families more than boys...they are policed by boys (and other girls) outside their family and they are policed by a male-centered language focusing on their sexuality."

Consequently, deinstitutionalization may not bring freedom to young women, as the status of "girl" is already subject to surveillance, discipline, and control in society (see Foucault, 1977). Young women may find themselves without social support or protection from the risks of living on the streets.

HITTING THE STREETS

A major hurdle in coping with street life is gaining an understanding of what constitutes appropriate behavior. Being tough, being independent, minding your own business, never reporting crime or violence to the police, keeping your personal belongings with you at all times, being loyal to mates, and above all being ever-vigilant are standard approaches to the challenges of the streets. The adoption of this disposition is essential to the survival of those youth who find themselves on the streets.

THE CODES OF THE STREET

In addition to this "attitude of the street" there are behavioral norms which the newcomer must quickly adopt in order to conform with established street etiquette. These are not rules, for on the street there are no rules. A young man living "on the streets" of a Northern New South Wales town said: "You just do your best. Try not to shit on anybody else that's on the street, watch your back, and keep out of trouble. Keep out of the way of the cops, but most important is 'watch your back.' One young woman told us: "You should always be on the alert to things happening around you. Be cool when the police come around. Just keep your mouth shut. Like if you know something's illegal you don't go to the police or nothing." Two young women in Northern New South Wales advised: "Don't tell anyone anything. It's pretty basic really...keep your fuckin' mouth shut and don't talk out of school." "I just act stupid...I know nothing. If I get questioned by anybody about anything, unless I know them real well, I just plead idiot."

SURVIVING ON THE STREET

Taking up illegal or deviant activities appears to be an integral part of a "street lifestyle." Deviance and crime may be directly related to survival mechanisms learned on the street. For example, homeless youth may rely on drug sales to provide an income and to support a drug habit. A Northern New South Wales youth told us:

> I'm not on the dole [social security] cause it's too much of a
> hassle to register and shit; besides that I need to have a
> permanent address and that. I sell a bit of pot [cannabis] and
> that keeps me going. Some of my friends deal also, but
> they're doing it to support habits. I've never touched the gear
> [heroin] so I don't have that problem.

Other youth speak of the means they have employed to obtain money:

> I prefer to thieve rather than anything else. Stereos out of
> parked cars and stuff, I've done a couple of bag snatches and
> stuff like that too. I also get a job search allowance [Social
> Security Payment], but you can't live on that. You can
> sometimes rip the tourists off on pot deals too, but you have
> to be a bit careful not to rip the wrong person.

A young person may have a prior history of conflict with the law.
Although many of the young women we spoke to in inner-Sydney were
more likely to be victims than to be offenders, contact with police,
court, and detention were fairly common occurrences. Seventy-eight
percent of the young women we interviewed had been involved with the
police, for a variety of reasons, for example, arrests for status offenses
or criminal acts, and for welfare/protection reasons.

Indeed, there are two possible interpretations of the relationship
between crime, violence and street life: deviance and illegal behavior
may be an outcome of running away and subsequent homelessness; or,
on the contrary, homelessness may be an outcome of previous deviant
and illegal involvement.

We can examine our data for an understanding of these two
alternatives. First, most of the young women we interviewed had
experienced some deviant involvement prior to leaving home and living
on the streets. For instance, before their movement into street life,
over half had engaged in shoplifting, 15 percent had sold drugs, 35
percent had stolen property worth $50 or more, and 19 percent had
committed forgery. This pattern of crime and deviance was especially
pronounced among the older homeless girls, and those girls sampled
while in the detention center.

Second, after moving to the streets, this pattern of illegal behavior
was exacerbated for many of the young women. Sixty-eight percent
admitted to shoplifting, 37 percent to regularly selling drugs, 56

percent to being involved in theft, almost 27 percent to having committed forgery, 70 percent to fighting, and most notably, almost 40 percent claimed to have used weapons.

Research on Canadian homeless youth conducted by McCarthy and Hagan (1992a, 1992b) points to the need to consider situational factors in making sense of delinquency and crime committed by street youth. For those youth who have been on the street for an extended period of time (six months or more), the absence of a permanent shelter, predictable supply of food or money is significantly associated with the commission of crime. In this regard, homeless youth resemble homeless adults. However, McCarthy and Hagan (1991) found that the relationship between crime and homelessness is complex. They reported that although a sizeable proportion of those surveyed participated in a number of illegal activities (most of them minor delinquencies) before leaving home, a significantly higher proportion of adolescents were involved in more serious criminal activities since leaving home. Levels of crime showed fairly serious increases for older street youth (16 years and up) and for those whose homelessness lasted more than a year. McCarthy and Hagan (1991) believe that street life is inherently "criminogenic" in that it provides both opportunities for criminal offending as well as the necessity to commit criminal acts in order to survive. McCarthy and Hagan (1991: 408) conclude that, "there is compelling evidence of an interactive relationship between illegal activity and the length of the current homeless episode." Hence, in general, the longer the time on the street, the greater the involvement in crime.

Whilst only a small proportion of the young women we interviewed stated that they were currently involved in sex work, about one out of three girls indicated that they had been involved in prostitution for money while on the streets, and nearly the same number had exchanged sex for drugs. It has been claimed that homeless youth constitute about three-quarters of all young people involved in sex work in the United States (Yates, MacKenzie, Pennbridge and Swofford, 1991). A 16-year-old Sydney girl stated:

> You do what you have to to survive. I left home at 12 because I couldn't handle it there any longer and I've been on the street ever since. I'm trying to support a heroin habit which costs me about $200 a day, and the only way I can do it is by cracking it [prostitution]. In the start, I needed money

> to survive, just to buy food and stuff. One of the other girls put me onto working, but I couldn't fuckin' do it unless I was stoned, it was just too sickening. At first I had to be stoned to work...now I have to work to get stoned.

This pattern contrasts with less street-wise girls who exchanged sex for food or shelter. Regardless of the specific motivation for selling sex, homeless young women involved in prostitution obviously constitute a high-risk group for health problems, especially HIV and the effects of drug abuse. As street prostitution is one of the most dangerous occupations a woman can pursue (Hatty, 1989), this activity places these young women at serious risk of physical and psychological injury, and even death.

Clearly, it is possible that there are two distinct modes of street adaptation regarding sex work. On the one hand, some young women may become involved in crime and deviance, but never or rarely in prostitution. These young women may seek protection from an older male and become part of a crime-dependent street culture. On the other hand, there are some young women who have rarely been involved in serious crime but instead use their bodies as "capital" to negotiate street life. Although only 2 percent of the sample identified themselves as "sex workers," girls who worked on a regular basis were apt to, first, not draw on welfare support; second, live primarily on their prostitution earnings; and, third, have chronic problems with illicit drugs. Indeed, national statistics on drug abuse in Australia show that homeless youth are particularly susceptible to drug and alcohol abuse, especially such illicit drugs as marijuana, barbiturates, cocaine, hallucinogens, heroin, inhalants, and ecstasy. Additionally, widespread use of tranquillizers (78% for "street kids" versus 9% for other youth) has been reported, as well as a very high incidence of self-injected drugs. The National Campaign Against Drug Abuse (NCADA, 1992) survey on "street kids" emphasized that acceptance of drug use was much higher among "street kids"; sixty-two percent of the "street kids" interviewed had self-injected drugs; and the preferred drug amongst the "street kids" was heroin (54%), followed by alcohol (17%) and amphetamines (11%).

The Street Children Project on Substance Abuse, sponsored by the World Health Organization (1993) has revealed that certain groups of children are exploited by local and international drug cartels that require them to participate in the trafficking of cocaine and heroin and hence engage in criminal activity. Further, the Street Children Project has shown that street children rely on licit and illicit drugs to deal with the violent and chaotic nature of their lives: "Everyday [the street children] search for food, shelter and care, often fearful for their lives....The use of drugs is often quoted as a means of coping with this stress, pain and suffering (WHO, 1993: 3)."

The interconnection between "street kids," illicit drugs and crime in the United States has been borne out by research conducted by Inciardi, Horowitz and Pottieger (1993) in Miami, Florida. The authors found that the greater the involvement in dealing in crack cocaine, the greater the involvement in violent crime. In terms of absolute numbers, the 254 youths (of a total of 611 sampled) were responsible for a total of 223,439 criminal offenses during the 12 months prior to the interview, including drug sales (61.1%), property offenses (23.3%), and major felonies (robberies, assaults, burglaries, and motor vehicle thefts) (4.2%) (Inciardi, Horowitz and Pottieger, 1993). The Miami crack trade and its intimate link with serious crime may be an exceptional case; our research shows the young female street population in Sydney to be less affected by deep involvement in a criminal lifestyle. Instead, most engage in episodic crimes, especially drug sales, prostitution and property crimes that sustain their life, as well as their lifestyle (see also Hirst, 1989; Robertson, 1991; Davis, 1992; Neil and Fopp, 1992).

The escalation in crime after a certain period of time on the street supports the assertion that crime may be adopted as a "conditional survival strategy" for coping with the economic and social strains which characterize homelessness (Cohen and Machalek, 1988; see also Stelf, 1987; and Wright, 1989). We need to bear in mind, however, that an overemphasis on criminality and drug abuse among these youth tends to draw attention away from the violent, exploitative and neglectful family and social conditions that precede and surround the criminal behavior.

STREET LIFE AND VIOLENCE

Life on the streets is a hazardous experience for young homeless people. Perhaps the *most* significant danger is the constant exposure to and involvement in violence.

Our interviews with homeless girls in Sydney showed that the most pervasive threat posed by living on the street is violence. The young women described witnessing hundreds of violent episodes "from street gang fights to fights between prostitutes to police beating kids to get them to break off fights." Brawls were commonplace and could erupt when one homeless youth took something from another, or when a young person was known to be associated with a perpetrator. "A girl came up to me and punched me in the face. Then a friend did the same thing. Another time my boyfriend ripped someone off, and we both got bashed up." Echoing the pattern of repeated violence, one young woman said: "Yes, I was forced to have sex. Heaps of times. Before the streets it was violent sex and bondage with my father."

Only 23 percent of our sample had not witnessed violence; over half had witnessed 10 or more violent acts. These were shootings, knifings, fights, beatings, rapes, muggings, death by overdose, and even a homicide. This street violence can come from numerous sources. Other homeless youth may prey on newcomers, clients may harass and assault young sex workers on the street, and drug dealers and others who operate within public space may intimidate and harass young people.

The following comments from the young women in inner-Sydney indicate the extent of the problem:

> I was crashing in a house and these guys broke in. The girl that said I could stay was dealing. The guys were raiding the joint for drugs.

> The most dangerous situation for me? Going to sleep at night, and not knowing if I'll wake up the next morning.

> It's dangerous on the streets. I don't care about anyone on the street—you worry about food, showers, clothes, everything.

VIOLENCE INFLICTED BY STREET PEERS

Often behavioral norms become obvious to the newcomer only when they are violated. Sanctions usually follow an infraction such as turning someone in to the police, stealing dope, crossing a "streetie" in any way. Punishment of a novice may be unexpected, swift, and, occasionally, lethal. Two Sydney girls stated:

Don't lag, don't tell anyone nothing. Don't spread around who's selling drugs, who's doing business. Don't tell police kids' nick-names. Just keep your mouth shut and your eyes open. The less you know the safer you are. Watch your own back, and never tell anyone anything.

For homeless girls living "on the street" the breaking of these codes of conduct means an end to the "adventure" of street life, and an increased awareness of the imminence of violence. This homeless girl spoke out about what happens to those who transgress: "They get punched out. They're not around for long, they just leave the streets or move to somewhere else. They can't handle it. Sometimes they're hurt real bad."

Recourse to violence and other criminal behavior may become essential elements of street survival (Crago, 1991). Thus, routine violence may be viewed as part of the experience of youth who are living on the street, and may involve peers, acquaintances, police, and strangers (Alder and Sandor, 1990; Alder, 1991; Davis, 1993).

VIOLENCE INFLICTED BY STATE AGENCIES

Young people may escape violent homes only to encounter further violence on the streets (Human Rights and Equal Opportunity Commission, 1989). Ian O'Connor (1989) reported to the Australian Human Rights and Equal Opportunity Committee that his research findings "were replete with descriptions of being attacked in all manner of situations and of the ever present danger of violence."

The intensive interviews with 51 homeless youth under the age of 18 conducted by Christine Alder (1991) in Melbourne, Australia, revealed that almost two-thirds had been physically assaulted and half had been sexually assaulted in the previous 12 months. Distinct gender differences in victimization were uncovered: violence between the males generally involved fights, whilst the girls' experience of violence often involved sexual assault (See also Hagen, 1987). Perpetrators of this violence were overwhelmingly male, including the police attackers reported by 47% of the females and 58% of the males (Alder and Sandor, 1990; Alder, 1991). One of the most disturbing findings of Alder's research was the extent to which these young people suffered their violent victimization in silence without seeking assistance or reporting the episodes to authorities.

A significant number of young women (34%) in our inner-city survey experienced police violence (bashings), a few on repeated occasions, especially if they were Aboriginal or members of other minority groups, or if they failed to behave in conventionally feminine ways (e.g. be polite, deferential, softly spoken, and so on). Forty-two percent had been held in custody or detention. Most of the young women reported that they had avoided contact with the police because the police response could be unpredictable. The young women were as likely to be arrested as helped, especially since many of them had been involved in episodes of street crime and violence.

Police harassment and brutality were frequently cited as major reasons why "you can never trust the police." A 16-year-old who reported having 30-40 police contacts talked about her experience of police violence, including the "phone book" technique, which reveals no external signs of injury, but can be extremely painful. She said: "The police bashed me heaps of times. Once they flushed my head down the toilet. They've kicked me in the stomach and threatened me with the phone book until I gave them what they wanted." Another young woman said: "Police bashed me 4 or 5 times. They bash the shit out of you. Keep you in cells. They put telephone books on you and then bash you so it doesn't leave bruises."

Aboriginal youth, in particular, report experiences of victimization at the hands of police. Recent research has revealed that Aboriginal youth state they are subjected to harassment, violence, and racist language during the course of their interaction with police. Aboriginal youth are over-represented in police custody (Cunneen, 1995). Not surprisingly, relations between Aboriginal youth and police are conflictual, and Aboriginal youth of both sexes report a fear of police. Research conducted by Cunneen (1995) showed that police violence directed at Aboriginal youth is endemic to relations between these groups. The majority of youth reporting assault stated that they had been hit by objects, especially police batons. Telephone books were also deployed as instruments of assault. Guns were sometimes produced, pointed at the young person in custody, and occasionally fired. Cunneen (1995: 122) characterized the violence as "often premeditated" and always fear-inducing. It is generally instrumental, aimed at generating admissions whilst the youth is in custody. Racist and sexist language frequently accompany these assaults.

Young people may be at risk of police intervention simply because they spend significant periods of time in public places. Young people who occupy the streets, parks, and commercial areas such as shopping malls may be targets for police intervention. These public places may be construed within law enforcement discourse as sites of danger requiring strict surveillance to prevent crime and violence. The police mandate of maintaining public order and the popular stereotype of young people in groups as potential or active criminals converge to produce police practices which often violate the civil rights of these young people. Police may engage in random "name checking," or officers may question and detain young people without legal justification. Watkins (1992: 31) describes such an incident: "[Police] take them out to the car park, split them up, ask them to stay there, and walk around and interview each one without arresting them, without giving them a reason."

Such techniques of harassment and intimidation can lead to confrontational challenges to the authority of the police. Once a young person demonstrates an apparently disrespectful attitude, the police are more likely to move beyond a simple caution. In a recent survey of the relationship between young people and the police in Australia, it was found that police decision-making was affected by these extra-legal factors. Almost all police officers interviewed (89%) claimed that a young person's "attitude" was an important determinant of the decision to arrest (Alder, O'Connor, Warner, and White, 1992). Consequently, structural factors such as homelessness, poverty, or membership of a youth subculture or a youth gang, may predispose a young person to police intervention, and to stigmatizing modes of informal or formal social control.

This situation is exacerbated for Aboriginal youth in Australia's cities. The police have historically engaged in the forcible removal of Aboriginal people from specific sites of occupation. Further, the police role of maintaining public order has frequently come into conflict with the use of urban, public space by Aboriginal people. Consequently, there is a long tradition of viewing the presence of Aboriginal people in public space as problematic. This renders Aboriginal youth who inhabit public space particularly vulnerable to police intervention. As we have already seen, this intervention is frequently violent and instils great fear within Aboriginal populations.

Indeed, the World Health Organization (WHO) argues that street children and adolescents are exposed to multiple forms of victimization in public places. Ironically, street behaviors involving drug abuse, prostitution, and property crime often jeopardize the youth's return to mainstream society. Regimes of social control, based upon violence, may submerge homeless youth and prevent them from extricating themselves from the street.

Violence perpetrated by State agencies against homeless youth is a staple feature of the political economy of some countries. In Brazil, impoverished children living on the street are routinely killed by agents of the State as well as professional and private citizens. During the period 1988-1991, over 7000 street children and adolescents were murdered. These killings were undertaken by police officers (on and off duty), private security police, and citizen "justicemakers." Contracts for prospective executions were acquired by the lowest bidder. Hit squads were kept on retainer by shop owners and commercial firms. Such activities are met with complacency within Brazil; there is little or no outrage at the extermination of the homeless youth (Huggins, 1993). The culling of street children by government-sponsored death squads continues in Brazil. In 1993, a group of street children were killed by off-duty police in the city of Rio de Janeiro. These children, who were sleeping in shop doorways, were roused from sleep by the promise of food. Upon approaching the individuals who had offered them food, they were shot (*Sydney Morning Herald*, 26 July, 1993). (Notably,the World Health Organization recently reported that fifty-five percent of the street children they had interviewed in Rio de Janeiro had attempted suicide.)

According to BBC television, a similar climate of terror and violence pervades Colombia. Here, death squads comprised of police or private assassins kill all those defined as Other including street children, petty criminals, prostitutes, and homosexuals. The list of target groups is increasing. Now, impoverished workers who earn a meager living from recycling garbage are vulnerable. In Colombia, where six million people live below the poverty line, the center of the capital Bogotá attracts the poor, the destitute, and the homeless. With unemployment at very high levels and no social welfare assistance, this heterogenous gathering of outcasts grows. There are now many thousands of unaccompanied children living within this area.

In Colombia, the poor, destitute, and homeless who inhabit the city streets are characterized as expendable. They are called the "disposables." The death squads which assassinate these people are engaged in what is euphemistically termed "social cleansing." The concept of the disposable human being is well understood by all. The

President of Colombia, Cesar Gaviria, recently defined "disposables" as (Buchanan, 1994): "People who earn no money, have no family, who have no place to live, who [have] no capacity to work.... There are quite [a lot] of people in that situation." Speaking of the extreme dangers facing street children and adolescents, a welfare worker, Father Rigoberto Ramirez recently commented (Buchanan, 1994): "It's the same as always. Boys who have been abused and assaulted, boys with infected wounds [from being shot], there's nowhere to treat them. The State does nothing to protect them. It's as if they are taking away their right to live."

The assassination of the "disposables" generally occurs after nightfall. These killings are undertaken by the police (on and off duty). The Deputy Attorney General of Colombia, Hernando Villa, recently admitted that most of the civil rights violations in Colombia are the responsibility of the police. Several thousand "disposables" are executed every year.

Now, with burgeoning crime rates arising from social dislocation, high unemployment, and a vacuum in social welfare, shop owners are taking matters into their own hands. Private assassins are being hired to "clean up" the streets, and rid districts of homeless people. Twenty death squads operate in the capital, Bogotá. Council vans pick up the corpses and deliver them twice a week to a pauper's graveyard. Here, they are interred in mass graves, their bodies barely covered.

The brother of one youth, killed by an assassin's bullet, said (Buchanan, 1994): "No one helps the disposables. People think by finishing them off, they are solving the problem." Indeed, the representation of the homeless street-dwellers as Other is evident in the following description of the disposables. One shopkeeper noted recently (Buchanan, 1994): "They are like animals. In fact, they are worse than animals." The depiction of the "disposables" as non-human distances the socially powerful group from its target and provides a rationale for social control through the most extreme form of violence—murder.

CONCLUSION

Why are so many children living on the streets of the world's cities? Why are so many children suffering assault, injury, and even death on the streets of the world's cities? What is the relationship between these two questions?

For answers to these questions, we need to refer to the hierarchical organization of society in which power and authority are unevenly distributed. The effect of this disparity in resources is that those with more social power are granted a license to engage in conduct which will secure and confirm their positional advantage. Those who are disadvantaged, by virtue of their lack of material or social assets, are vulnerable to the intrusion of sanctioning behaviors. Women, the poor, the disenfranchised and children are particularly at risk of exposure to behaviors intended to influence and sometimes constrain their belief systems, their self-perceptions, and their ability to exercise freedom of choice. This receives its expression in the regimes of social control which range across a continuum of violence (from minimal to severe, sporadic to constant) and which shape and limit the behaviors of homeless persons, especially homeless youth.

Homeless young people are subjected to multiple forms of social control. Within the family of origin, many of these youth are abused. Violence—physical, sexual, and emotional—is often the mechanism used to exert control over their behavior. This violence engenders long-lasting traumatic effects. Attempting to escape from the source of abuse is a typical response to the constant application of control through violence. Leaving home may thus be a gesture of resistance to the imposition of violent forms of social control.

The street is an environment in which sanctioning practices proliferate. Street codes—defined by the inhabitants of the street—mold behaviors; infraction of these codes brings swift retribution. Of course, males who inhabit the street exert various forms of control over other males, women, and children to ensure both behavioral predictability and conformity to gender-appropriate norms. Drug dealers, and others involved in the illicit economy, utilize a hierarchy of punitive sanctions to underscore their authority and induce obedience to the codes of the street. For young, minority males, the streets may prove to be an extremely hazardous location (see Davis and Hatty, in press). For young women, there are few places of belonging or of safety. Permitted only conditional access to public space and subjected to strategies of violence and control, young women continue to be victimized.

Official state agencies impose bureaucratic forms of social control upon young people. Law enforcement agents and welfare workers intervene frequently in the lives of homeless youth. Police patrol public space and regulate behavior according to the dictates of public law and order agendas. Young homeless people report that police use various mechanisms to contain and control youth behavior—questioning youth, asking for identification, moving youth from place to place, interrogating youth regarding deviant and criminal activity, and, of course, arrest and charging of the young person. For some youth, especially Aboriginal youth, these interactions with the police involve violence. Indeed, these routinized forms of intervention may be viewed as the institutionalized expression of instrumental violence; that is, violence enacted to achieve particular outcomes, ranging from a "confession" to the dispensing of summary justice. Some commentators contend that the criminalization of Aboriginal youth may be regarded as an extension—in both political, social, and historical terms—of the earlier state policies of genocide (see Cunneen, 1995).

Welfare agencies also police the street, scouring the streets for runaways and youth "lost to the system." The large number of state wards living on the streets of the inner-Sydney rarely intersect with these welfare professionals, and the welfare system, in general, has little or no official knowledge regarding the whereabouts of these youth.

Further, youth in some countries are exposed to a public culture of terror. State regimes, through their military and police forces, may . dispense violence in the streets as a means to subdue and control citizens. Individuals bearing the stigmatized label of Other may be defined as expendable—as "disposables."

Homeless youth may be subjected to a myriad of violent behaviors —from assault by individuals to State-sponsored extermination campaigns. This cluster of victimization experiences extends from the home to the street, enclosing the young person within a web of violence extending over time and space.

Youth living on the street resist these forms of social control in a variety of ways. These acts of resistance are sometimes successful, permitting the youth to define and articulate their own reality and enact the behaviors that they deem appropriate and rewarding. Other times, these strategies of resistance are less successful and young people may find their opportunities and behaviors severely curtailed. This applies particularly to the less socially powerful members of the homeless youth population, for example, the very young and those from minority groups. These individuals are less equipped to successfully resist the various forms of social control applied to them and are more likely to be victimized. These forms of victimization may range from abuse meted out by street peers, pimps, dealers and others to extreme violence perpetrated by police and other agents of social control. It may even include death at the hands of the State.

The formalized authority vested with police and, to a lesser extent, welfare authorities, is more difficult for youth to resist. Once in the clutches of police whether on the street or at the station—youth are caught up in an almost inevitable process of deviance amplification. Criminalization of homeless youth is one outcome of this dialectical process of control and resistance. The execution of homeless youth represents the victory of State agencies of social control—and sometimes "community" groups—over the defiant and resistant strategies of youth. The production of "disappearances," and the construction of the "space of death" (see Taussig, 1984), confirms the ascendancy of the State dedicated to obedience, conformity, and "clean streets."

NOTE

1.   This paper is a revised version of that presented at the American Society of Criminology conference, Miami, Florida, November 9-12, 1994.

REFERENCES

Alder, C. 1991. Victims of Violence: The Case of Homeless Youth. *Australian and New Zealand Journal of Criminology* (March) 24:1-14.

Alder, C. and Sandor, D. 1990. Homeless Youth as Victims of Violence. Report available from Criminology Department, University of Melbourne.

Alder, C. O'Connor, I. Warner, K., and White, R. 1992. Perceptions of the Treatment of Juveniles in the Legal System. Canberra: National Youth Affairs Research Scheme.

Barak, G. 1990. Resisting State Criminality and the Struggle for Justice, in Barak, G. (ed.). *Crimes by the Capitalist State.* New York: State University of New York Press.

Barak, G. 1991. *Gimme Shelter: A Social History of Homelessness in Contemporary America.* New York: Praeger.

Barak, G. 1994. Homelessness, in M. Adams (ed). *Magill's Survey of Social Science: Sociology.* New York: Salem.

Belcher, J.R., Scholler-Jaquish, A. and Drummond, M. 1991. Three Stages of Homelessness: A Conceptual Model for Social Workers in Health Care. *Health and Social Work.* 16, May, 87-93.

Buchanan, E. 1994. The Disposables: Social Cleansing in Colombia. *News and Current Affairs, BBC Television.*

Burgess, A., Janus, M., McCormick, A., and Wood, J. 1986. Canadian Runaways: Youth in Turmoil and Running for Their Lives. Paper presented at the Symposium on Street Youth, Toronto.

Burke, S., and Hatty, S.E. 1994. Victimizing Deviant Youth: The Case of Ferals in Northern New South Wales. Paper presented at the 8th International Symposium on Victimology, Adelaide, Australia, 21-26 August.

Campbell, A. 1993. *Men, Women and Aggression.* New York: Basic Books.

Campbell, A., and Muncer, S. 1987. Models of Anger and Aggression in the Social Talk of Women and Men. *Journal for the Theory of Social Behaviour,* 17: 489-512.

Campbell, A., and Muncer, S. 1994. Men and the Meaning of Violence, in J. Archer (ed). *Male Violence.* London: Routledge.

Chamberlain, C., and McKenzie, D. 1993. Temporal Dimensions of Youth Homelessness. Paper presented at the conference, Rethinking Policies for Young People: Towards a National Perspective. Melbourne, Australia, 14-16 April.

Chesney-Lind, M., and Shelden, R.G. 1993. *Girls, Delinquency, and Juvenile Justice.* Pacific Grove, California : Brooks/Cole.

Coffey, M., and Wadelton, D. 1991. *Shelter and the Streets: A Statistical Survey of Homeless Youth in New South Wales.* Youth Accommodation Association, NSW.

Cohen, L., and Machalek, R. 1988. A General Theory of Expropriative Crime: An Evolutional Ecological Approach. *American Journal of Sociology,* 94: 465-499.

Crago, H. 1991. Homeless Youth: How the Solution Becomes Part of the Problem. *Quadrant,* 35(9): 26-32.

Cunneen, C. 1995. Aboriginal Young People's Experiences in Police Custody. C. Simpson and R. Hall (eds.). *Ways of Resistance.* Sydney: Hale and Iremonger.

Dadds, M.R., Braddock, D., Cuers, S., Elliott, A., and Kelly, A. 1993. Distress of Homeless Adolescents. *Community Mental Health Journal*, 29(5): 413-422.

Davis, N.J. 1992. Offender as Victim: The Case of Homeless Female Youth. Public Lecture, Institute of Criminology, University of Sydney, Australia, May 5.

Davis, N.J. 1993. Systemic Gender Control and Victimization Among Homeless Female Youth. *Socio-Legal Bulletin*, Number 8 (Summer).

Davis, N.J., and Hatty, S.E. 1990. Violence Against Prostitute Women: A Paradigmatic Case of Sexism. Paper presented at the Annual Meeting of the American Society of Criminology, Baltimore, Maryland.

Davis, N.J., and Hatty, S.E. (in press). Revisioning Justice: The Case of Young African American Men. *Journal of African American Men.*

Davis, N.J., Hatty, S.E., and Burke, S. 1995. Rough Justice: Social Control and Resistance Amongst Homeless Youth, in Simpson, C. and Hil, R. (eds.). *Ways of Resistance.* Sydney: Hale and Iremonger.

Elliot, M., and Krivo, L.J. 1991. Structural Determinants of Homelessness in the United States. *Social Problems*, 38(1): 113-131.

Farrow, J.A., Deisher, R.W., Brown, R., Kulig, J.W., and Kipke, M.D. 1992. Health and Health Needs of Homeless and Runaway Youth. *Journal of Adolescent Health*, 13: 717-726.

Foscarinis, M. 1991. The Politics of Homelessness. *American Psychologist*, 46, 11, 1232-1238.

Foucault, M. 1977. *Discipline and Punish.* New York: Vintage Books.

Goodman, L., Saxe, L., and Harvey, M. 1991. Homelessness as Psychological Trauma. *American Psychologist*, 46(11): 1219-1225.

Graycar, R., and Morgan, J. 1989. *The Hidden Gender of Law.* Annandale: Federation Press.

Grossberg, L. 1992. *We Gotta Get Out of This Place: Popular Conservatism and Postmodern Culture.* New York: Routledge.

Hagen, J.L. 1987. Gender and Homelessness. *Social Work*, 32(4): 312-316.

Hanmer, J., and Maynard, M.(eds). 1987. *Women, Violence and Social Control*. London: Macmillan.

Hanmer, J., Radford, J., and Stanko, E.A.(eds). 1989. *Women, Policing, and Male Violence*. London: Routledge.

Hatty, S. E. 1989. Violence Against Prostitute Women: Social and Legal Dilemmas. *Australian Journal of Social Issues*, 24(4): 235-251.

Hatty, S.E. 1992a. The Continuum of Unsafety: Violence Against Women. Proceedings of the Local Domestic Violence Committees Conference Sydney: Women's Co-ordination Unit, NSW Ministry for Education, Youth and Women's Affairs.

Hatty, S.E. 1992b. The Social Structural Context of Violence, in T. Jagenberg and P. D'Alton (eds). *Four Dimensional Social Space: Class, Gender, Ethnicity and Nature*. Sydney: Harper Educational.

Hatty, S.E. 1993. Invisible Lives: Women, Dependence and the Law, in P. W. Easteal and S. McKillop (eds). *Women and the Law*. Canberra: Australian Institute of Criminology.

Hatty, S.E., and Davis, N.J. 1994. No Exit: Violence, Gender and the Streets. Paper presented at the 8th International Symposium on Victimology, Adelaide, Australia, 21-26 August.

Hirst, C. 1989. Forced Exit: A Profile of the Young and Homeless in Inner Urban Melbourne, Melbourne. Report of the Salvation Army Youth Homelessness Policy Development Project, Melbourne.

Honig, M., and Filler, R.K. 1993. Causes of Intercity Variations in Homelessness. *The American Economic Review*, 83: 248-255.

hooks, b. 1990. *Yearning: Race, Gender and Cultural Politics*. Boston: South End Press.

Howe, A. 1990. Sweet Dreams: Reinstitutionalizing Young Women, in Graycar, R. (ed.). *Dissenting Opinions, Feminist Explorations of Law and Society*. Sydney: Allen and Unwin, 40-57.

Huggins, M. 1993. Lost Childhoods: Assassinations of Youth in Democratizing Brazil. Paper presented at the American Sociological Association Conference.

Human Rights and Equal Opportunity Commission (1989). Report of the National Inquiry into Homeless Children. Canberra: Australian Government Publishing Service.

Inciardi, J.A., Horowitz, R., and Pottieger, A.E. 1993. *Street Kids, Street Drugs, Street Crime.* Belmont CA: Wadsworth Publishing Company.

Jones, L.P. 1988. A Typology of Adolescent Runaways. *Child and Adolescent Social Work Journal*, 5(1): 16-29.

Keane, L. 1993. Back to the Brink. *New Statesman and Society*, 6, April 2, 1012 (supplement).

Knightley, P. 1994. Goodbye to Great Britain. *The Australian Magazine, The Australian Newspaper*, April 2-3,8-18.

Kurtz, P.D., Kurtz, G.L., and Jarvis, S.V. 1991. Problems of Maltreated Runaway Youth. *Adolescence*, 26(103): 543-555.

Leavitt, J. 1992. Homelessness and the Housing Crisis, in Robertson, M.J., and Greenblatt, M., (eds.). *Homelessness: A National Perspective.* New York: Plenum Press, 19-35.

Marcus, J. 1991. Under the Eye of the Law. *Journal for Social Justice Studies*, 4: 117-132.

McCarthy, B., and Hagan, J. 1991. Homelessness: A Criminogenic Situation? *British Journal of Criminology*, 31 (4): 393-410.

McCarthy, B., and Hagan, J. 1992a. Mean Streets: The Theoretical Significance of Situational Delinquency Amongst Homeless Youths. *American Journal of Sociology*, 98(3): 597-627.

McCarthy, B., and Hagan, J. 1992b. Surviving on the Street: The Experiences of Homeless Youth. *Journal of Adolescent Research*, 7(4): 412-430.

Morse, G.A. 1992. Causes of Homelessness, in Robertson, M.J., and Greenblatt, M. (eds.). *Homelessness: A National Perspective.* New York: Plenum Press, 3-19.

National Campaign Against Drug Abuse (1992). Street Kids: Survey Findings. Statistics on Drug Abuse in Australia. Commonwealth of Australia: Department of Health, Housing and Community Services.

Neil, C. and Fopp, R. 1992. *Homeless in Australia: Causes and Consequences.* Victoria: C.S.I.R.O. Division of Building, Construction and Engineering.

O'Connor, I. 1989. Our Homeless Children: Their Experiences. Report to the Human Rights and Equal Opportunity Commission, Sydney.

Perdue, W. 1989. *Terrorism and The State : A Critique of Domination Through Fear.* New York: Praeger.

Podschun, G.D. 1993. Teen-Peer Outreach Street Work Project. *Public Health Reports*, 108, Mar/April, 150-155.

Powers, J.L.L. 1990. Survivors of Abuse Tell Their Stories. *Human Ecology Forum*, 18:8-11.

Quixley, S. 1990. *Whose Children? Responding to Homeless Under 16 Year Olds.* Adelaide: South Australian Youth Housing Network Inc.

Radford, J.L., King, A., and Warren, W.K. 1990. *Street Youth and AIDS.* Kingston, Ontario: Queen's University.

Robertson, M.J. 1991. Homeless Youth: An Overview of Recent Literature, in J.H. Kryder-Coe, L.M. Salamon, and J.M. Molnar (eds). *Homeless Children and Youth: A New American Dilemma.* New Brunswick, N.J.: Transaction Publishers.

Robertson, M.J., and Greenblatt, M. 1992. Homelessness, in M.J. Robertson and M. Greenblatt (eds). *Homelessness: A National Perspective.* New York: Plenum Press.

Rossi, P.H. 1987. No Good Applied Research Goes Unpublished. *Social Science in Modern Society*, 25: 73-80.

Rossi, P.H. 1989. *Down and out in America: The Origins of Homelessness.* Chicago: University of Chicago Press.

Rotherum-Borus, M.J., Koopman, C., and Ehrhardt, A.A. 1991. Homeless Youth and HIV Infection. *American Psychologist*, 46(11): 1188-1197.

Shinn, M. 1992. Homelessness: What Is a Psychologist to Do? *American Journal of Community Psychology*, Vol. 20(1): 1-24.

Shlay, A.B., and Rossi, P.H. 1992. Social Science Research and Contemporary Studies of Homelessness. *Annual Review of Sociology*, 18: 129-160.

Simons, R.L., and Whitbeck, L.B. 1991. Running Away During Adolescence as a Precursor to Adult Homelessness. *Social Service Review*, 65: 224-247.

Stelf, M. 1987. The New Homeless: A National Perspective, in R.D. Bingham, R.E. Green, and S.B. White (eds). *The Homeless in Contemporary Society.* Newbury Park, CA: Sage.

Taussig, M. 1984. Culture of Terror — Space of Death. *Comparative Studies in Society and History*, 26(3): 467-497.

Toro, P.A., and McDonell, D.M. 1992. Beliefs, Attitudes and Knowledge About Homelessness: A Survey of the General Public. *American Journal of Community Psychology*, 20(1): 53-80.

Watkins, J. 1992. Youth and the Law. Discussion Paper No. 3, Select Committee into Youth Affairs. Perth: Western Australian Government Printer.

West, C. 1993. The New Cultural Politics of Difference, in S. During (ed). *The Cultural Studies Reader*. London: Routledge.

White, R. Underwood, R., and Omelczuk, S. 1991. Victims of Violence:World Health Organization (1993). A One Way Street? A Report on Phase 1 of the Street Children Project. Program on Substance Abuse, WHO, Geneva March 26, Issued by Regional Office for the Western Pacific, P.O. Box 2932, Manila.

Wright, J.D. 1988. The Worthy and Unworthy Homeless. *Society*, 25: 64-69.

Wright, J.D. 1989. Address Unknown: The Homeless in America. New York: Aldine.

Yates, G.L., MacKenzie, R.G., Pennbridge, J., and Swofford, A. 1991. A Risk Profile Comparison of Homeless Youth Involved in Prostitution and Homeless Youth Not Involved. *Journal of Adolescent Health*, 12(7): 545-548.

Zide, M.R., and Cherry, A.L. 1992. A Typology of Runaway Youths: An Empirically Based Definition. *Child and Adolescent Social Work Journal*, 9(2): 155-168.

CHAPTER 10

Aboriginal Australia*
Current Criminological Themes

Rick Sarre**

BACKGROUND: THE BRITISH COLONIZATION OF AUSTRALIA

When the first white settlers set sail for Australia from England late in 1787, it was for the purpose of establishing a South Seas penal settlement. The English prison system was to be relieved by this process of its unwanted felons, an historical story of much interest to contemporary researchers (Hughes, 1986).

But what law was to apply to them upon arrival? For two centuries legal scholars recorded that Australia was uninhabited when the first fleets arrived, and thus English law, in so far as it was applicable, was assumed to have been brought with the settlers. In a British legal decision a century later, the Privy Council (the Queen's own court that received appeals from the colonies) confirmed that the Australian colony had " ...consisted of a tract of territory practically unoccupied, without settled inhabitants or settled law, at the time when it was peacefully annexed to the British dominion" (*Cooper v Stuart* [1889] 14 AC 291). This judgment was of great significance for the treatment of indigenous peoples in colonial Australia and in the contemporary life of this nation.

The international law position at the time permitted a colonizing country to ignore the legal status of the indigenous people if the country were to be deemed "unoccupied." By contrast, if the country were *conquered*, local laws prevailed until the conquerors installed a new legal order. Australia was deemed to be unoccupied (*terra nullius* or "land of no-one"), and thus a legal vacuum existed.

Furthermore, colonizing countries were also at liberty to claim as theirs any land that was not, in their opinion, being used appropriately. As the early international European jurist Vattel wrote in 1758:

> There is another celebrated question which has arisen principally in connection with the discovery of the New World. It is asked whether a Nation may lawfully occupy any part of a vast territory in which are to be found only wandering tribes whose small numbers can not populate the whole country....[W]hen the Nations of Europe, which are too confined at home, come upon lands which the savages have no special need of, they may lawfully take possession of them and establish colonies in them... (Vattel Book 1, Chapter 18).

Furthermore,

> But now that the human race has multiplied so greatly, it could not subsist if every people wished to live after that fashion [as hunters and gatherers]. Those who still pursue this idle mode of life occupy more land than they would have need of under a system of honest labor, and they may not complain if other more industrious Nations, too confined at home, should come and occupy part of their lands (Vattel Book 1, Chapter 8).

Historians are now discovering that English administrators and their lawyers were aware of the existence of at least locally sovereign native or customary laws early as the 1830s but preferred to ignore them for the difficulties such recognition would have created politically, both retrospectively and prospectively (Reynolds, 1992: 9). Australian legal history therefore "...proceeded on the assumption that [the] indigenous people did not have a system of rights to land, with the most horrendous consequences when Aborigines tried to defend those rights against the settlers. [It was] an error born in ignorance and racial arrogance..." (Wootten, 1993: 3).

Whatever the historical excuse, the legal result was the same. The English Crown, upon settlement, "legitimately" deprived the indigenous peoples of their land in all of eastern Australia, defined by the first governor of the Sydney cove settlement as all the country inland westward at least to longitude 135 degrees east. On February 7, 1788 (the date of the official pronouncement of the governor's "Commission"), then, tens if not hundreds of thousands of Australia's "first" peoples became subjects of the British sovereign at the time, King George III. As ludicrous as that may sound, this official legal position continues to this day.

The colonial settlers began, officially, with cordial relationships with the local tribes, preferring to ignore them as far as possible. There was no professional police force in colonial Australia until well into the nineteenth century and thus the military performed policing roles. When trouble began brewing between the Aborigines and the settlers, an unofficial policy of *eradication* began to unfold amongst the military peace-keepers. The history of this phase of Australia's colonial settlement is replete with stories of savagery, waterhole poisonings and shootings (e.g. Elder, 1988). But as rural settlements expanded and farming prospered, it became clear that Aboriginal labor was cheap and accessible, and eradication shifted to a nineteenth century policy of *protection*.

The racism of the colonial past has not been confined to the eighteenth and nineteenth centuries. Along with policies of *assimilation* (from about 1937) and *integration* (about 1962) came the widespread practice of taking "half-caste" children from their families and placing them in "proper" Christian homes. This policy was carried out with the most honorable social and religious intentions. The consequences for social and familial upheaval are well documented and continue to this day in many communities around Australia (e.g. Cummings, 1990).

Disenfranchisement of Aboriginal peoples continued well into the twentieth century. Aborigines could not vote in federal elections until as recently as 1962. Each of the six States finally granted the vote to all of their constituents, regardless of race, in 1965. It was not until 1967 that section 51 (xxvi) of the Australian Constitution was altered to allow the federal government to make special laws for Aboriginal peoples. In that same referendum section 127 was partially deleted so that Aboriginal people could be counted in a census. Universal suffrage and the recognition of the worth of all races in Australia, therefore, has only officially occurred in the last thirty years.

It has only been in the last decade that there has been a formal shift to a policy of *multi-culturalism* in Australia, a position that eschews former integration policies in favor of the recognition of the inherent right of all people to preserve and cherish their cultural and traditional heritage. *Self-determination* and *self-management* by virtue of the *Aboriginal and Torres Strait Islander Commission Act* (Cth) 1989 are key concepts in current Australian political life. Indeed, the official terminology is changing as well. The 1788 "settlement" is now more commonly referred to as "occupation" (Commonwealth Parliament, 1988). Indeed, the term "invasion" is commonly used amongst Aboriginal Australians.

A major legal judgment in 1992 had the effect of challenging the official colonial position on *terra nullius*. The Australian High Court's ruling in *Mabo v Queensland* (1992) 107 ALR 1 recognized the inherent right of first ownership to land in indigenous Australian peoples. This right to title preceded colonization and survived the assertion of sovereignty by colonizers in some situations (Sarre, 1994a). The High Court also successfully challenged many of the legal and moral assumptions of British settlement, and largely overturned the common law view regarding the legal foundations of the Australian colonies.

> If it were permissible in past centuries to keep the common law in step with international law, it is imperative in today's world that the common law should neither be nor be seen to be frozen in an age of racial discrimination. The fiction by which the rights and interests of indigenous inhabitants in land were treated as non-existent was justified by a policy which has no place in the contemporary law of this country (1992) 107 ALR 1 at 27 per Brennan J.

In re-writing legal history, the court placed international human rights concerns above the simple distinction between idle and industrious people that had been made by Vattel.

The common law does not necessarily conform with international law, but international law is a legitimate and important influence on the development of the common law, especially when international law declares the existence of universal human rights. A common law doctrine founded on unjust discrimination in the enjoyment of civil and political rights demands reconsideration ...(1992) 107 ALR 1 at 28 per Brennan J.

There will be few indigenous peoples in Australia, however, who will be able to benefit directly from the *Mabo* decision, perhaps fewer than ten per cent. The idea that there may be others who should *in*directly benefit from the decision is one which exercised the minds of the members of the Australian federal parliament in passing the *Native Title Act* (Cth) in December, 1993 and including in that Act a social justice package designed to compensate those members of Aboriginal communities who would not be able to show a surviving "native" title.

The *Mabo* judgment brought Australia further into the mainstream of international thinking on the rights of indigenous peoples. One might argue, of course, that there are still many bridges to cross. The International Commission of Jurists, for example, has painted a picture of black Australia of which few can feel anything but shame (Cunneen, 1992a). Nevertheless, for two hundred years Aboriginal Australians were regarded as legally irrelevant. The legacy of that period is a damning social and economic indigenous landscape.

THE SOCIAL PICTURE OF CONTEMPORARY ABORIGINAL AUSTRALIA

While the *Mabo* judgment was of great significance in altering the legal status of indigenous law, one must hasten to add that little has changed since that High Court decision in contemporary life in Aboriginal Australia. In the past decade there has been no shortage of evidence of poor health, education and employment for Aboriginal Australians. Commission after commission, study after study, has concluded that Aboriginal Australians are at vastly greater risk of threat to life and health than non-Aboriginal Australians (Sarre, 1994b: 43). The sociologist Tatz, for example, paints a pessimistic picture of the personal violence, child neglect, destruction of property and alcoholism that currently pervades many communities (Tatz, 1990). The effect of monoculturalism led to the demise of Aboriginal spiritual and legal restraints and drastically eroded the security, cultural integrity and self-esteem of the Aboriginal peoples.

Aboriginal Australians face the risk of becoming a victim of homicide, for example, at a rate far greater than that which is borne by the general Australian population. In South Australia and Queensland that rate could be as high as ten times greater if past figures are any guide (South Australia, 1981: 6; Wilson, 1982: 4), and in New South Wales at least seven times greater, noting also in that State that 87% of Aboriginal deaths by homicide occur at the hands of other Aboriginal persons (Bonney, 1987).

> When it is remembered that these figures are a gross under-estimation of the true state of violence, their implications are startlingly clear: black men and women are killing each other at a rate which far exceeds their counterparts in other sectors of the State and nation (Wilson, 1982: 4).

Three major Australian reports in recent years are worthy of particular mention in this context. They allow an impression of contemporary life in many Aboriginal communities to emerge.

The Findings of the Royal Commission into Aboriginal Deaths in Custody

A Royal Commission was established in 1987 to undertake a three-year investigation into the deaths of 99 Aboriginal people who died in police lock-ups, prisons and juvenile detention centers between 1980 and 1989, 11 of whom were women. The release of the US$20 million five-volume Final Report (along with 27 companion volumes) in May 1991 had the potential to establish a renaissance in Aboriginal/non-Aboriginal legal and social relations. But while the report stressed "...that underlying issues such as racism, alienation, poverty and powerlessness resulting in hopelessness and alcoholism all contributed more significantly to the imprisonment of Aboriginal people than any degree of criminality" (Payne, 1992: 33), the Royal Commission placed little emphasis upon etiological explanations, preferring description to explanation (Lincoln and Wilson, 1994: 61). Nevertheless, the Final Report made 339 recommendations covering, amongst other things, police training, court and prison practices, government reform initiatives and counseling services. The Commissioners suggested the creation of an implementation "watchdog" to ensure that the Report was properly acted upon.

The Royal Commissioners found, somewhat surprisingly, that, once in custody, Aboriginal people die at the same rate as non-Aboriginal Australians. However, when comparing deaths in custody with population generally, a different picture emerged. Taking Australia as a whole, there were 75 Aboriginal deaths in custody per 100,000 of the adult Australian population compared to 3.3 non-Aboriginal deaths in custody per 100,000 population. Aboriginal deaths, on this reckoning, were at a rate 23 times higher (Biles et al., 1990). The disproportionalities of Aboriginal deaths in custody, therefore, is chiefly due to the disproportionate number of Aboriginal people received daily into custody. At June 30, 1992 there were 2,200 Aboriginal and Torres Strait Islanders in prisons around Australia in a total prison population of 12,940, or a rate of 1,391 per 100,000. This makes them approximately 14 times more likely than non-Aboriginal people to be in prison Australia-wide (Walker, 1994: 13). There is little difference between adult and juvenile figures (Wundersitz et al., 1990).

Criticisms were also levelled in the Report at the bureaucracies that administer Aboriginal affairs. The Royal Commissioner responsible for the Final Report, Mr Elliott Johnston QC, found that he:

> ...had no conception of the degree of pin-pricking domination, abuse of personal power, utter paternalism, open contempt and total indifference with which so many Aboriginal people were visited on a day to day basis (ATSIC, 1993: 21).

Despite evidence that some police and prison officers were flexible with the truth in their evidence and that many Aborigines had been unlawfully arrested, detained and assaulted, no criminal charges were ever laid. Anger continues to simmer in some Aboriginal communities whose members believe that official stalling and prevarication denied justice to the 99 deceased persons, along with families and loved ones.

According to the first Annual Report on the implementation of the recommendations of the Royal Commission released February 27, 1994, the picture of deaths in custody remains virtually unchanged. While indigenous people account for approximately 1.2% of the Australian population, they still make up more than 8% of the custodial deaths. Since the number of indigenous people in prison continues to increase, there is still an average of 10.5 Aboriginal deaths in custody annually, the same as the average during the period covered by the Royal Commission (Australian Institute of Criminology, 1994: 2).

In many respects the Final Report and the implementation report confirmed what was well known anyway; that Aboriginal Australians are grossly over-represented in police lock-ups and prisons and are far more likely than non-Aboriginal people to be drawn to the attention of police and taken into custody.

> Aboriginal people in their many submissions and in consultations conducted during this inquiry have most frequently identified their relations with police officers as the most serious and constant indicator of the injustice and prejudice which they experience in society (Royal Commission into Aboriginal Deaths in Custody, 1991, Vol 2: 207).

The intersection of Aboriginality and gender in criminology is an area that is only now receiving the academic attention it deserves. A 1988 study found a higher degree of disproportionality in Aboriginal women's imprisonment rate compared to the imprisonment rate of Aboriginal men. Aboriginal women are in prison at a rate of 150 per 100,000 compared to 9.3 per 100,000 for non-Aboriginal women, a disproportionality of approximately 16 times (Howe, 1988). This is notwithstanding an environment where authorities tend to favor *non*-custodial sanctions for low-risk offenders (the majority of women prisoners).

Aboriginal women are among the least employed and the least economically secure groups in Australia, borne out by the evidence that the most frequent offenses committed by Aboriginal women involve non-payment of fines, drunkenness and social welfare fraud. They are victims who can rarely escape the victimizing process.

> Aboriginal women are often ashamed to report rapes and be subjected to the sneering interrogation of young white male policemen with their sexist and racist questions. And if Aboriginal women do take their cases to the judicial system they have to listen to sexist and racist arguments being condoned by the courts. Rape and assault of Aboriginal women is not seen to be as serious as rape of non-Aboriginal women (Paxman and Corbett, 1994: 4).

Many Aboriginal women today are portrayed as passive victims of non-Aboriginal and Aboriginal men, and of assimilationist policies of the past (for example, those that sponsored forced adoption and fostering of Aboriginal children). The effect of colonization and latterday patriarchy has been to undermine the status of Aboriginal women in contemporary Australia. Traditionally, women in Aboriginal culture have a status equal to that of men, with their own ceremonies, sacred knowledge, family laws and secrets. When the voices of Aboriginal women are more widely heard than currently is the case and when Aboriginal women are again included in decision-making and in defining and articulating the mechanisms of their social organization, Aboriginal Australian communities will be significantly farther down the road towards self-management and self-determination (Paxman and Corbett, 1994: 5).

The Findings of Amnesty International

A report released by the international human rights watchdog Amnesty International in 1993 characterized the Australian criminal justice system as one which makes Aboriginal Australians vulnerable to "highly disproportionate levels of incarceration and to cruel, inhuman or degrading treatment" (Amnesty, 1993: 5). Indeed, one somewhat unexpected implication of the Australian government's implementation of Recommendation 333 of the Final Report is that prisoners in Australian jails now have the right to make a complaint to the United Nations if they are subjected to what they believe can be regarded as torture or other cruel, inhuman or degrading treatment or punishment (Lofgren, 1994).

Recommendation 333 stated that:

> while noting that in no case did the Commission find a breach of the Convention Against Torture and Other Cruel, Inhuman or Degrading Treatment or Punishment, it is recommended that the Commonwealth Government should make a declaration under Article 22 of the Convention...in order to provide a right of individual petition to the *Committee Against Torture*....

On January 28, 1993 Australia lodged a declaration with the UN accepting its obligations under the *Convention Against Torture and Other Cruel, Inhuman or Degrading Treatment or Punishment* which came into force in Australia on September 7, 1989. It will be interesting to observe whether this official act will heighten the resolve of Australian governments to bring about a political and legal solution to the current unacceptable levels of Aboriginal incarceration. One can only speculate, in the absence of test cases, how broadly "cruel, inhuman, or degrading treatment or punishment" will be interpreted in the context of prisoners' rights, and the rights of *groups* of peoples who find themselves so remarkably over-represented in prisons. The threat of international attention being drawn to Australia's record of imprisonment of its indigenous peoples might prompt all Australian governments, State and federal, to pursue their commitment to the implementation of the Royal Commission recommendations with renewed vigor.

The Findings of the Australian National Committee on Violence

This committee was established in Australia in October 1988 by the then Australian Federal Minister of Justice after extensive negotiations between federal, State and territorial governments. In February 1990 it submitted its report of its research and findings to the Federal Government. It gave an overview of the state of violent crime in Australia today. It reviewed a great number of issues associated with violence, including causes and effects, the impact of drugs and alcohol on violent behavior, and the vulnerability of victims (and especially children and family members) to aggressive conduct. It was also concerned with strategies to deal with the causes of violent conduct including the treatment of violent offenders. The committee made over 130 recommendations for governments, public sector agencies, private enterprise, as well as religious and professional groups and associations.

The National Committee on Violence had the following to say on the subject of violence by and upon Aboriginal Australians:

> [I]t is possible to state with conviction that the level of violence existing in some Aboriginal communities is of a scale that dwarfs that in any sector of white Australia ....It is generally accepted that this level of violence amongst Aboriginals is a manifestation of a more complex malaise relating to loss of traditional culture and authority structures, boredom, overcrowding, unemployment and despair. Wilson (1982) has written graphically of the consequences of cultural disintegration and has demonstrated that the greater the disintegration, the greater the rate of violence. He observes that displacement from traditional homelands and the lack of community cohesion deriving from mobility and the mixing together of people from different groups all contribute to escalating rates of crime and violence (Australian National Committee, 1990: 165).

The National Committee made a number of recommendations concerning Aboriginal peoples, insisting generally that policies be put in place that acknowledge unequivocally the dignity of Aboriginal Australians, and that appropriate allocations of funding should remain a government priority.

The Human Rights and Equal Opportunity Commission Report on Racist Violence (1991) and the Australian Law Reform Commission Report on Multi-Culturalism and the Law (1992) were other reports which were instrumental in placing Aboriginal issues on the current social, political and legal reform agendas.

CAUSAL ANALYSIS: THEORIES OF ABORIGINAL CRIMINALITY

It might be easy to conclude from the above evidence that there is something within the Aboriginal Australian community, almost intrinsically, which aligns them inevitably with a life of crime and violence. The temptation of such a conclusion should be resisted.

[T]he superficial conclusion could well be that colour and criminality are indeed blended—or that deprivation goes hand in hand with delinquency...but the fact that not all or even most people so afflicted find their way to courts belies any causative link. Rather has it been suggested that the real problem is not Aboriginal or social at all but lies with the discriminatory operation of the criminal justice system...conversely [the system] is overloaded with Aboriginals (sic) or the poor simply because it is burdened by society with a number of social and political problems which society cannot solve (Clifford, 1981: 4-5).

This statement from the then director of the Australian Institute of Criminology develops the two key theoretical areas which have been of increasing interest to Australian criminologists in the last decade.

- o The legal factors: the effect upon Aboriginal criminality of the criminal justice system
- o The political and social factors: the effect upon Aboriginal criminality of economic and cultural forces

The former topic has attracted more attention than the latter in Australian criminological circles, primarily because criminologists who are interested in Aboriginal issues tend to align themselves with critical thinkers rather than mainstream sociologists. The following discussion provides an overview of the current work being conducted in Australia.

The Legal Factors: The Effect upon Aboriginal Criminality of the Criminal Justice System

Examples and descriptions of over-policing, racism and discrimination in Australian policing abound in the criminological literature (eg. Wootten, 1993b: 281). Many complaints regarding police conduct by Aboriginal and other minority groups are directed, however, not so much at misconduct by individual police officers as at systematic patterns of policing. Often these patterns are a product of a failure by police, through inappropriate or inadequate training, to understand indigenous cultural values (Royal Commission into Aboriginal Deaths in Custody, 1991, 2: 209).

The *Royal Commission into Aboriginal Deaths in Custody* found that "[m]ost of the conflict with Aboriginal people arises from police endeavors to enforce 'street offenses' legislation, which seeks to impose on Aboriginal people the views of the European culture about the appropriate use of public space" (Royal Commission into Aboriginal Deaths in Custody, 1991, 2: 199). "Deviant" behavior is drawn to the attention of police often because of the highly public manner in which Aboriginal Australians socialize. Add the influence of alcohol and conflict between police and Aboriginal Australians becomes almost inevitable (McCorquodale, 1984: 17).

A great many of the problems can be located in the sheer weight of numbers of police. The Amnesty International report referred to above (Amnesty, 1993: 23) found many Aboriginal communities burdened with very high police-community ratios. For example, in the outback (and largely Aboriginal) New South Wales town of Wilcannia there is one officer per 73 population while the average for New South Wales is 1 per 459 population. Disproportionate levels of surveillance, arrest and detention are very likely to follow such intense over-concentrations of police power. Furthermore, Aboriginal persons are less likely than non-Aboriginal Australians to have access to legal counsel, family and societal support structures as they confront police.

Complaints concerning systemic difficulties should not hide the racism which is all too evident in the attitudes of many Australian police officers. A 1991 study was conducted by Sydney University criminologist Chris Cunneen (Cunneen, 1991a, 1991b) into the extent of police violence against Aboriginal Australian juveniles held in detention in New South Wales, Queensland and Western Australia. He found that an overwhelming majority of them (88 per cent) reported being physically assaulted by police, with just less than two-thirds reporting being hit with an object, usually a police baton. Over 80 per cent reported being abused by racist language (and, in the case of females, by sexual insults) and 21 per cent of respondents in Western Australia stated that police officers had either made threats or suggestions relating to hanging or suicide.

> [T]he processes of criminalization entail subjecting individuals to varying degrees of violence. Those same processes selectively discriminate against Aboriginal youth. In addition, the over-representation has racist outcomes. Aboriginal people are seen to be in some way "naturally" criminal. Thus there are structural reasons for regarding the violence against Aboriginal youth as constituting racist violence (Cunneen, 1991a: 9).

Cunneen (1992b) and Thorpe (1987) have also written extensively on aspects of judicial life in Australia (individually and institutionally) which they regard as racist. These allegations give much cause for concern.

The Political and Social Factors: The Effect upon Aboriginal Criminality of Economic and Cultural Forces

A range of sociological theories has been explored in the search for causal explanation. There is evidence for social control theorists that traditional control mechanisms in Aboriginal community life have become vastly more complicated than those which proved appropriate in the past. "Such complexity means that people's ability to deal with disorder is impaired. It also means that what was once culturally appropriate behavior may now, in the face of new factors such as easy access to alcohol, produce unintended consequences such as uncontrolled, as opposed to controlled, violence" (Edmunds, 1990: 3).

Strain theorists might note that until only very recently, Australian Aborigines' feelings of powerlessness have been exacerbated by official neglect and discrimination. As a result

Aboriginal mobility has been reduced and access to land has been restricted. Health policies have increased state control over young children in a culture of misplaced benevolence. The relaxation of restrictions on alcohol has overridden rule-governed fighting. White managerial bureaucratic models of Aboriginal policy-making leave Aboriginal people as powerless as before and some types of offending have been isolated as a consequence of this (Lincoln and Wilson, 1994: 80).

It was discovered in the *Royal Commission into Aboriginal Deaths in Custody* that of the 99 persons who died in custody 43 had been charged with an offense prior to the age of 16 and 74 before the age of 19. These offenders became caught up in the vortex of the criminal justice system from which they never escaped, concluded the Commissioners. Labeling theorists would find much of interest in these findings. Policy-makers have indeed created structures within the justice system (for example, the "caution" and new bail laws) to keep as many indigenous people out of the system as possible. Fortunately, the media stereotyping of Aboriginal offenders has, for the most part, been eliminated by the strict guidelines now in place in the various media codes of conduct. Prior to these guidelines becoming commonplace, however, media excesses were under fire from commentators (e.g. *Human Rights and Equal Opportunity Commission*, 1991: 117).

Conflict theorists have noted the attempts by Aborigines to exercise control over their own lives in opposition to police attempts to contain their communities according to non-Aboriginal values. This conflict often leads to rule-breaking. To that end crime becomes a political activity. The dimensions of this phenomenon have received renewed interest since the Royal Commission (e.g. Hogg and Brown, 1990: 865).

EXPLORING APPROPRIATE RESPONSES

It is clear that any policy shifts and reform processes must begin with political initiatives which concentrate upon the two key issues discussed above. Change must be orchestrated at the level of the justice system and within the social structure of Australian life.

Changes required to the criminal justice system (police, courts and prisons)

i) Changes to policing practice

The success of the "professional partnership policing" in the Australian context (where Aboriginal people are given a key role in controlling anti-social behavior, minor infractions and serious breaches of the law) has been reported widely (eg. Etter, 1993: 11). Other schemes involving police aides and newly devised multi-racial recruitment practices, training in non-racist attitudes and cultural awareness programs have received much attention since the Royal Commission. Attitudes will not change overnight, but the desire is apparent amongst senior police policy-makers to root out police racism where it appears. Once distrust and antipathy dissipate, there is hope for the future of police/Aboriginal relations.

ii) Exploring "shame and reintegration" as models of sentencing

The concept of "shame and reintegration" developed by Australian criminologist John Braithwaite as an alternative punishment model (Braithwaite, 1989) is worth exploring in this context. "Reintegrative shaming" is a system of "restorative" justice where there is a clear acknowledgment of wrongdoing by the offender and a desire to rebuild links with his or her community. Braithwaite contrasts the notion of "disintegrative shaming," that is, where condemnation of the wrongdoer is not followed by the rebuilding of social bonds, thereby setting up potentially serious tensions within the community. The criminal trial and "corrections" process provide examples of disintegrative shaming where familial and social bonds are more likely to loosen.

The model of restorative justice through family conferences, victim/offender mediation or community accountability conferences provides for new possibilities for policy-makers and legislators alike to overcome the dilemmas posed by the contemporary criminal justice system culture.

iii) Moving towards greater recognition of Aboriginal customary law

It is not possible, said the Supreme Court of New South Wales in *R v Wedge* [1976] 1 NSWLR 355, for Australia to have two sets of criminal laws. Aboriginal defendants, it was confirmed, were subject to the law of New South Wales whether or not both victim and offender were Aboriginal and whether or not they were to be subject to customary law as well. This case confirmed some older legal precedents. In *R v Neddy Monkey* [1861] VLR (L) 40 the court determined that they would not compromise the general rules of evidence in order to take judicial notice of "vague rites and ceremonies" (at 41). Furthermore, in *R v Cobby* (1883) 4 NSWLR 355, the Supreme Court of New South Wales determined that they would not and could not recognize a marriage of "these aborigines, who have no laws of which we can have cognizance" (at 356). For almost two hundred years the Australian courts gave no credence to customary law and ignored the few calls for it to be implemented into the Australian civil or criminal justice system.

In the landmark decision, *Milirrpum v Nabalco Pty Ltd and the Commonwealth* (1971) 17 FLR 141 Justice Blackburn of the Northern Territory Supreme Court decided that there had been a system of law in existence in Australian Aboriginal societies in 1788. It was:

> ...a subtle and elaborate system highly adapted to the country in which people lived their lives, which provided a stable order of society and was remarkably free from the vagaries of personal whim or influence ..."a government of laws not of men" (at p 267).

Justice Blackburn, however, tied to the precedent then existing of *Cooper v Stuart,* could not recognize customary law despite the remarks he made in the course of the judgment. *Milirrpum* was overturned by the *Mabo* decision twenty years on (but only in relation to title to land). The High Court vindicated Justice Blackburn's feeling ill at ease with the decision he was bound to reach in 1971.

Indeed, the Australian Law Reform Commission's report on Customary Law released in 1986 (Australian Law Reform Commission, 1986) and the Northern Territory Legislative Assembly Committee on Constitutional Development (Northern Territory,

1992) recommended a careful yet piecemeal approach to such recognition. Other academics have expressed agreement (e.g. Clifford, 1981: 20; Hennessy, 1984; Crawford, 1992) including the editor of a criminal justice journal in the months following the passage of the Native Title Act:

> Present-day legislators can help to heal [the] wounds inflicted by their predecessors by returning some form of native criminal jurisdiction back to Aboriginal communities. Such a reinstatement would also be in line with an emerging international trend towards providing indigenous peoples with the right to self-determination or self-management (Editorial, 1994: 196).

iv) Keeping people out of jail

Recommendation 92 of the Royal Commission Report states that "governments which have not already done so should legislate to enforce the principle that imprisonment should be utilized only as a sanction of last resort." There appears to have been some effort in each State to adopt this recommendation, but one might suspect that lip-service has predominated over true reform (Smith, 1992). Implementation of the recommendations concerning rehabilitation programs should be a matter of priority for federal and State governments (Australia, 1994; Royal Commission, 1994: 101 ff).

Changes required to the fabric of Australian political life

i) Education and employment

Walker discovered that the chance of a person who is both indigenous and unemployed being in prison is over 250 times the chance of the non-indigenous, non-unemployed person (1994: 14; Walker and Salloom, 1993). He concluded that unemployment and levels of education are far more powerful predictors of imprisonment than Aboriginality. Since Aboriginal Australians are more likely than non-Aboriginal Australians to be unemployed and poorly educated, the consequences for contact with the criminal justice system are obvious.

If unemployment amongst Aboriginal and Torres Strait
Islander people were reduced to that of the non-
indigenous population, and if rates of imprisonment
reflected this change...the indigenous prison population
could fall from over 2,200 down to around 530...If
levels of education amongst Aboriginal and Torres
Strait Islander people were improved to that of the non-
indigenous population and if rates of imprisonment
reflected this change...the indigenous prison population
could fall...to 262 (Walker, 1994: 15).

These predictions are worthy of serious further exploration for
criminologists and policy-makers alike.

ii) Rising above the levels of despair

The conclusion could be drawn from much of the above
discussion that many Aboriginal communities are incapable of rising
above their powerlessness and associated difficulties, thereby
providing fuel for racist assumptions. Lincoln and Wilson recognize
the dilemma of describing the pain of Aboriginality without at the
same time demeaning the key Aboriginal protagonists and peoples
generally.

[T]here are those who see that Aborigines have been
alienated and dispossessed and are therefore not coping
with contemporary European constructs. Then there are
others who see Aboriginal society and culture as
enduring and continuing in the face of extensive change
and enormous external pressure. We would argue that
both positions have some merit and should not be seen
as cancelling each other out. That alienation and
oppression took place for Aboriginal societies in the
past is undeniable; that social pathologies currently
abound in many communities is also undeniable; that
discrimination and structural inequalities exert influence
on Aboriginal people today is also apparent; yet the
sum of these elements does not deny a distinct
Aboriginal way of being and acting upon those forces
(Lincoln and Wilson, 1994: 79).

The challenge for those committed to developing meaningful responses to the dilemmas faced by all Australians in this regard is to incorporate these sentiments. Only in that environment will the most appropriate responses be developed to ensure that Australia's indigenous peoples are able to enjoy the fruits of Australian life which should be available to all.

CONCLUSION

Two hundred years of colonial paternalism has eroded much of the spiritual and cultural life which preceded European colonization of Australia in the eighteenth century. The legacy is a present-day disenchantment with the justice system and massive over-representation in that system by Aboriginal peoples. What has emerged from the social and criminological studies and the literature is a stark warning. The criminal justice system will have to change (and in particular police racism) and social, educational and political opportunities will have to emerge for indigenous Australians for there to be any movement away from the grim realities of contemporary life for Aboriginal peoples. Above all, concepts of self-determination and community-based development (Hazlehurst, 1987; Brennan, 1991) will need to be made national priorities if the future relationship between Aboriginal and non-Aboriginal Australians is to be one of harmony and justice. In the process, some serious de-regulation must occur.

> By definition, self-determination cannot exist if it is supported and thereby controlled by government policy, funding or bureaucracy in any shape or form. That is not to suggest that governments at all levels can sit back and let a rule of absolute non-intervention prevail (Lincoln and Wilson, 1994: 85).

Justice cannot exist in Australia unless there is justice for all.

NOTES

* The term "Aboriginal peoples" includes the Torres Strait Islander peoples, although the mainland Aboriginal Australian is racially quite different from Torres Strait Islanders. According to the 1991 census the adult (over 15) Aboriginal population in

Australia was 160,000 compared to 13 million non-Aboriginal adults. (Adult numbers are used to make imprisonment rates comparisons more meaningful). Torres Strait is the waters which separate northern Australia from Papua New Guinea.

The word "Aboriginal" is an adjective that has come to describe Australia' s "first" or " indigenous" peoples generally. It should be used as an adjective and not a noun. The term "Aborigine" is a commonly used description, but preferable at the local level is the customary name. In my own city, Adelaide, the first people were the *Kaurna* people. An Aboriginal person is, for the purposes of the law in Australia, one who aligns himself or herself with an Aboriginal community and is accepted by that community.

**The author is a senior lecturer in law at the University of South Australia. He would like to thank Paul Martin of the Legal Practice Course library, University of South Australia for his research assistance.

Australian spellings have been preserved in the quotations.

REFERENCES

Amnesty International. 1993. *Australia: A Criminal Justice System Weighted Against Aboriginal People*, Sydney: Amnesty International.

ATSIC (Aboriginal and Torres Strait Islander Commission). 1993. Social Justice for Indigenous Australians 1993-4, Canberra AGPS.

Australia. 1994. *Implementation of the Commonwealth Government's Response to the Recommendations of the Royal Commission into Aboriginal Deaths in Custody:* First Annual Report 1992-3, Canberra: AGPS.

Australian Institute of Criminology. 1994. *Deaths in Custody Australia,* No. 6 Australian Deaths in Custody 1992-3.

Australian Law Reform Commission. 1986. *The Recognition of Aboriginal Customary Laws, Report No. 31* Canberra: AGPS (together with Discussion Paper no 17, 1980, *Aboriginal Customary Law — Recognition?*).

Australian Law Reform Commission. 1992. *Multi-culturalism and the Law, Final Report No. 57.* Canberra: AGPS (together with Issues Paper No. 9, January 1990, and Discussion Paper No. 48, May, 1991).

Australian National Committee. 1990. *Violence: Directions for Australia*, Australian National Committee on Violence, Canberra: Australian Institute of Criminology.

Biles, David, David McDonald, and J. Fleming. 1990. Aboriginal and Non-Aboriginal Deaths in Custody. *Australian and New Zealand Journal of Criminology*, 23(1):15-2 3.

Bonney, Roseanne. 1987. *Homicide II*, Sydney: Report of the NSW Bureau of Crime Statistics and Research (published 1988).

Braithwaite, John. 1989. *Crime, Shame and Reintegration*, Cambridge: Cambridge University Press.

Brennan, Frank. 1991. *Sharing the Country: The Case for an Agreement Between Black and White Australians*, Ringwood, Victoria: Penguin.

Clifford, William. 1981. An Approach to Aboriginal Criminology. (The John Barry Memorial Lecture, 1981), Canberra: Australian Institute of Criminology (reprinted in the *Australian and New Zealand Journal of Criminology*, March, 1982 15 (1): 3-21.

Commonwealth Parliament. 1988. Commonwealth Parliamentary Resolutions on the Aboriginal Occupation of Australia. *Australian Law Journal*, 62: 978-980.

Crawford, James. 1992. The Recognition of Aboriginal Customary Laws: An Overview, in Cunneen, Chris, *Aboriginal Perspectives on Criminal Justice*, The Institute of Criminology Monograph Series No. 1, Sydney: Institute of Criminology, pp. 53-75.

Cummings, Barbara. 1990. *Take This Child: From Kahlin Compound to the Retta Dixon Children's Home*, Canberra: Aboriginal Studies Press.

Cunneen, Chris. 1991a. Aboriginal Young People and Police Violence. *Aboriginal Law Bulletin*, 2(49): 6-9.

Cunneen, Chris. 1991b. Aboriginal Juveniles in Custody. *Current Issues in Criminal Justice*, 2(2): 204-218.

Cunneen, Chris. 1992a. Commentary on the Report of the Aboriginals and the Law Mission, International Commission of Jurists (Australian Section). *ANZ Journal of Criminology*, 25: 186-191.

Cunneen, Chris. 1992b. Judicial Racism. *Aboriginal Law Bulletin*, 2(58): 9-11.

Editorial. 1994. *Criminal Law Journal,* 18(4): 193-196.

Edmunds, Mary. 1990. Doing Business: Socialization, Social Relations and Social Control in Aboriginal Society. *Discussion Paper for the Royal Commission into Aboriginal Deaths in Custody,* Canberra: AGPS.

Elder, Bruce. 1988. *Blood on the Wattle: Massacres and Maltreatment of Australian Aborigines Since 1788,* French's Forest NSW: Child and Associates.

Etter, Barbara. 1993. The Police Culture: Overcoming Barriers. *Criminology Australia,* 5(2): 8-12.

Hazlehurst, Kayleen. 1987. Widening the Middle Ground: The Development of Community-Based Options, in Kayleen Hazlehurst (ed.), *Ivory Scales: Black Australia and the Law,* Kensington, NSWUP, Chapter 12, pp. 241-281.

Hennessy, Peter K. 1984. Aboriginal Customary Law & The Australian Criminal Law: An Unresolved Conflict, in Bruce Swanton (ed.), *Aborigines and Criminal Justice,* Proceedings of the AIC Training Project 27/1/5, pp. 336-349.

Hogg, Russell, and Brown, David. 1990. Violence, Public Policy and Politics in Australia, in David Brown, David Farrier, David Neal, and David Weisbrot. *Criminal Law: Cases and Materials,* Leichhardt: Federation Press, reproduced in Ian Taylor (ed.), *The Social Effects of Free Market Policies,* 1990. New York: St. Martin's Press.

Howe, Adrian. 1988. Aboriginal Women in Custody. *Aboriginal Law Bulletin,* 30: 5-7.

Hughes, Robert. 1986. *The Fatal Shore: A History of the Transportation of Convicts to Australia 1787-1868,* London: Collins Harvill.

Human Rights and Equal Opportunity Commission. 1991. *Report of the National Inquiry into Racist Violence in Australia,* Canberra: AGPS.

Lincoln, Robyn, and Wilson, Paul. 1994. Aboriginal Offending: Patterns and Causes, in Duncan Chappell and Paul Wilson (eds.), *The Australian Criminal Justice System: The Mid 1990s,* Sydney: Butterworths, Chapter 3, pp. 61-86.

Lofgren, Neil. 1994. Complaint Procedures Under Article 22 of the Convention Against Torture and Other Cruel, Inhuman or Degrading Treatment or Punishment, 1(1) *Australian Journal of Human Rights,* pp. 401-408.

McCorquodale, John. 1984. Alcohol and Anomie: The   Nature of Aboriginal Crime, in Bruce Swanton (ed.), *Aborigines and Criminal Justice,* Proceedings of the Australian Institute of Criminology Training Project 27/1/5, pp. 17-42.

Northern Territory. 1992. *Recognition of Aboriginal Customary Law,* Discussion Paper no 4, Sessional Committee on Constitutional Development, Legislative Assembly of the NT pp. 7-11.

Paxman, Marina, and Corbett, Helen.   1994. Listen To Us: Aboriginal Women and White Law.   *Criminology Australia,* 5(3): 2-6.

Payne, Sharon. 1992. Aboriginal Women and the Law, in Chris Cunneen (ed.), *Aboriginal Perspectives on Criminal Justice,* Institute of Criminology Monograph Series No 1, Sydney University, pp. 31-45.

Reynolds, Henry. 1992. Mabo and Pastoral Leases. *Aboriginal Law Bulletin,* 2(59): 8-10.

Royal Commission. 1994. *Royal Commission into Aboriginal Deaths in Custody, 1993 Implementation Report,* South Australian Government, Department of State Aboriginal Affairs.

Royal Commission into Aboriginal Deaths in Custody. 1991. *National Report* (Commissioner Elliott Johnston) Canberra: AGPS (5 volumes).

Sarre, Rick. 1994a. The Concept of Native Title to Land: An Australian Perspective. *Humanity and Society,* 18 (1): 97-104.

Sarre, Rick. 1994b. Violence: Patterns of Crime,   in Duncan Chappell and Paul Wilson (eds.), *The Australian Criminal Justice System — The Mid 1990s,* Sydney: Butterworths, pp. 37-60.

Smith, Margaret. 1992. They Take Them Away: The Problems of Aboriginal Youth Who "Criminally Offend." *Criminology Australia,* 4(2): 25-28.

South Australia. 1981. *Homicide and Serious Assault in South Australia,* Report of the Office of Crime Statistics, Adelaide: Government Printer.

Tatz, Colin. 1990. Aboriginal Violence: A Return to Pessimism. *Australian Journal of Social Issues*, November 1990, Volume 25(4): 245-260 (with response by Lee Sackett), *Australian Journal of Social Issues*, 26(1): 68-70.

Thorpe, David. 1987. Structures of Judicial Racism in Australia. *The Howard Journal*, 26(4): 259-271.

Vattel. 1758. *The Law of Nations or the Principles of International Law* (English Translation, 1916 by Lapradelle), London.

Walker, John. 1994. The Over-representation of Aboriginal and Torres Strait Islander People in Prison. *Criminology Australia*, 6(1): 13-15.

Walker, John, and S. Salloom. 1993. *Australian Prisoners, 1992*, Canberra: Australian Institute of Criminology.

Wilson, Paul. 1982. *Black Death White Hands*, Sydney: George Allen and Unwin.

Wootten, Hal. 1993a. A Cheer for the Mabo Nudgers. *Aboriginal Law Bulletin*, 3(62): 3.

Wootten, Hal. 1993b. Aborigines and Police. *UNSW Law Journal* 16(1): 265-301.

Wundersitz, Joy, Rebecca Bailey-Harris, and Fay Gale. 1990. Aboriginal Youth and Juvenile Justice in South Australia. *Aboriginal Law Bulletin*, 2(44): 12-14.

CHAPTER 11

An Examination of Disposition Decision-Making for Delinquent Girls

Jody Miller

INTRODUCTION

With the relatively recent emergence of feminist criminology, scholars have documented extensive gender bias within the fields of criminology and criminal justice (Cain, 1989; Campbell, 1981; Daly and Chesney-Lind, 1988; Gelsthorpe and Morris, 1990; Leonard, 1982; Smart, 1976, 1977). Recently, feminist scholars have expanded our work to include critiques of our own universalizing tendencies and have recognized the need to examine gender within the contexts of race, class, sexuality and age (Daly, 1991; Joe and Chesney-Lind, forthcoming; Klein, 1991; Rice, 1990). The goals of this body of literature are to build theoretical frameworks which recognize the intersecting nature of these phenomena in the experiences and treatment of females involved in crime and the justice system, in order to more successfully enhance change.

The goal of this paper is to contribute to this process of theory-building by exploring the relationship of race to disposition decision-making processes for adjudicated delinquent girls.[1] While limited in scope, the current research provides further empirical evidence of the intersecting nature of gender, race and class and shows that an emphasis solely on gender discrimination provides a simplistic and insufficient account of the treatment and handling of delinquent girls. I will begin with a brief review of current research on gender and racial bias in juvenile justice.

RELATED LITERATURE

A number of studies have documented the existence of gender discrimination within the juvenile justice system (Alder, 1984; Canter, 1982; Chesney-Lind, 1977, 1978, 1988; Figueira-McDonough, 1985; Gelsthorpe, 1989; Krohn et al., 1983; Mann, 1984; Sarri, 1976; Visher, 1983; but see Teilmann and Landry, 1981). Discriminatory treatment has been reported in varying degrees at all levels of the system, including police arrest and diversion decisions, disposition decisions, and treatment within placement facilities.

For example, while type of offense is a strong predictor of arrest for both male and female suspects, females believed to have committed property crimes have been found to receive harsher treatment by the police than males suspected of similar offenses (Visher, 1983). However, females who interact with police officers in stereotypically feminine ways (e.g., crying, apologizing) are less likely to be formally arrested than females who do not display "femininity" (Chesney-Lind and Shelden, 1992; DeFleur, 1975; Gelsthorpe, 1986, 1989; Krohn et al., 1983; Visher, 1983).

In addition, girls have averaged approximately 40% of referrals to diversion programs while they constitute a maximum of 25% of those youths processed through the juvenile justice system (Alder, 1984: 402). A higher proportion of girls than boys are placed in diversion programs for non-offense behaviors, and those diversion programs that specifically deal with non-offense behaviors have a higher percentage of female clients (Alder, 1984: 405). As a result, these programs have served to widen the net of social control over girls more than boys. There is also evidence that girls placed in detention face longer lengths of stay than boys (Krisberg et al., 1986: 17-21). Girls placed in institutional settings often face behavioral expectations of stereotypical femininity (Chesney-Lind and Shelden, 1992; Gelsthorpe, 1989; Kersten, 1989), as well as fewer visitation privileges than boys and fewer institutional programs than boys (Chesney-Lind and Shelden, 1992; Mann, 1984).

In addition to gender bias, much research within the field of criminology indicates the existence of racial bias within the juvenile justice system (Bondavalli and Bondavalli, 1981; Dannefer and Schutt, 1982; Feyerherm, 1981; Krisberg et al., 1986; Laub and McDermott, 1985; Rice, 1990; Sarri, 1983; Visher, 1983). For example, in a comparative analysis of juvenile processing by race in police agencies and courts, Dannefer and Schutt (1982) found evidence of discrimination within police agencies, as well as some evidence of better treatment for white than African American or Latino juveniles within the court, with Latinos receiving the harshest treatment. Similarly, Bondavalli and Bondavalli (1981) report discrepancies in placement by race, with a larger percentage of Latino youth placed in public institutions and a smaller percentage in private institutions than either white or African American youth.

As this review shows, much criminological research has analyzed race or gender separately, rather than recognizing and examining their interactive nature. Visher's (1983) analysis of police-suspect encounters is rare in that she examines the interconnection between gender and race in the treatment of female suspects. Consistent with prior research (DeFleur, 1975; Krohn et al., 1983), Visher found that the demeanor of the suspect influences arrest decisions for both sexes. However, she indicates that race and gender interact in shaping this process, so the race of the suspect (as well as age, class and demeanor) has a greater impact on arrest decisions for females than males. She notes:

> In encounters with police officers, those female suspects who violate typical middle-class standards of traditional female characteristics and behaviors (i.e., white, older, and submissive) are not afforded any chivalrous treatment during arrest decisions. In these data, young, black or hostile women receive no preferential treatment, whereas older, white women who are calm and deferential toward the police are granted leniency (Visher, 1983: 21-23).

Likewise, Sarri's analysis of court decisions revealed interactive effects of race, gender and class in the processing of juvenile offenders, with "white males having the best chance for dismissal; white females for diversion; black females for probation; and black males for the most formal processing and the severest sanctions" (1983: 390). In fact, "white middle class youth were far more often referred to their parents and to private treatment agencies" (Sarri, 1983: 390).

Similarly, Krisberg et al. report "growing disproportionate representation of minorities in juvenile correctional facilities" (1986: 11). At the same time that African Americans and Latinos have increased in proportion to whites in both detention centers and training schools, expenditures within these facilities have been declining, and overcrowding has increased (Krisberg et al., 1986). These disparities by race also hold for girls. According to Chesney-Lind, while the incarceration rate for white girls increased 14% between 1979 and 1982, "the incarceration rate for Hispanic and Black girls increased by 29%. Moreover, Black girls' incarceration rate in 1982 was more than double the incarceration rate for white girls" (1988: 155).

These findings all demonstrate that researchers who are concerned with the treatment of delinquent girls in the juvenile justice system must not simply treat girls as "girls"; rather they must be recognized as individuals whose lives are shaped interactively by gender, race, and class, as well as by other contexts of their lives. In this investigation, I will examine the impact of race on disposition decision-making for adjudicated delinquent girls in one regional probation office of Los Angeles county. I will use both quantitative and qualitative analyses to do so. Before describing the research setting and methods, I will first explain the proposed hypotheses.

RESEARCH HYPOTHESES

1. On average, African American and Latina girls will be recommended to receive harsher dispositions than those recommended for white girls, controlling for prior record and demeanor. Given research indicating that African American and Latino youths face harsher treatment in juvenile court than white youths generally (see above), it is predicted that this relationship will exist for girls, and will result in a smaller percentage of white girls on formal probation and placement than African American or Latina girls, and a larger percentage of white girls placed on informal probation. In addition, I predict there will be a disparity in institutionalization, with white girls more likely to be found in treatment facilities and African American and Latina girls more likely to be found in detention centers.

2. Regardless of race and prior record, girls who are perceived as having a negative demeanor will be recommended to receive harsher dispositions than girls who are not perceived as having a negative demeanor. Likewise, girls who are perceived as having a positive demeanor will be recommended to receive less severe dispositions than other girls. As previously discussed, research has consistently revealed a relationship between demeanor and police decisions to arrest and forward cases to the juvenile courts. For girls, the impact of demeanor also relates to police officers' beliefs about appropriate gender expectations, whereby girls who behave in stereotypically feminine ways tend to be treated more leniently (Gelsthorpe, 1986, 1989; DeFleur, 1975; Visher, 1983). It is hypothesized that the influence of demeanor is not exclusive to the police, but will be similarly influential for the probation officers who make disposition recommendations.

3. African American girls will be perceived more frequently as having a negative demeanor than Latina or white girls. Latina and white girls will more frequently be perceived as having a positive demeanor. Thus a portion of the total effect of race on disposition recommendation will be an indirect effect based on the relationship between race and perceived demeanor. Much of the interpretation of girls' demeanor within the juvenile justice system is based on whether they are perceived as conforming to (middle class white) feminine gender expectations. However, research conducted on the gender orientations of African American girls shows that they are less likely to exhibit stereotypical feminine qualities than their white counterparts (Higginbotham, 1982; Malson, 1983; Rice, 1990; Smith and Stewart, 1983). In addition, cultural imagery of white women depicts them as "tender, warm, quiet and gentle" while depicting African American females as "aggressive, rebellious, rude and loud" (Smith and Stewart, 1983:2). Likewise, popular images of Latinas present them as submissive and dependent, a counterpart to Latino men's perceived machismo (Baca Zinn, 1982). Given different cultural and situational expressions of gender (shaped by socio-economic and historical contexts), and given cultural imagery that differently depicts African American, Latina, and white females, probation officers' perceptions of demeanor will be shaped in part by racialized gender expectations.

DATA AND METHODS

Data for this project were gathered from the investigation reports of adjudicated delinquent girls on probation in one area office of the Los Angeles County Probation Department. Data were collected from July 1992 through March 1993. There were 198 girls on probation, with a total of 244 investigation reports. Each report represents one formal contact with the juvenile court, and these were recorded as separate cases. The area office was chosen because it is located in a racially mixed region within the county, with significant populations of African Americans, Latinos, and white, and therefore provides a useful sample for comparative analysis of girls by race.

I will be utilizing log-linear[2] analysis of the entire sample (n=244), chi-square analysis of the entire sample and portions thereof, and detailed content analysis of the investigation reports of a smaller portion of the sample (n=30). For the statistical portions of this analysis, the following information was extracted from the case files[3]: race, prior record, disposition recommendation[4], and demeanor. Prior record was coded as (1) no prior history of police contact, and (2) prior arrest(s) and/or adjudication(s). This allowed me to compare first offenders with those with lengthier records, while simultaneously maximizing cell frequencies.

Disposition recommendations were coded as follows: (1) informal probation, (2) formal probation, and (3) institutional placement. Formal probation includes stayed institutional placement orders. Stayed placement orders function as formal probation orders in that the juvenile remains in the community, but these orders give the probation officer more power to remove the youth from the community at a later date for violations of probation conditions. There are two basic types of institutional placement: treatment facilities and detention facilities. The former (hereafter referred to as suitable placements, in keeping with the language used in probation reports) consist of group homes, non-secure treatment facilities, and secure treatment facilities. The latter refers to the probation department's camp community placement facilities, which are detention centers located in the mountains north of Los Angeles, as well as California Youth Authority (CYA) placements.

For the statistical portion of the analysis, demeanor was coded specifically in terms of the probation officers' perception of the juvenile's attitude toward the officer and the court, and expressions of remorse or lack thereof. Three categories were utilized: (1) no mention, (2) positive demeanor, and (3) negative demeanor. An example of a statement coded as positive demeanor was: "When seen the minor was accepting of her responsibility believe [sic.] that she could make an effort to improve her behavior at home and indicates a desire to follow all court orders without subsequent problems." A typical investigation statement coded as negative was: "At the time of the interview, the minor's attitude and cooperation were very poor.

The probation officer could not detect any extent of remorse." Coding of demeanor indicators was limited to those appearing in the report in the voice of the investigating officer. While there were occasional quotes from parents, school officials or police officers about the girl's demeanor, unless the probation officer openly agreed with these descriptions in her or his analysis, these were coded as "no mention."

Log linear analysis was utilized to examine the main relationships between race, prior record, disposition recommendation, and demeanor. This analysis was supplemented with chi-square tests of significance to explore the relationship between race and class and the relationships between race, class and type of placement setting, as these were not included in the log linear analysis.[5]

For the qualitative portion of the research, I stratified the population of girls by race, then randomly selected 30 case files (ten each of African American, Latina, and white girls) for close content analysis of the investigation report. In addition, I analyzed these cases by subdividing them into four categories: AFDC recipients, non-AFDC recipients with family income under $20,000, family income between $20,000 and $45,000, and family income exceeding $45,000. This allowed me to also explore within-group differences by class.[6] My interest was in carefully examining the discursive frameworks used to describe girls' behavior, motivations, and attitudes, and to examine the similarities and differences in constructs used to describe girls of varying race and class backgrounds.

FINDINGS

Table 1 provides a descriptive breakdown of the characteristics of delinquent girls in the sample. Latinas are the largest percentage of the sample, followed by whites and African Americans. The majority of cases involve formal probation recommendations, and a slight majority of cases make no mention of girls' demeanor. Before presenting the best fitting log linear model of the relationship between these variables, I will briefly discuss the relationship between race and social class in the data. While class had to be excluded from the log linear analysis (see note 1 for an explanation), I did examine the relationship between income level and race for those cases in which the information was available (n=205). Tables 2 and 2a show that there is a significant relationship between income level and race for delinquent girls.

Table 1 *Characteristics of Delinquent Girls* (n=244)

VARIABLE	Number of Cases	Percentage of Cases
Race		
Latina	105	43%
White	83	34%
African American	56	23%
Prior Record		
Yes	123	51%
No	121	49%
Demeanor		
No Mention	132	54%
Positive	65	27%
Negative	47	19%
Disposition Recommendation		
Informal Probation	35	14%
Formal Probation	152	62%
Institutional Placement	57	23%

Table 2 *Race by Family Income among Delinquent Girls* (n=205)

INCOME LEVEL	RACE			
	Latina	White	African American	TOTAL
AFDC Recipient	18	17	25	60
Under $20,000	43	13	9	65
$20,000-45,000	20	22	11	53
Over $45,000	4	21	2	27
TOTAL	85	73	47	205

$X^2 = 50.09$; df = 6; p < .001

Table 2a *Race by Family Income: Column Percentages*

INCOME LEVEL	RACE			
	Latina	White	African American	TOTAL
AFDC Recipient	21.2	23.3	53.2	29.3
Under $20,000	50.6	17.8	19.1	31.7
$20,000-45,000	23.5	30.1	23.4	25.8
Over $45,000	4.7	28.8	4.3	13.2
TOTAL	100	100	100	100

While white girls tend to be most evenly distributed between income levels, they are clearly and markedly over represented in the over $45,000 income level as compared to African American and Latina girls. African American girls are over represented among AFDC recipients, and Latinas among the working poor (under $20,000/no public assistance). The significance of this relationship between race and income as a class indicator suggests that caution must be taken in interpreting the relationship between race and the other variables in the log linear analysis, as some of the effects may be the result of class rather than or in conjunction with race. While these relationships need further exploration, the log linear analysis nevertheless provides important information regarding the relationships between the variables examined. It is to this analysis that I now turn.

Table 3 *Log Linear Analysis for Best Fitting Model* (n=244)

PARAMETER	Independence Model	Best Fitting Model
MAIN EFFECTS		
Mean	1.161****	0.9860**
Formal Probation	1.469****	1.944****
Placement	0.4877*	-0.5502
Latina	0.2351	0.3497
African American	-0.3935*	-0.9280***
Prior Record	0.01639	-0.8689*
Positive Demeanor	-0.7084*** **	0.7802*
Negative Demeanor	-1.033****	-10.20
2-WAY INTERACTIONS		
Formal Probation/Prior Record		0.4347
Placement/Prior Record		2.593****
Latina/Prior Record		-0.2544
African American/Prior Record		0.9027*
Formal Probation/Positive Demeanor		-1.642****
Formal Probation/Negative Demeanor		8.875
Placement/Positive Demeanor		-3.116****
Placement/Negative Demeanor		9.898
L^2		33.602
df		38
BIC		-118.018

*p<.05; **p<.01; ***p<.001; ****p<.0001

Table 3 shows the independence model and the best fitting model for the log linear analysis.[7] There is a significant relationship between prior record and severity of disposition. This relationship was expected, as prior record has consistently been found to have a strong impact on disposition decisions (Empey and Stafford, 1991). Specifically in this case, girls who were ordered into placement facilities were very likely to have prior records (p < .0001). The relationship between being placed on formal probation (as opposed to informal probation) with a prior record is positive but not significant.

Race and Prior Record

Table 3 also shows a significant relationship (p < .05) between race and prior record, wherein African American girls are more likely to have prior contact with the system than Latina and white girls. This finding may be explained in several ways. This relationship partially may reflect higher rates of crime for African American girls, resulting in a greater likelihood of law enforcement and juvenile justice intervention. However, research comparing rates of crime for African American and white girls does not reveal higher rates of crime for African Americans, but some differences in the patterns and types of crimes committed.

For example, Ageton's (1983) analysis of National Youth Survey data reveals significant racial differences in the incidence of theft, with white girls reporting higher frequencies of involvement. She found no significant race differences in the incidence of crimes against persons, but significant differences in the prevalence, with "substantially higher proportions of black...females reporting involvement in violent behavior for three of the five years" (Ageton, 1983: 555).

Young's (1980) analysis of National Crime Survey data reveals differences in crime rates by race for girls when they offend within groups as opposed to alone. For lone female offenders, Young found that African American and white girls had similar rates of crime, with simple and aggravated assault comprising the bulk of offenses reported. However, in comparing multiple offenders, there were considerable differences:

> Black female offender groups differed substantially from white female offender groups in some specific offense categories. Assault (simple and aggravated) made up 72%

of total victimizations by white offenders but only 44% of
the total by black offenders. Theft (robbery and larceny
with contact) accounted for 56% of the victimizations by
black female offender groups but only about 28% of those
by white female offender groups (Young, 1980: 30).

Thus the greater number of African American girls with prior records
might be a partial result of law enforcement practices which prioritize
certain types of offenses over others.

It may also be partially accounted for by the preferential treatment
granted white female offenders by the police (Dannefer and Schutt,
1982; Visher, 1983). Thus, the likelihood of a prior record is
increased for African American girls by the greater likelihood of formal
intervention resulting from their contacts with the police. In addition,
research on the relationship between class and juvenile justice also
reveals discriminatory treatment, as well as differences in offense
patterns, for youths from lower socio-economic backgrounds, where
African American youths are disproportionately found (Empey and
Stafford, 1991). Thus class differences may also account for a portion
of the variation between African American and other girls, particularly
given their greater likelihood in this sample of coming from families
who receive public assistance.

There has been little prior research examining and comparing
crime rates of Latinas to other girls, or examining police interactions
with Latina girls. My findings, though not statistically significant,
suggest that Latina girls may be the least likely to have a prior record.
This could be a result of lower crime rates, in addition to police
perceptions of Latina youth as more traditional than their African
American and white counterparts. These relationships clearly highlight
the interactive nature of race, class and gender, and reveal the need for
further investigation into these connections in future research.

Demeanor and Disposition Recommendation

As predicted in hypothesis two, there was a significant
relationship between girls' perceived demeanor and their disposition
recommendations. However, it was significant only in relation to girls
with positive demeanor, who were less likely than other girls to receive
formal probation supervision ($p < .0001$) and less likely to receive
placement ($p < .0001$). It appears, then, that girls who displayed

remorse and were perceived as cooperative by the investigating officer were treated more leniently than girls for whom no demeanor displays were recorded or who were perceived as having negative attitudes. This is consistent with research about police leniency towards girls (Gelsthorpe, 1986, 1989; DeFleur, 1975; Visher, 1983), and suggests that demeanor is influential at higher levels of the juvenile justice system as well.

However, hypotheses one and three, which predicted a significant relationship between race and demeanor leading to an indirect effect of race on disposition, as well as a direct significant effect of race on disposition, were not confirmed. Neither the relationship between demeanor and race nor the relationship between race and disposition were significant in the log linear analysis, and did not appear as relationships which accounted for considerable variance in the best fitting model (although the relationships were in the predicted directions). However, I will explore each of these hypotheses further below in different ways.

First, there are several possible reasons for these particular results. It may be that certain differences by race do not exist in significant ways among the population of girls in the region I investigated specifically because of its demographics. For example, Dannefer and Schutt (1982) found that racial bias in police and court handling varied by the racial composition of the community. Of two regions compared, racial bias in police handling was more severe in the region where African Americans made up a larger percentage of the population, while there was a stronger relationship between race and court disposition in the region with a smaller population of African Americans. This raises questions about the regional influences on girls' disposition.

It may also be that the ways in which race interacts with both demeanor and disposition is not captured by the log linear analysis. For example, it may be that only when girls' behaviors are seen as serious enough to warrant significant intervention (such as removal from the home and community) does race become a decisive interpretive factor in the handling of delinquent girls. To investigate this further, I examine the interaction of race with type of placement recommendation to see which girls were recommended for treatment facilities and which were recommended for detention.

The Interaction of Race and Placement Recommendation

While the log linear analysis did not show a significant relationship between race and disposition recommendation, a further breakdown of the category "institutional placement" does reveal a significant relationship between race and type of placement recommended for adjudicated girls. This relationship is shown in Tables 4 and 4a. There is a significant skew in placement recommendations, wherein white girls are much more likely to be recommended for suitable placement than African American or Latina girls, particularly African American girls (75% of white girls, versus 20% of African American, and 34.6% of Latinas). Likewise, African American girls are the most frequent recipients of a camp placement recommendation (80%, versus 25% for white girls and 65.4% for Latina girls).

Table 4 *Race by Placement Recommendation* (n=57)

PLACEMENT RECOMMENDATION	RACE			
	White	Latina	African American	TOTAL
Suitable Placement	12	9	3	24
Camp/CYA	4	17	12	33
TOTAL	16	26	15	57

$X^2 = 10.7$; df = 2; p < .01

Table 4a *Race by Placement Recommendation: Column Percentages*

PLACEMENT RECOMMENDATION	RACE			
	White	Latina	African American	TOTAL
Suitable Placement	75.0	34.6	20.0	42.1
Camp/CYA	25.0	65.4	80.0	57.9
TOTAL	100.0	100.0	100.0	100.0

Interestingly, class was not significantly related to whether a girl was recommended for suitable placement versus camp community placement. In fact, there was a relatively even distribution of girls by class within the placement categories, particularly in comparison to the skewing of placement recommendation by race (see Table 5). Given the strong relationship between race and class among the sample revealed in Tables 2 and 2a, and the lack of its reproduction in placement recommendations, it appears that race is the overriding characteristic affecting probation officers' decisions. Suitable placement facilities are explicitly treatment oriented, while the camp community placement facilities and CYA are detention oriented. In the interpretation of girls as "criminal" or as "in need of treatment," race appears to be quite significant: middle class African American girls are more likely to be labelled "criminal," while poor white girls are in need of "help."

Table 5 *Class by Placement Recommendation* (n=45)

	PLACEMENT		
INCOME LEVEL	Suitable Placement	Camp/CYA	TOTAL
AFDC Recipient	7	10	17
Under $20,000	3	7	10
$20,000-45,000	3	6	9
Over $45,000	6	3	9
TOTAL	19	26	45

There are clear differences by race, then, in the treatment of girls who are more seriously delinquent-involved. This is consistent with other research findings presented earlier (Chesney-Lind, 1988; Krisberg et al., 1986; Sarri, 1983), and may partly be a result of probation officers' interpretations of girls, as shaped by their notions of race and gender. Perhaps one means by which the phenomenon of differential placement recommendations operates is in the interpretive frameworks used by probation officers to understand girls' actions. Below I will use a more nuanced approach to examining probation officers' perceptions of delinquent girls that goes beyond measures of demeanor as usually used within quantitative research.

Race, Class, and Perceived Roots of Female Delinquency

It may be that the narrow definition of demeanor as remorse-related does not capture the subtleties in categorizations of girls. To further explore this, I have examined a portion of the investigation reports (n=30) to build a detailed analysis of the discursive frameworks drawn upon to describe the nature of delinquent girls and their behaviors, and to justify the court's decisions about their handling.

Within the investigation reports, there was a consistent discursive pattern among probation officers of emphasizing the causes of girls' delinquent behaviors removed from their social contexts and wider social, political or economic causes. Officers did not attempt to search for answers to the questions of why girls committed offenses beyond the individuals' perceived nature, emotional health, family dynamics, or peer group influences. Often these interpretations appeared to be shaped by racialized gender expectations.

The most striking difference in the framing of delinquent girls by race was in the discursive constructs used to describe the roots of their delinquent activities. African American girls' behavior was often framed in terms of inappropriate "lifestyle" choices. On the other hand, white girls' delinquent acts were frequently described as resulting from low self esteem, their being easily influenced by negative peers, or, less frequently, as a result of abandonment issues. Significantly, these discursive constructs were not used in *any* of the analyses of African American girls. Latina girls were framed using both those constructs typically used to describe African American girls and those used to describe white girls. In the following sections, I will provide examples of these discursive constructs.

Inappropriate "Lifestyle" Choices

Janice[8], an African American AFDC recipient, was arrested after she lied to the police "in order to protect her brother." In making recommendations to the judge, the probation officer stated, "she needs to participate in counseling so that she can explore her current lifestyle and set positive goals for the future." These discursive constructs— "positive goals" and "lifestyle"—appear to function as codes for class expectations. In a more blatant example, Diana, a middle-income African American girl, was harshly criticized for failing to assimilate into a middle class lifestyle when provided with the opportunity. According to the probation officer, Diana resented her mother for divorcing her father. However, the officer was very critical of Diana's feelings, and her criticism was steeped in class-based value judgments:

> [Minor] knows that when her mother and father were together the family was on welfare and living in the inner city. In the process of *lifting her family up*, the mother has found that she is not at all in touch with minor's stated desires, which seem to be to return to the *insidious place* they left [my emphases].

In both Diana's and Janice's cases, social class was reflected in the probation officers' recommendations. For Diana, non-conformity to proper class position appeared at the heart of the sanctions the probation officer recommended. Diana was defined as "manipulative" and "self-centered," and the officer stated that "the minor needs to delve into why she finds it necessary to behave as she does." The probation officer pathologized her behavior, rather than examining what values or relationships her mother might have left behind in the "inner city" that Diana might legitimately choose not to abandon.

Like Diana, Tonia, an upper-middle income African American girl, was judged harshly for rejecting the upper-middle class expectations that came with her family's position: "Minor is spoiled and immature. She lives for the moment and is not goal oriented." According to Tonia's mother, she "gravitates towards losers." However, the twist in Tonia's case, which was not found in the descriptions of lower income African American girls, but was found consistently among Latina and white girls of all income levels, was the label "self destructive" rather than having negative "lifestyle" choices. In being framed as "self destructive," she was in need of help and protection. Girls with poor "lifestyle" choices were framed instead as deviant, as when Leanne, a lower income Latina, was described by the probation officer as "devoid of values" for her participation in a gang.

Low Self-Esteem and Negative Peer Influences

Except for the label "self destructive," even Tonia was not afforded the explanations frequently drawn upon to describe white girls. In contrast to the above examples, the delinquent acts of a number of white girls were framed in ways that emphasized their vulnerability to the "corrupting" influences of others, or their fragility as a result of emotional problems. In these cases, the girls weren't delinquent because of some "badness" within them, but from some weakness or from external sources. Becky, a white AFDC recipient arrested for vandalism, was described as having a difficult time "withstand[ing] the negative influence" of her peers. In addition, the probation officer theorized that Becky had "an unhealthy blocking of feelings and growing rage." As a result, the officer concluded:

It is very doubtful that she would commit this type of offense on society again but probation officer believes that she is very capable of becoming self-destructive without intense therapy. This destruction might begin as simply as failing her classes but would then progress into poor, destructive relationships and any negative activity that might result from those relationships.

In addition to negative peer influences and self-destructive tendencies, several white girls were described as also having low self-images. Nowhere did such a construct appear to describe African American girls. For example, Cathy, a lower income white girl, was characterized as "easily influenced by others." She has "a tendency to pick the wrong kind of friends, but she does not seem to be delinquently sophisticated." As a result, the probation officer recommended that "participation in counseling might help her develop a more positive self-image and ability to think for herself." Cathy's behavior was not characterized as originating from her own delinquent proclivities, but rather from those of negative peers.

Similarly, Marsha, a middle income white girl, "does not appear inordinately delinquent...[but] can best be described as a teenager unable to set limits for herself....Minor has low self-esteem and has continually re-involved herself with less than positive peers." Her need for help was framed as stemming from "low self-esteem" rather than from lifestyle choices; the discourse drawn upon described her as influenced by negative peers, rather than being inherently delinquent herself. Likewise, Karen was a middle income white girl who was involved with gangs. While Leanne was described as "devoid of values" for her gang involvement (see above), Karen's gang involvement was framed as a consequence of "family dysfunction":

Although in a relative sense, this is not a serious offense [shoplifting], there are numerous severe problems in this minor's life which need ongoing supervision. Her stepfather is an alcoholic and her mother is an enabler....Minor denies that she is self-destructing by her ongoing truancy, gang associations, et cetera....Minor must become involved in some type of self-help group to deal with her feelings regarding her alcoholic stepfather, her natural father's abandonment of her and her anger towards her mother for her own codependency.

Interestingly, Latina girls were framed in ways that paralleled those found in the descriptions of both African American and white girls. Some Latinas were characterized by drawing upon paternalistic discourses similar to those describing white girls, as "self-destructive," having a "negative self-image" and "negative peers." For example, of Dora, the probation officer said, "[a]lthough this offense should not be taken lightly, it appears as though she may have been acting from emotions rather than in a delinquent manner."

Other Latinas were framed in more punitive ways. For example, Sylvia, a lower income Latina, was framed by the probation officer in very negative terms due, in part, to the officer's perception of her as a bad mother. The officer noted that "the minor has set a pattern of living on the streets generally abandoning her child to associate with car thieves." It was stressed several times in the report that Sylvia had "left her child," who remained in the care of her mother. According to the probation officer, Sylvia "generally rationalized her socially deviant behavior...[and] failed to acknowledge the seriousness of her actions." It is perhaps significant that the only minor who was explicitly labeled "deviant" in any of the investigation reports was one whose deviance was clearly linked to being a bad mother and abandoning her child.

This dichotomized treatment of Latina girls may be related to probation officers' interpretations of gender norms in Latino culture. Perhaps Latinas who violate gender norms by participating in offenses deemed particularly masculine (in the above cases, car theft, burglary, and gang membership) face harsher treatment than those girls who commit offenses perceived as feminine or commit offenses as a result of their involvement with a boyfriend. These complexities should be studied further.

DISCUSSION AND CONCLUSION

The data I have analyzed allude to the complexities of the relationships between race, gender and juvenile justice for delinquent girls. While research has consistently shown racial bias in police handling of youths (Dannefer and Schutt, 1982; Visher, 1983), the evidence of bias within the courts is more limited, except when examining placement (Bondavalli and Bondavalli, 1981; Chesney-Lind and Shelden, 1992; Krisberg et al., 1986; Sarri, 1983). The results of my analyses were mixed. I hypothesized that there would be clear and significant relationships between race and disposition recommendations, with Latina and especially African American girls being treated more punitively than white girls. I also hypothesized that demeanor would enter in as an interactive variable, being significantly related to both disposition recommendation and race. The log linear analysis showed no overall pattern of racial bias in the treatment of delinquent girls.

However, my findings add credence to claims of differential placement by race of delinquent girls, revealing a clear disparity between treatment versus detention placement recommendations. While the data support the possibility that disposition patterns are not racially biased when the supervision does not require out-of-home placement, when girls are seen as in need of more intense supervision, the placement recommendations observed raise fundamental questions about how notions of gender are shaped by race in ways that influence which girls are perceived as needing "help" and which are perceived as deserving punishment.

The preliminary content analysis of investigation reports points to the need for further investigation of the contexts of probation officers' perceptions of girls' behaviors, in addition to perceptions of demeanor. The relationship between race and demeanor (as defined by remorse and cooperative attitudes towards juvenile justice or the lack thereof) was not statistically significant in the statistical analysis. However, when a more nuanced approach was explored in examining the interpretive frameworks used by investigating officers, many complexities were revealed which appear linked to race. Patterns of discursive constructs emerged which categorized African American, white and Latina girls in varying ways; these types of constructs, and their links to officers' perceptions of girls, may help explain differences in placement.

The discursive shifts that took place within specific race (and class) contexts were often subtle, but revealed themselves in significant ways. Paternalistic discursive frameworks were frequently called upon to explain the behavior of white and Latina girls, while punitive constructs were more likely to be used to describe African American girls. In addition, middle class girls were expected to appreciate their class privilege and behave accordingly, while lower income girls were expected to aspire to middle class values and goals. These findings represent general patterns in the data, rather than universals.

In this paper, I have drawn on recent trends in feminist criminology which emphasize that unitary analyses of gender and gender discrimination, divorced from the contexts of factors such as race and class, miss the complexities of both the social world and the treatment of delinquent youths within it. My study of disposition decision-making specifically examines the intersecting dimensions of race and gender, and as such, it remains limited in scope and preliminary. Nonetheless, this study offers strong support for the argument that only by examining the interactive effects of race, class and gender can we begin to truly understand the multiple and contradictory experiences of delinquent girls. We must continue to build our knowledge of the relationships between race, class and gender at all levels of the juvenile justice system, in order to more effectively document existing discrimination and affect change.

AUTHOR'S NOTE: An earlier version of this paper was awarded second place in the Gene Carte Student Paper Competition, American Society of Criminology, 1994. Thanks to Malcolm Klein and Barrie Thorne for guidance and feedback during the research process, Dragan Milovanovic for comments on an earlier draft, Tim Biblarz for instruction in the use of log linear analysis, and the Los Angeles County Probation Department and its probation officers for providing me with access to girls' case files.

NOTES

1. My specific focus in this paper is limited to the relationship of race to the treatment of adjudicated girls. Given a small sample size (n=244) and a number of case files with missing data on class indicators (16 percent, n=39), I have excluded a variable measuring class from the main statistical analysis. Recognizing this as a serious limitation, I will discuss the relationships between race and class prior to presenting major findings, and in the qualitative portion of the analysis.

2. Log linear analysis was chosen over multiple regression analysis after carefully weighing the benefits and limitations of each. With log linear analysis I was limited in the number of variables I could examine

at one time because of the concern with cell size. However, using multiple regression would have resulted in losing information crucial to my research concern with the collapse of key nominal variables into dichotomous categories. With log linear analysis, I was able to examine disposition recommendation, race and demeanor without losing the most important features of each.

3. In preliminary analyses using both log linear analysis and chi-square tests of significance, the type of offense (coded as misdemeanor versus felony) was used as a variable as well. However, it was subsequently dropped from the final log linear analysis because it was not found to be significantly related to the other variables, and dropping it provided a means to increase cell sizes.

4. I have chosen to use disposition recommendation rather than the actual disposition as the dependent variable because of my interest in exploring demeanor indicators. Since the indicators are generated by the investigating officer rather than the judge, I find greater continuity in focusing on the investigating officers' disposition recommendation rather than the judges' orders. While there is occasional deviation between the disposition recommended and that ordered by the court, it is typical for judges to concur with the recommendations put forth by probation investigators. Nevertheless, my results do not reflect sentencing patterns, but sentencing recommendations.

5. Small cell frequencies place constraints on the analysis. A small percentage of the overall sample of girls were placed in institutionalized settings (23 percent, $n=57$), so further breakdown of this category was not desirable for the log linear portion of the analysis.

6. While this does not provide a comprehensive measure of social class, it provided a fruitful way of examining disparities in the ways that girls were discussed by income levels, and allowed me to examine the possible stigmatizing effects of being welfare recipients. My specific interest is how factors such as class are related to the investigating officers' perceptions of girls, and I would argue that they also adopt a rough measure of social class, based on the limited data points available to them. For the sake of continuity, I use this measure as well when I discuss the relationships of race and placement to class in the entire sample.

7. With larger sample sizes and a greater number of variables, the search for the best fitting model must be theory-driven and trial/error. However, it was possible in this case to run every possible combination of relationships to determine the model that best accounts for the variation in the data, using the BIC criterion. There was no residual greater than two.

8. All names are fictitious.

REFERENCES

Ageton, Suzanne S. 1983. "The Dynamics of Female Delinquency, 1976-1980." *Criminology.* 21: 555-584.

Alder, Christine. 1984. "Gender Bias in Juvenile Diversion." *Crime & Delinquency.* 30(3): 400-414.

Baca Zinn, Maxine. 1982. "Mexican-American Women in the Social Sciences." *Signs.* 8(2): 259-272.

Bondavalli, Bonnie J., and Bruno Bondavalli. 1981. "Spanish-Speaking People and the North American Criminal Justice System." In R.L. McNeely and Carl E. Pope, eds. *Race, Crime and Criminal Justice.* Beverly Hills: Sage.

Cain, Maureen. 1989. "Feminists Transgress Criminology." In Maureen Cain, ed. *Growing Up Good: Policing the Behavior of Girls in Europe.* London: Sage.

Campbell, Anne. 1981. *Girl Delinquents.* New York: St. Martin's Press.

Canter, Rachelle J. 1982. "Sex Differences in Self-Report Delinquency." *Criminology.* 20: 373-393.

Chesney-Lind, Meda. 1977. "Judicial Paternalism and the Female Status Offender: Training Women to Know Their Place." *Crime & Delinquency.* 23: 121-130.

Chesney-Lind, Meda. 1978. "Young Women in the Arms of the Law." In Lee H. Bowker, ed. *Women, Crime and the Criminal Justice System.* Lexington, MA: Lexington Books.

Chesney-Lind, Meda. 1988. "Girls and Status Offenses: Is Juvenile Justice Still Sexist?" *Criminal Justice Abstracts.* 20(1): 144-165.

Chesney-Lind, Meda, and Randall G. Shelden. 1992. *Girls, Delinquency and Juvenile Justice.* Pacific Grove, CA: Brooks/Cole Publishing Company.

Daly, Kathleen. 1991. "Impact of Feminist Theory on Studies of Law and Crime." Paper presented at the annual meetings of the American Society of Criminology.

Daly, Kathleen, and Meda Chesney-Lind. 1988. "Feminism and Criminology." *Justice Quarterly.* 5(4): 497-538.

Dannefer, Dale and Russell K. Schutt. 1982. "Race and Juvenile Justice Processing in Court and Police Agencies." *American Journal of Sociology.* 87: 1113-1132.

DeFleur, Lois B. 1975. "Biasing Influences on Drug Arrest Records: Implications for Deviance Research." *American Sociological Review.* 40: 88-103.

Empey, LaMar T., and Mark C. Stafford. 1991. *American Delinquency: Its Meanings & Construction.* Belmont, CA: Wadsworth Publishing Company.

Feyerherm, William. 1981. "Juvenile Court Dispositions of Status Offenders: An Analysis of Case Decisions." In R.L. McNeely and Carl E. Pope, eds. *Race, Crime and Criminal Justice.* Beverly Hills: Sage.

Figueira-McDonough, Josephina. 1985. "Are Girls Different? Gender Discrepancies between Delinquent Behavior and Control." *Child Welfare.* 64: 273-289.

Gelsthorpe, Loraine. 1986. "Towards a Skeptical Look at Sexism." *International Journal of the Sociology of Law.* 14: 125-152.

Gelsthorpe, Loraine. 1989. *Sexism and the Female Offender: An Organizational Analysis.* Aldershot, England: Gower.

Gelsthorpe, Loraine, and Allison Morris, eds. 1990. *Feminist Perspectives in Criminology.* Milton Keynes/Philadelphia: Open University Press.

Higginbotham, Elizabeth. 1982. "Two Representative Issues in Contemporary Sociological Work on Black Women." In Gloria T. Hull, Patricia Bell Scott, and Barbara Smith, eds. *But Some of Us Are Brave.* Old Westbury, NY: The Feminist Press.

Joe, Karen, and Meda Chesney-Lind. Forthcoming. "'Just Every Mother's Angel': An Analysis of Gender and Ethnic Variations in Youth Gang Membership." *Gender & Society.*

Kersten, Joachim. 1989. "The Institutional Control of Girls and Boys: An Attempt at a Gender-Specific Approach." In Maureen Cain, ed. *Growing Up Good: Policing the Behavior of Girls in Europe.* London: Sage.

Klein, Dorie. 1991. "Dilemmas of Diversity for Feminist Criminology." Paper presented at the annual meetings of the American Society of Criminology.

Krisberg, Barry, Ira M. Schwartz, Paul Litsky, and James Austin. 1986. "The Watershed of Juvenile Justice Reform." *Crime & Delinquency.* 32: 5-38.

Krohn, Marvin D., James P. Curry, and Shirley Nelson-Kilger. 1983. "Is Chivalry Dead?" *Criminology.* 21: 417-439.

Laub, John H., and Joan McDermott. 1985. "An Analysis of Serious Crime by Young Black Women." *Criminology.* 23: 81-98.

Leonard, Eileen. 1982. *Women, Crime and Society: A Critique of Theoretical Criminology.* New York: Longman.

Malson, Michelene Ridley. 1983. "Black Women's Sex Roles: the Social Context for a New Ideology." *Journal of Social Issues.* 39(3): 101-113.

Mann, Coramae Richey. 1984. *Female Crime and Delinquency.* University, AL: University of Alabama Press.

Rice, Marcia. 1990. "Challenging Orthodoxies in Feminist Theory: A Black Feminist Critique." In Loraine Gelsthorpe and Allison Morris, eds. *Feminist Perspectives in Criminology.* Milton Keynes/Philadelphia: Open University Press.

Sarri, Rosemary. 1976. "Juvenile Law: How It Penalizes Females." In Laura Crites, ed. *The Female Offender.* Lexington, MA: Lexington Books.

Sarri, Rosemary. 1983. "Gender Issues in Juvenile Justice." *Crime and Delinquency.* 29: 381-397.

Smart, Carol. 1976. *Women, Crime and Criminology: A Feminist Critique.* London: Routledge & Kegan Paul.

Smart, Carol. 1977. "Criminological Theory: Its Ideology and Implications Concerning Women." *British Journal of Sociology.* 28(1): 89-100.

Smith, Althea, and Abigail J. Stewart. 1983. "Approaches to Studying Racism and Sexism in Black Women's Lives." *Journal of Social Issues.* 39(3): 1-15.

Teilmann, Katherine S., and Pierre H. Landry, Jr. 1981. "Gender Bias in Juvenile Justice." *Journal of Research in Crime and Delinquency.* 18: 47-80.

Visher, Christy A. 1983. "Gender, Police Arrest Decisions, and Notions of Chivalry." *Criminology.* 21: 5-28.

Young, Vernetta D. 1980. "Women, Race and Crime." *Criminology.* 18: 26-34.

CHAPTER 12

Controlling Homeless Mothers: The Surveillance of Women in a Homeless Shelter

Victoria Pitts

This article examines the social control of poor women—particularly, poor mothers—in a homeless shelter that houses women and children. My discussion of shelters identifies three important aspects of the social control of poor women: first, the direct, immediate control of women's activities in such institutions via rules and authority structures; second, the use of surveillance (the search for and gathering of information about poor women's lives, personalities, and behaviors); and finally, the indirect control of homeless mothers through the use of that information to intervene in their lives beyond the limited arena of the institution itself. My own study of a family homeless shelter is the focus of this article, but I also locate these three social control activities in the reported findings of other researchers who have examined shelters.

The notion of social control that I use in describing homeless women's experiences is one that is highly relevant to criminology. It is a notion that assumes a "transinstitutional" nature to social control—that social policy institutions such as jails, mental hospitals, and welfare institutions are not insular, separate entities but rather intersect and form connections (Lowman et al., 1987)—and that recognizes that at least some of the tools of social control are shared by institutions. The research that I present is also relevant to criminology in that many of the women in family homeless shelters are survivors of domestic violence and domestic violence is a significant cause of homelessness among poor women (Hagen, 1987). Homelessness that results in shelter use is often relevant to class and race issues even when the cause of homelessness is domestic violence, even though much of the domestic violence literature argues that the problem cuts across class and racial barriers, because "in practice shelters cater only to a specific population of women, that is poor women who have no other means of escape from abusive situations" (Murray, 1988). Shelters house those who have little or no access to other housing alternatives, and poor women, some whom are women of color, have the least alternative resources. Family homeless shelters (that are not designed only for battered women) almost exclusively house those who are poor. It is poor women that are clients of social welfare institutions and thus poor women who are vulnerable to the social control practices of institutions like homeless shelters.

The dominant ideology of social policy "as a purely humanitarian enterprise" (Higgins, 1980) is not supported by the disciplinary tactics, interventions and attempts to resocialize clients by social service institutions that have been reported by researchers of the radical social work perspective. Welfare policy has been identified by critics with several modes of social control, including repression, exploitation, co-optation, integration, and paternalism (Higgins, 1980) and has been regarded as an "institution for social control and subjugation" in radical critiques of social work (Schillinger, 1988; see also Piven and Cloward, 1975; Dobash and Dobash, 1979).

Social control is then a concept that has been developed to describe the practices of social service institutions as well as those of official criminal justice institutions. Cohen's notion of social control expands the use of the concept beyond the realm of crime control. This notion of social control recognizes welfare institutions as part of a network of sites of control. Social control here is constituted by:

> organized responses to crime, deviance and allied forms of
> deviant and/or socially problematic behavior which are
> actually conceived of as such, whether in the reactive sense
> (after the putative act has taken place or the actor has been
> identified) or in the proactive sense (to prevent the act).
> These responses may be sponsored directly by the state or
> by more autonomous professional agents in, say, social
> work and psychiatry. Their goals may be as specific as
> individual punishment and treatment or as diffuse as 'crime

prevention', 'public safety', and 'community mental health' (1985, quoted in Lowman et al., 1987).

Lowman et al., starting with Cohen's definition of social control, emphasize the role of language and classification as tools of surveillance and discipline by social service, mental health, and criminal justice institutions. This approach to social control examines the "cross-institutional" nature of control and the use of information gathering (what Foucault calls surveillance) as a "technology of discipline" (Lowman et al., 1987; Hewitt, 1983). This use of the concept of social control allows for the discussion of controlling and intervening practices on the part of welfare institutions in addition to those of criminal justice and focusses on the role of surveillance as a controlling practice.

The radical social work literature has documented contemporary social control practices of welfare institutions (Higgins, 1980) and feminist historians have researched the intersection of social control and the development of social policy (Gordon, 1986). Few researchers, however, have investigated the practices of homeless shelters in particular (Berk et al., 1986; Hagan, 1987), with the exception of battered women's shelters, which often are organized around an explicitly feminist orientation cognizant of at least some of the controlling aspects of bureaucratic institutions that serve poor women. Little research is available on family homeless shelters, which house poor mothers and children and are not designed explicitly to address domestic violence. Family homeless shelters are welfare institutions and are connected with and often funded by public agencies. This article describes my observations of a family homeless shelter and in particular attempts to explicate three aspects of shelter life which I believe constitute social control practices: direct control of mobility, activity and privacy within the institution, surveillance, and intervention that utilizes information and networks between the shelter and other institutions.

DIRECT CONTROL

Evidence of the direct control of women within shelters has been documented by researchers of battered women's shelters. In many shelters the policies regarding lifestyles are expansive, are not determined collectively, and carry official sanctions (Murray, 1988;

Wharton, 1989; Schillinger, 1988). Murray's (1988) study of a shelter noted that the house rules emphasized control rather than the health and safety of its residents. Staff members in shelters are encouraged to establish their authority in shelters in order to enforce the rules and control is maintained through an "a priori rejection of clients' ability to legitimately challenge the staff" (Ferraro, 1983). The rules of shelters limit activity, set guidelines for everyday practices, and display uneven distributions of power between the staff and the residents. Because of the expansiveness of the policies, their undemocratic nature, and the power that is used in enforcing them, Wharton compares shelters to Goffman's "total institutions" (Wharton, 1989). Researchers have not emphasized one of the functions that the rules may serve, which is to increase the institution's knowledge about the behaviors and personalities of the residents. I will argue below that this function is a major effect of the rules and authority structure of the shelter I studied.

INFORMATION GATHERING

Higgins (1985) compared the human service worker with a "detective, who gathers, organizes and uses information in order to make sense out of the client's situation." Studies of shelters are replete with references to the staff logs in which information is documented about residents. Women do not have access to their own files, and as Murray (1985) notes, "control over personal information involves power." Murray's discussion of a battered women's shelter identifies the asymmetry involved in the situation where staff members can know personal information about residents but the residents know nothing of the staff. This "sets residents apart from the staff and reinforces asymmetrical power and hierarchal relations." Murray argues that intake forms should be changed to limit information procured to a woman's immediate situation. Wharton argues that staff bring assumptions with them to their detective work and that these assumptions need to be questioned. She concludes that "shelter staff must become better 'detectives' in discovering their clients' needs and perceptions" (Wharton, 1989). The discussions in the literature about what I am calling "surveillance" vary in their critical stances, but not all of them emphasize information-taking as central to the activities of shelters and as contributing to control or discipline. Piven and Cloward (1975) call social workers' logs "dossiers of the state." In my discussion of the operations of a shelter, I also regard the files and logs and forms written about shelter residents as crucial to the use of power in shelters. It is important to remember, more broadly, that it is poor people who are most likely to be the targets of the social worker's "detective" notes.

INTERVENTION

Interventions—shelters' use of the knowledge gathered about clients to affect their clients' lives beyond the simple control of activity within the shelter—have been documented at battered women's shelters in the form of socialization (Schillinger, 1988; Ferraro, 1983) and therapeutic intervention (Ferraro, 1983; Loseke, 1992). Schillinger (1988) argues that welfare institutions targeted their resources and priorities to the "correction and control" of the women they serve, and Murray (1988) states that the staff at the shelter she studied perceived the institution to be both a "people-processing" and a "people-changing" organization. "People-changing" in shelters and other welfare institutions has a wide variety of meanings for poor women: empowerment, therapy, psychiatric medication, job training, child care, greater involvement with the welfare system, influence over child-rearing practices and lifestyles, and so on. The interventions are sometimes perceived by clients as positive and sometimes as negative (one of Murray's (1988) interviewees said that "Once you've been identified as weak or deficient or having no one to protect you, they go after you like a pack of wolves.") What I am most interested in, regardless of whether the interventions are ultimately perceived as benefitting the women or not, is the process in institutions whereby information is collected that facilitates these interventions.

RACHEL'S HOUSE

The shelter I studied, which I am calling Rachel's House (all names have been changed including that of the institution), is a family shelter that houses families of mothers and children. Rachel's House is located in a small city near the metropolitan area of a major U.S. city. My discussion of the operations of the shelter come from the field notes that I kept while working there as a part-time staff member over six months (I varied between 16 and 40 hours a week). My observations come from my own experiences in the shelter as a staff member enforcing the rules and policies as well as from conversations with other shelter workers and residents, from reading the daily log notes and files, from staff meetings, and the written instructions given during staff training. My known role there was not one of a researcher but of a worker, and my notes were normally taken in the hours immediately after I left.

Rachel's House houses six to seven families that range in size. Fathers are eligible to live with their children at the shelter but to my knowledge, less than five have done so in the past six years. Nearly all of the families that have lived there are headed by single mothers. The shelter is managed by a private, non-profit agency (as many shelters are) and receives the majority of its funding from the state's Department of Public Welfare budget. The agency maintains that the average stay for families is three to four months. Many of the women at Rachel's House have left batterers, but the shelter is not organized as a battered women's shelter. (The shelter houses many families who are there due to poverty only and not domestic violence; the shelter does not take families on an "emergency" basis, who have immediately left batterers and who have not been referred through the local welfare department; and the house does not have the security measures in place that battered women's shelters do.) The residents are of a variety of races and ethnic backgrounds. Because old residents are often moving out and new residents are moving in, it is difficult to make claims about the average racial and ethnic makeup of the shelter. Some families were themselves racially mixed. Usually at least half the mothers were Caucasian. Others were of a variety of racial or ethnic backgrounds, including African American, Latina, and African Caribbean.

My discussion of the social control aspects of life at Rachel's House will focus on the three elements I have already discussed: first, the direct control of the women's activity, mobility, and privacy through the rules and authority structure; second, the surveillance activity of the institution that is facilitated by the direct control within the shelter; and third, the interventions that rely upon information gathering and direct control and that are felt beyond the limited arena of the shelter itself. My emphasis in this article is on describing surveillance because I believe it is a major aspect of poor women's experiences of the controlling nature of welfare institutions as well as an important part of the "transinstitutional" nature of social control. Although I do not discuss other institutions in great detail, it is intervention which relies on information gathering that may connect welfare institutions with those of mental health, criminal justice and so on.

DIRECT CONTROL OF RESIDENTS' DAILY LIVES

Life at the shelter is constructed around rules that govern many aspects of residents' lives. The rules are a point of contention among the residents, who often express resentment against the direct control that the shelter exerts over their daily lives. This direct control is often seen by the residents as punitive. Residents have described the shelter as "oppressive" and "like jail." One resident told me, "I don't like living under so much control...I've been out on my own for a long time now and it's hard under so much control." Another described living at the shelter as "being incarcerated."

The shelter's system of rules limits the spacial mobility of the residents: they have an evening curfew; they must be upstairs in their rooms at 12:30pm; they must sleep at the shelter at least six days a week; they must be at the shelter to attend several meetings per week; they must be at the shelter daily to have their chores checked by the staff. The rule system also addresses their activity: visitors are allowed on the first floor only, in the common living areas; chores must be done every day; cooking is not allowed after 10pm; residents must sign in and out every time they leave and enter the shelter; they must ask for their medications, which are kept in the staff office, and so on. In addition, at Rachel's House as in other shelters (see Wharton, 1989), there are many rules regarding parenting.

The atmosphere of the shelter serves to remind residents that they are not living on their terms. A description of the signs posted on the kitchen walls illustrates this well. The walls are covered with instructions about daily life, in addition to posters advertising social services, the battered women's hotline number, and fire escape plans. One week I counted 27 signs posted in the kitchen, and 17 of them were instructions—for example, "Please Sign up for Meetings with [Case Worker]" and "All Residents Must Actively Participate in Housing Search." Some of them were accompanied by reminders of the institution's expectations: for example, "All Meetings Are Mandatory"; "Failure to Comply with This Policy Will Be Reported to the DPW and May Result in Termination from the Shelter," and so on.

The rules are enforced by a punitive system of "warnings" and termination. Three written warnings given by the staff results in the resident and her children being "asked to leave" the shelter. One of the resources of power that the institution has is its ability to take away what it has given (shelter), which can induce anxiety and insecurity in the residents. The "gift" of shelter is conditional, both by Rachel's House, which can terminate residents, and by the welfare department which issues emergency assistance benefits. If the shelter's conditions are not met the residents can be terminated from that specific location, and if the welfare department's conditions are not met, the residents can be denied access to all shelters that it funds. The conditional nature of the relationship Rachel's House has with its residents was made explicit by one worker to Greg, a resident's adolescent son who was complaining about the rules. She reported telling him, "Look, it's not like you have to live here. You agreed to the contract, if you don't want to follow the contract you don't have to stay here." The conditional nature of assistance can have serious consequences. During the first two and a half months I was at the shelter, three of the four residents who left did so because they were terminated for breaking the rules. After six months, a total of 6 out of the 11 residents who had left did so involuntarily.

The staff members expressed ambivalent feelings about the rules, and there is some selectivity in their enforcement. Staff members have a lot of discretion in enforcing the policies for two reasons. First, some are designed with the staff's judgments in mind. For example, staff members can make "quiet hour" earlier if they feel that the shelter is "out of control." Second, they have discretion because to some extent can choose to look the other way if they catch a resident breaking the rules. This happened to my knowledge several times when a resident was in danger of being terminated from the shelter. However, staff discretion is not always to the benefit of residents. Staff members can create "potential violators" out of residents who are not cooperating or who are assessed by the staff to need psychological help. I was instructed by other staff members to pay particular attention to certain residents because it was assumed that they would break the rules.

The "rule enforcer" role of workers contributes to what is often an adversarial relationship between staff members and residents. Workers often assume that residents will take advantage of a situation. When residents have a legitimate reason for being late for curfew, for example, they must procure written documentation that explains their tardiness, because residents are regarded as challengers of the rule system and thus potential liars. Residents, for their part, challenge the rules (asking for exceptions to be made for them, or criticizing the logic of the rules) and thus workers are continuously in the position of enforcing rules in the face of challenge.

The rules exist for several reasons. Some are explicitly justified by safety standards. The "sign in/sign out" rule, for example, lets staff members know in the event of a fire who is in the house. Some rules also serve the convenience of the staff, and sometimes the residents, in coordinating necessary tasks like cleaning the house. They also exist so that the shelter can "set boundaries" for the residents because, according to the director, "they don't know how." This includes curfews and bedtimes as well as setting limits for interactions between residents (for example, no yelling or hitting).

Whatever the reasons for the rules, they create a system of direct control over resident mobility and activity. In this sense the rules contribute to a system of simple "social control" over the residents—the social control in the literature that has been described as "paternalism" or even "repression" (Higgins). But this simple, direct control has another effect: it also serves to increase institutional awareness of the lives and personalities of the residents. The rules facilitate the *surveillance activity* of the institution (Foucault, 1979).

SURVEILLANCE

Residents of the shelter live under constant surveillance—where they go and for how long; what feelings they emote; what medicine they're taking; their past history of drug and alcohol use, or psychological counselling; how they're getting along with family members—all of these aspects of their lives and others are potential subjects to be monitored and documented. Such information about shelter residents is collected through both formal procedures and informal observation, and is used to create an unofficial profile of each resident that influences the institution's treatment of its clients.

There are at least five methods of obtaining information about the residents. As stated above, some of the rules of the shelter serve to increase institutional awareness about the activity of the residents. Second, incoming residents must fill out an extensive "intake" form upon entering the shelter. Third, the staff are expected to both solicit information from the residents themselves and to record their own observations on the activity of residents. Fourth, mandatory weekly meetings are held where residents divulge information about themselves to the shelter staff. Finally, other agencies participate in information sharing.

Rules and Policies

The many rules around which life at the shelter is constructed serve to increase the institution's awareness about resident activity. As is the case with many of the rules, the "sign out" policy is explicitly designed to increase the safety of the shelter, but implicitly serves as a tool to monitor residents. The "sign out" list, which on several occasions during my work became a point of contention between the residents and staff, has a place for the resident's name and "destination." This ensures that staff members know at least when residents come and go.

Another policy that increases staff knowledge about residents' lives is one that prohibits residents from keeping medicine in their rooms. All medicine is kept in the office, and the staff member on duty is supposed to hand out the medication when requested. Although the rationale for this rule is safety (keeping medicine out of the possible reach of children in the house), one result is that staff are aware at all times which residents are on the pill or taking Prozac, for example, and a resident who wanted to keep such information private would not be able to do so.

Spatial privacy at the shelter is limited. Residents' bedrooms are generally off limits to staff, but the staff can and do search the rooms if the staff has reason to suspect that the residents are breaking the rules (e.g., keeping food, alcohol, or medicine in the rooms). During one of these checks, the staff found a roach clip and a marijuana joint in two residents' rooms (in one room, hidden under the floorboards), and the residents were terminated and the police were called. (Also, a child abuse report was filed with the social services department.) During another check, a resident's room was found to be unsafely unsanitary, and the information was reported to the resident's state social worker.

Some of the policies of the shelter put formerly private areas of life—relationships with friends and family outside the shelter—into public view. Visitors to the shelter must stay in the common areas, to which staff members have access. Phone calls to the shelter must be made from a pay phone in a hallway that is immediately outside the staff office door. Incoming calls cannot come through the pay phone but must come through the office, where staff members take messages. This policy is designed to prevent the pay phone from ringing constantly and the residents from arguing over using the phone, but one effect is that the staff are aware of every phone call the residents receive. If the caller is of interest to the staff—for example, if he or she is rude or sounds drunk—the call is often reported in the log.

Drug and alcohol use is prohibited at the shelter, and is also prohibited off shelter grounds. To enforce this, residents can be drug tested if a staff member suspects that she has been drinking or using illegal drugs. During the time I was collecting data a resident was drug tested. Selective confidentiality (which will be described below) was applied in this instance—while she had left the shelter before the results came back from the lab, the resident's state social worker shared the results with the shelter staff anyway.

Intake Form

Murray's (1988) findings that shelter intake forms solicit information that pertains to issues far beyond residents' immediate situations and that it is shared with all staff members are supported in my study. The intake form is filled out by the resident and the case manager or director prior to the resident's placement in the shelter. The form is designed to document information about the resident's personal history and current social and economic situation. The form provides the staff with a sort of profile of each resident and is also used to screen out potential residents (ones that may be using drugs, for example). At the top of the intake form is clearly printed the mandatory status of the question: statements must be accurate and truthful, and omittance or dishonesty may result in the denial of entrance to the shelter. Questions asked at the intake include financial ones (savings accounts, employment history, source of income) and information about the cause and history of the family's homelessness. They also include medical and psychological concerns; past surgery and current medications; past and present drug and alcohol use (including "experimentation") and mental health history and counselling. The form also inquires about involvement with the state (court involvement, history of child abuse charges filed with the social services department) as well as marital status, education, military history, and interest in returning to work. As Murray states, the wealth of knowledge insisted upon by the institution about residents creates a clear separation between them and the staff, who create "professional boundaries" by revealing little information about themselves in exchange (Murray, 1988).

Weekly Meetings

Residents are required to give several hours of their time to the weekly meetings that take place at the shelter. The shelter mandates that the residents attend house meetings and individual meetings with the case manager and the housing advocate. (This does not include meetings with other institutions that clients of the welfare system often must attend.) All of these meetings generate documentation about the residents and their lives: there are "housing updates" from the housing meetings; "family life files" that document the case manager meetings; and notes from the house meetings often show up in the logs. The meetings are mandatory and residents are expected to participate, which involves engaging in discourse concerning the resident herself or her children. The latter brings to mind Foucault's "confessional," because residents are encouraged to disclose information about themselves. One resident told me, "I hate these meetings, because they stick their noses into everything." "Everything" for this resident, according to the notes from one "Family Life" meeting, includes the following issues: how the children are doing in school; whether or not the children need counselling; whether or not the resident is saving money and how much; and how she feels about divorcing her abusive husband.

Staff

The staff members at the shelter are expected to keep written documentation of the activities of residents. Much of the staff member's job revolves around the staff logs. There is a daily log and a log with a separate file for each resident. According to one worker, "You can tell what kind of problems they have by how thick their personal file is." What are spotted as residents' personal troubles by the staff are recorded in shelter logs (See Loseke, 1992, and Murray, 1988). Residents are not permitted to read either log and are not supposed to know of their existence. The secret and inaccessible status of the logs facilitates what is their main function, which is the recording of information about the residents and the circulation of it among the staff.

Information written in the logs by staff members is procured mainly in two ways. First, staff indirectly solicit information by being available for "supportive listening." "Supportive listening," according to written instructions given to new staff members during the staff orientation, is the staff's "main responsibility." The object of supportive listening is, according to the instructions, "not to pry but to encourage people to feel listened to and supported," which staff can encourage "by drawing different residents into conversations." Information from those conversations is recorded in the residents' files.

Secondly, staff comment in the logs on what they observe in the shelter, which, given the rules of the shelter that limit privacy, is a great deal. If there is particular interest in a resident, staff seem to observe more frequently and to write more extensively about her. For example, when staff members were concerned that one resident was neglecting her infant, one staff worker told me that "She [the resident] knows what we're doing...we're monitoring her and she knows that...staff comes out every time the baby cries." In the case of parenting issues, staff members are compelled by state law to report the abuse or neglect of children. This encourages staff members to document interactions that they see or hear between parents and children, even if they don't meet a legal definition of abuse. In addition, information about residents' lives outside of the shelter obtained through hearsay is recorded. (For example, "MaryEllen visits her boyfriend in prison at least two times per week.")

The observations of the residents by shelter workers are communicated through the logs and help to create a shared profile of what residents are like and what they need. At the staff meetings I attended there was much consensus about the residents. The latter were often labelled "manipulative," "nosey," or "uncooperative" if the consensus had a negative quality.

Other Agencies

Residents are involved with other social service institutions, psychiatrists, lawyers, doctors, and so on. The release forms that residents are asked to sign are used to obtain information from these institutions and also to give information to these institutions. Since residents are often counselled to get involved with more social services (such as early childhood intervention programs, family counselling, and so on), the information net that is cast can get wider during the resident's stay at the shelter. Once residents give consent to the shelter to share information with other agencies, they are not privy to the information that is shared (Also see Murray, 1988). The information shared can have serious consequences for residents' lives because of the institution's practice of intervention into the lives of residents, which will be discussed below.

A selective confidentiality exists at the shelter. Confidentiality is selective in at least two ways. First, it is selective in that "confidentiality" at the shelter often means that members of the general public, other residents, the press, family members and even the resident herself are not privy to a resident's files or to information circulated about her by shelter workers, but that on the other hand the staff members unrestrictedly share information about residents among themselves and to a more limited extent share information with other agencies and professionals. The shelter is normally required to have the resident sign a release form allowing the institution to communicate with other institutions, but this form does not allow residents to have access to the information shared. In addition, the form is not deemed necessary in many instances that are considered "crisis" situations by the staff. The shelter has shared information with the police, with the crisis team at the local psychiatric hospital, and with the welfare department in charge of monitoring child abuse and neglect without consent. The ethic of confidentiality at the shelter is selective in another way. While mechanisms are in place to obtain consent from residents for the sharing of information between agencies, at times this agreement is broken even in non-crisis situations. For example, other agencies shared information with the shelter several times after the residents' consent forms were no longer valid.

INTERVENTION

Rachel's House is not a neutral haven. Its mission statement lists help with "issues related to homelessness" as one of its three goals, which is indicative of its function of intervention. The institution seeks not only to provide material resources to homeless women and their children, but also to train them in what the mission statement calls "daily living skills," to counsel them, and to increase their involvement with social service agencies. Its intended interventions are based on the same assumption of many other shelters (even many self-identified feminist shelters)—the assumption that individual problems contribute to homelessness (Murray, 1988; Loseke, 1992; Ferraro, 1983; Schillinger, 1988.) It is the poverty of the women, their financial dependence upon assistance, that makes them available as targets of intervention, and it is this financial dependence that structures the intervention by giving the institution its power.

The persons who come to the shelter are not entering a disinterested space that serves solely to give them temporary housing. The institution is not neutral territory; persons who seek its assistance cannot therefore be anonymous, and they cannot live private lives. One of the functions of the institution is to intervene in their lives, and to do so it operates with an *insistence on knowing*. Its rules both establish what I am calling "simple control"—direct limitations on mobility and privacy in the shelter—and facilitate surveillance. The information procured through surveillance not only shapes staff treatment of residents, but also facilitates intervention, which can be a more complicated and sometimes indirect control that reverberates *beyond shelter life.*

Susan Murray, in her work on a battered women's shelter, states that "control over personal information involves power" (1988). In addition to the uneven relationship between residents and the institution regarding personal information inside the shelter, one of the power resources that the shelter has on its side is its sharing of information with other institutions, including welfare departments, mental health institutions and the criminal justice system. Social control that is not simple, direct control, is "transinstitutional" (Lowman et al., 1987). The most serious interventions into the lives of the residents at Rachel's House involved the state agency that handled child abuse and neglect reports, the local police, and in one instance, the psychiatric ward of a local hospital.

One of the ways in which the institution intervenes is in its use of information about the residents to file reports with the state agency that handles child abuse and neglect. The reports, even though they are usually not serious enough for the agency to take action, are sometimes enough for the agency to declare "protective" custody over children, which allows them to mandate social services like mental health counselling and early childhood intervention programs. Such reports were filed on at least five of the residents during the six months of research. The residents very often expressed fear regarding this state agency, and one resident in particular often charged that the shelter was "trying to get my kids taken away." Reports were filed for a variety of reasons, from evidence or suspicions of violence against children to insanitary living to residents' not taking their children's medicine with them when they leave the shelter. The range of charges filed against women regarding parenting is probably not simply a reflection of the [middle class] biases of social workers (see Gordon's 1986 criticism of this social control explanation), but might be partly attributable to the highly public, scrutinized life that residents must live in the shelter.

The criminal justice system also has a relationship with the shelter regarding information. The personal files of residents can be (and have been) subpoenaed, and shelter workers are expected to keep this in mind when they write case notes. In addition, the local police are resources for the shelter. For example, during two instances of residents being terminated from the shelter the police were called to keep peace in case of violent disputes. In addition, the shelter reported women to the police who were found to have illegal drugs in their rooms.

One resident's experience at the shelter involved a crisis team from the psychiatric ward of a local hospital, the police, and the state agency who had protective custody of her infant. Thelma, who had a psychiatric evaluation in her file that labeled her as having "homicidal or suicidal tendencies," was being monitored because it was suspected by staff members and other agency workers that she was neglecting her infant, who had gained only one pound in the previous month and who was kept in the resident's dark bedroom for many hours every day. After weeks in which the shelter and other agencies collected information regarding Thelma's patenting, the state agency who had protective custody decided to take physical custody of the child. During the ensuing confrontation at the shelter where Thelma was told her child would be taken away, Thelma was restrained by a police officer who had been called and, after threatening violence to the shelter staff, was involuntarily committed to a local psychiatric hospital. The information that was collected by the shelter on Thelma—including many notes on her habits and activities—which was substantial, was shared with all of the institutions involved.

The latter example was one of the most extreme that I found regarding the shelter's intervention into the lives of its residents. Other actions, such as pressuring residents to get counselling or other services, holding interagency meetings to discuss clients without their knowledge, and reporting terminated residents to the police, were less extreme, but nonetheless affected the lives of residents beyond the walls of the shelter, and possibly for longer than their shelter residency. Many of the interventions I discussed here were cast negatively. Other interventions, such as assisting residents in getting restraining orders on their abusive husbands, were considered more helpful by the residents themselves. In addition, many interventions—especially those regarding child rearing—are defensible in the eyes of many, and some are legally mandated, such as the reporting of child abuse and neglect.

CONCLUSION

Much of the intervention of shelters like Rachel's House in the lives of its clients relies upon information gathering. The staff at Rachel's House operate like other shelter workers, who are "detectives" gathering information (Higgins, 1985). The information gathering— what I am calling surveillance, taking from Foucault (1979)—is an operation that benefits from simple, direct control over resident activity and privacy. *Whether or not this direct control is intended* to increase institutional awareness of residents' lives, it often has this effect. The intervention that evolves from direct control and surveillance often has serious consequences for the lives of residents.

The notion of social control that I have discussed in relation to shelters is one that benefits from the linking of "power, knowledge, and language to bureaucratic control over women," which Ferguson does in relation to Foucault's discourse theory (Schillinger, 1988; see Ferguson, 1984). The relationship between information and "cross-institutional arrangements and dynamics" (Lowman et al., 1987) is central in this analysis and places it within what Lowman et al. refer to as a "revisionist" analysis of social control, which recognizes broad connections between institutions of formal control, such as criminal justice institutions, and welfare, educational and mental health institutions.

There is an important class and racial element in social control aspects of social policy. Much of the literature on social control argues that poor women, often minority, have been subjected to far greater social control by the welfare state than other women (Gordon, 1986; Murray, 1988). Women of color are more likely to be in class positions which make them vulnerable to social control (and social control is sometimes enacted or made possible because of racism). But it is only in this broad sense that my study is relevant to issues of race. My study makes little of the racial differences between the staff of the institution (Caucasian) and the residents (mixed, both Caucasian and minority) for several reasons. All of the residents, regardless of race, were subjected to surveillance; in fact, surveillance is built in, formally and informally, to the operations of the shelter and transcends the stays of individual, racially specific families. In addition, it seemed to me that the residents were unified by the staff in their status as "residents," as people subject to the power of the institution, and as homeless people with problems that caused or contributed to their homeless status. (The most significant exception, which I did not discuss in the body of this article, was the distinction between those who spoke English as their first language and those who did not, which included both Caucasian people and people of color.) It was the class circumstances of the women which united them as targets of social control.

Literature which discusses the social control of poor women often cites the imposition of middle-class values on poor people via social workers. The power relationships in shelters are certainly affected by the class backgrounds of residents and shelter workers (Murray, 1988). But again, broader issues than the specific class statuses of the staff and residents are important. The workers, regardless of their own classes (and races) represent a primarily middle-class and white welfare bureaucracy and follow policies that are designed by or modelled after it. In addition, my analysis relates social control with surveillance regarding the intimate parts of people's lives—with their emotions, mental health, relationships, activities—and the connection of that surveillance with discipline. Here a class analysis becomes easier. It is poor people, and more specifically poor mothers, who come into contact with disciplining welfare institutions the most, and who live more of their lives in the public space of places like shelters. It is for the most part economically vulnerable women who end up in family shelters, even battered women's shelters (Murray, 1988). To live in these places, which have been compared to "total institutions" (Wharton, 1989), means to live a public life that is documented in logs and files, and to be vulnerable to the institutions which collect and distribute such information.

REFERENCES

Berk, R.A., P.J. Newton, S.F. Berk. 1986. What a Difference a Day Makes: An Empirical Study of the Impact of Shelters for Battered Women. *Journal of Marriage and the Family,* 48: 481-490.

Dobash, R.Emerson and Dobash, Russell P. 1979. *Violence Against Wives.* New York: Free Press.

Ferraro, Kathleen. 1983. Negotiating Trouble in a Battered Women's Shelter. *Urban Life,* 12:3.

Foucault, Michel. 1979. *Discipline and Punish: The Birth of the Prison.* New York: Vantage Books.

Gordon, Lisa. 1986. Family Violence, Feminism, and Social Control. *Feminist Studies,* 12:3.

Hagen, Jan. 1987. Gender and Homelessness. *Social Work,* 23.

Higgins, Jan. 1980. Social Control Theories of Social Policy. *Journal of Social Policy,* 9:1.

Higgins, Jan. 1985. *The Rehabilitation Detectives: Doing Human Service Work.* Newbury Park, CA: Sage.

Loseke, Donileen. 1992. *The Battered Woman and Shelters: The Social Construction of Wife Abuse.* Albany: SUNY Press.

Lowman, John, Robert F. Menzies, and T.S. Palys. 1987. *Transcarceration: Essays in the Sociology of Social Control.* Brookfield: Gower.

Murray, Susan. 1988. The Unhappy Marriage of Theory and Practice: An Analysis of a Battered Women's Shelter. *NWSA Journal,* 1:1.

Piven, Frances Fox, and Cloward, Richard A. 1975. "Introduction" in *Radical Social Work,* Roy Bailey and Mike Brake, eds. New York: Pantheon.

Piven, Frances Fox, and Cloward, Richard A. 1971. *Regulating the Poor: the Functions of Public Welfare.* New York: Vintage/Random House.

Schillinger, Elizabeth. 1988. Dependency, Control and Isolation: Battered Women and the Welfare System. *Journal of Contemporary Ethnography,* 16:4.

Wharton, Carol. 1989. Splintered Visions: Staff/Client Disjunctures and Their Consequences for Human Service Organizations. *Journal of Contemporary Ethnography,* 18:1.

CHAPTER 13

Adolescence and the Socialization of Gendered Fear

Jo Goodey

INTRODUCING UNHEARD VOICES

Criminology tells us that men are the criminals, men and women are the victims, and women are the fearful. Inverting this statement, victimological research proceeds to inform us that, firstly, most people are fearful, secondly, they are victims, and, thirdly, they are offenders. However, fear of crime and the fearful are still relegated near the bottom of a criminological hierarchy which perceives the offense, the offender and *his* place in the criminal justice system as being of most interest to academic researchers in the discipline. This stance fails to address the majoritive experience of crime, that of "fearful," and the process by which this position, quintessentially a gendered position cutting across race and class, is attained. It is this most unglamorous area of criminological research, fear, and its largely untapped population of informants, children, that this chapter will introduce. The centrality of childhood fear to a comprehensive understanding of its adult expression, and an understanding of childhood fear itself, is forwarded in the next few pages. Using evidence from the author's research with the aim (ultimately) of filling a theoretical void, the chapter examines the socialization of fear during childhood; its gender, class and racial connotations.

Turning to the book's title, the variable "age" is noticeable for its absence. Like the category "able-bodiedness," age does not conjure up romantic illusions to struggles which have spawned political debates and academic investigation. To capture the imagination of radical criminology, discussion has tended to surround the triumvirate of "race, gender, and class" (Taylor, Walton, and Young [1974],

Schwendinger and Schwendinger [1975], Hall and Scraton [1989]—to name but a few) to the neglect of age and the lifetime experiences, starting in childhood, that society brings to these tenets of criminological interpretation. The research on which this chapter is based is equally guilty of this process. Gender initially formed the cornerstone for investigating fear, with the under 16s providing the fodder for understanding its adult expression. However, the research went on to be titled "The Socialization of Gendered Fear Among 11-16 Year Olds"[1] with the childhood or, more appropriately, the adolescent experience ultimately viewed as a life period worthy of study in its own right. Drawing on the work of childhood sociologists and anthropologists James and Prout (1990), Blitzer (1991) and Qvortrup et al. (1994), the significance of childhood as the underutilized research base or the new "paradigm shift" for '90s sociology (criminology), was gradually appreciated. Similarly, the homogeneity of the research population—white, working class and from a British council (public sector) housing estate—is both the beauty and limitation of the undertaking. Here, gender and age are the variables which are examined in the analysis of fear; removing the demographic complexity of race, ethnicity, religion, class, geography (etc.), while providing insights that could be construed as narrow in their comparative scope.

Few research initiatives can claim to speak for everyone. The present research provides a detailed base for an investigation of the numerous influences upon gendered adolescent fear of crime amongst one group, in one place and at one time. The analysis does not stop here though, for having documented and theorized these findings, the gaps, the variables of class and race, become the basis for a critique of the research while providing suggestions for future initiatives. This chapter presents a stepping stone to a comprehensive understanding of fear, primarily through its work with children. The anomalies have become the arena for new questions. Having cursorily introduced where this chapter might fit in a book attempting to incorporate the broad categories of race, gender and class in criminology, one needs to turn to the work which has been undertaken on fear to appreciate the present attempt at filling a theoretical niche.

FINDING A NICHE AND FILLING THE GAP

The United States' National Crime Survey spawned its British counterparts in the early 1980s with the British Crime Survey (B.C.S.)

and localized investigations of crime, victimization and fear such as the Merseyside Crime Survey (Kinsey, 1984), the Islington Crime Survey (I.C.S.) (MacLean, Jones and Young, 1986) and the Edinburgh Crime Survey (Anderson, Smith et al., 1990). With this emphasis on the victim and non-criminalized fear evoking incidents, a new era was born in British criminology. What is revealed by surveys such as these, regardless of their location, is the striking importance of an individual's "make-up" (their race, gender, class, and age) when examining the nature of fear and victimization.

Highlighting the I.C.S. findings on fear, for the purposes of this chapter, the researchers state (1986: 5.11) "Women are much more likely to perceive risk for themselves when going out after dark than men do, and this difference holds across all groups investigated." These "groups" are focused on race and age (with the London borough of Islington predominantly classified as a low income or working class area). In the I.C.S., the percentage of males and females (respectively), "feeling worried about themselves, after dark," is 27% and 73.3% of whites, 23.7% and 68.6% of Afro-Carribeans and 33.2% and 67.4% of Asians[2]. Maxfield (1984), Hough and Mayhew (1985), and Boers (1991) (to name but a few) cursorily attempt to explain the extreme gendered nature of fear, which holds for various demographic indicators. Vulnerability, rated in terms of the individual's physical, psychological and economic ability to cope with victimization, is forwarded as central to an understanding of differential fear levels, with women (and particularly elderly women) the most vulnerable. Fear is also affected by the diurnal and environmental circumstances in which people find themselves. However, it is "who" the individual is, rather than "where" they are and "when," that centrally informs the experience of fear. Above all, it is one's gender, within the make-up of "who," that determines fear. Gender specifies the crimes to which one is thought vulnerable, with the female sex allotted the dominant share of victimization potential for those most fear evoking crimes after murder; sexual assault and rape. Women's fear of sex crimes may differ according to race[3], class, geography and age, but their overall fear levels are consistently and proportionately higher than their male peers because of the specific threat they suffer.

References to the irrationality of female fear, in lieu of women's victimization potential, have been readily displaced by feminist criminologists (Smart and Smart, 1978; Hanmer and Saunders, 1984; Stanko, 1985). Drawing on victimization surveys such as the I.C.S., life histories (Kelly, 1987) and documentary analysis (Brownmiller, 1975), feminist work has highlighted the precautionary measures that women undertake to avoid the dire experience and consequence of becoming a victim of sex crime. Feminist studies have opened up the narrow interpretations of fear evoking situations to locate the sexual threat in a continuum from home to workplace and (most significantly for the purposes of this study) from childhood to adulthood. Although gendered appraisals of fear can be applauded for their refreshing analysis, they can be criticized on a number of levels which relate to the central concerns highlighted in this chapter.

While feminist studies have brought home the reality of fear as a gendered phenomenon, the accusation of reductionism can be thrown at their endeavors. Women's experiences of fear and crime may be different to men's but women (like men) do not respond as a homogeneous whole. Rather than pitch findings on male fear "against" those on female fear, research must account for the heterogeneity of gender. Dependent on the population under study, the effects of gender, age, class and race should be incorporated in the research undertaking or (at least) acknowledged as significant variables in the fear equation. Feminist criminology has made significant progress with its recognition of gender's diversity, or the individualization of gender; however, danger lies in characterizing women as the "fearful sex" if victimological research (in particular) fails to monitor its goals, questions and resultant findings. If anything, the documentation of women's fear has underplayed the significance of childhood and adolescent girls' fear. Acknowledgement of women's fear has seen a call for wider recognition of the limits fear places on women's lifestyles; but the stereotypical response to this burgeoning wealth of information is to hand out leaflets to women on how to stay safe and feel safe, while piecemeal attempts are made at the local government level to design out fear and crime with women in mind. Consciousness raising enterprises are worthwhile in themselves but, too often, many endeavors can be described as cosmetic alterations to the complexities of fear (here one might include the likes of lighting and crime projects, motoring organization campaigns etc.). Advice to women to travel by car or fit window locks to their homes to enhance their safety, and reduce their fear, often negates the diversity of women's lifestyles and experiences.

There is nothing amiss with tactics that aim to reduce women's fear but, returning to the neglected research on girls' fear, one sees the gaping hole left by an absence of childhood and adolescent research leading to preventative measures against the formulation of gendered fear. The niche that needs filling is research on children. Specifically needed is research on children and for children, and the gap that needs filling is the false boundary between childhood, adolescence and adulthood which, in reality, is a seamless progression. These studies can aid interpretation of gendered fear. To reassess gendered fear, long-held assumptions concerning children under 16 need challenging. Most children are not young offenders (a stereotypical view of many boys' "roles" in criminological investigations), nor are they victims of sexual abuse (a stereotypical view attributed to younger children and particularly girls). This is not to deny the experiences of a significant minority of children but, like adults, the majority's primary concern, in relation to crime, is fear. If one looks to work on fear, the bulk is undertaken with those aged 16 and over; the exceptions being the likes of Anderson, Kinsey et al.'s "Cautionary Tales" in Edinburgh (1990) and the 1992 B.C.S. (Home Office), although even these studies combine victimization research with examination of children's offending behavior and their attitudes towards drugs and the police.

The convenient dividing line, between child and adult, simplifies the research process while negating the under 16 experience. This bounded analysis could imply that either the child's life world is so very different from the adult's or, more simply, that the child is not worthy of studying to the same extent as the adult. Extending the analogy further, one is almost inferring that at age 16 women suddenly become the victims of unwanted sexual threat and the fear it induces. The reality is females *do not* become afraid of sexual assault and rape upon obtaining adulthood, but rather their fear is progressively learnt through the broad influences of socialization from watching television and parental influence [see Schlesinger et al.'s (1991) comments on mothers' attitudes to their daughters viewing violence on television] to personal experience of victimization; as supported by Gordon and Riger's in-depth interviews with 299 women from three cities in the United States (1989: 3): "Personal experiences women have as young girls are especially influential in forming their attitudes toward sexual assault and in initiating female fear." The silent but central theme in this process is sexuality. Having recognized the need to connect childhood with adult research on women's heightened fear of sexual assault and rape, one has to locate this suggestion within the gendered and essentially sexualized socialization processes that define the sexes' appropriate actions and reactions to crime and fear.

THE SEXUALIZATION OF GENDERED FEAR

Sex role theory and social learning theory have directed gender-specific criminogenic explanations away from the confines of biological determinism. Gendered behavior, whether as victim or offender, is readily explained by feminist literature as the result of differential socialization between the sexes. Rape is a product of society's abuse of power, and power, as males and females learn, has historically been in the hands of men (Kennedy, 1992); as Brownmiller said in her much-quoted book (1975: 15): "It [rape] is nothing more or less than a conscious process of intimidation by which *all* men keep *all* women in a state of fear." One can begin to comprehend the stranglehold that fear of rape has over women, and girls, when one acknowledges that all men are not rapists—but it is the threat of rape that determines females' heightened fear across continents, race, and class. However, misconceptions and reactionary references to fear of rape remain in analogies to the biological variables of strength and the "ability" to rape, particularly in reference to race. One has only to consider the western myth of the insatiable black, male rapist as highlighted by the recent case of Mike Tyson in the United States (see also Brownmiller, 1975: 210-255, on race and rape).

It is society's sexual stereotyping (not strength or race) that allows the reality and myth of male rape to flourish. Nowhere is this better illustrated than in cases of "acquaintance rape" or "wife rape." The pervasiveness of "wife rape" is illustrated by Russell's (1982) research on the lifetime experiences of 644 married women which found that 12% had been "forced to have sex with their husband"; similarly, Finkelhor et al.'s (1983) research on the life experiences of 326 women found that 10% who had been married or living as married had had physical force, or its threat, used by their partners to make them have sex.

Emphasis on polarized gender roles cuts across class and race and instills a sense of sexual vulnerability among women which men, typically, see themselves as immune from; as Stanko says of the B.C.S.

which, as a reflection of its randomly sampled population average of 10,000 households, is both inter-racial and inter-class (1990: 122): "In the 1984 British Crime Survey, for example, only 13% of interviewed men said they felt 'a bit or very unsafe,' where 48% of women revealed they did so when walking alone after dark. It may be that women's as well as men's assessments of safety lie in their assessment of sexual danger. And because men are not subjected to the day-in and day-out sexual intrusion so common in women's lives, they are able to report feeling largely secure."

Society places fear of sexual assault and rape squarely on the shoulders of women with the daily sexual intrusion of their lives, while men are taught to fear for the safety of women they know rather than acknowledge their own sexual vulnerability as potential victims (and offenders). This pervasive and "normalized" female fear is not the sole product of adult experience; its origin can be firmly located in the pre-adult experience. Girls and boys progress on a different path towards fear because they are socialized within gendered parameters. As Burt and Estep (1981: 520) concluded in their much neglected article entitled "Learning Sexual Vulnerability": "Adolescence thus appears to be the period during which family and friends inculcate awareness of potential sexual danger in women, but not in men."

Returning once more to biological determinates of sexualized fear, one can point to puberty as the period when the individual becomes sexualized by society. Puberty is a physical marker on the road from childhood to adulthood, but, as a significant life stage, western society prefers to closet the physicality of this time to concentrate on puberty's meanings for the young person's social world. The biology of puberty is hijacked by a society which distorts and emphasizes the changes it sees as appropriate for future gender roles. Hence girls are typically defined and learn to define their blossoming sexuality in terms of their attractiveness and sexual desirability, while boys are defined and must develop their sexuality in the classic guise of machismo's strength and aggressiveness. These dual roles have been eroded *at the edges* by the late 20th century's media hyperbole in the guise of the 1980's "new man" and the 1990's "Tank Girl" (a dubious "feminist" superhero) (see Burrell and Brinkworth's 1994 report in the U.K.'s *Sunday Times*). However, the gendered reality of sexual aggressor, or offender, and sexual victim, remains firmly embedded in patriarchal constructions; glancing at victimization surveys and offender/victim demographics from the U.K.'s Home Office illustrates this point only too clearly (Barclay, 1993).

The reality of puberty as a period of change, confusion, and adjustment, for girls and boys needs reassessment. Above all, the social construction of the individual in terms of his or her gendered sexuality requires deconstruction. Puberty is more than the creation of a "sexual being" whose "sexy" label is disproportionately assigned to the female sex. However, patriarchal society can only deal with the complexities of multiple and transitory gender identities in any individual, or group, by "boxing" behaviorisms into expected gender norms. Connell's (1987) work on hegemonic masculinity defines the dominant assertion of an ideal type in society; that is, male, white and heterosexual. To this one can add western, middle-class, wealthy, and (probably) aged 30-something. Hegemonic masculinity can be viewed as a form of hierarchical boxing which places significance and power with this ideal type, while others such as gay men, colored men and *all* women, fall below and outside this ideal. Within the boxed categories of age, puberty is currently (Aries, 1973) a convenient boxing point for western society but, in puberty's neat compartmentalization of gender, the similarities of male and female become lost while the extremes of experience in any one gender (as influenced by race, class, and sexuality) are often ignored. Western society currently constructs puberty as the period when the values and social roles of hegemonic masculinity are learnt to the exclusion of the multiple variables of experience (such as race). In particular, the socialization of sexualized fear, which is perhaps the most fitting title for this brief theoretical introduction, simplifies the sexes to the point where the study of "masculinities," or multiple and equally significant types, has been "reinvented" to verify the discovery that boys are different and do, in fact, cry.

Having circumnavigated a number of core issues which question the findings to date on gendered adult fear: its sample population, the role of socialization processes and a skewed emphasis on sexuality, this chapter will turn to some research findings which examine gendered fear with the above considerations in mind. The central assumption on which the research is based lies with the recognition that gendered fear is a product of socialization processes which have adolescence, puberty, and the construction of the "sexual being" as pivotal in the development of female fear and male threat. Theory and speculation aside, one needs to let the under 16s "tell it like it is."

RESEARCH WITH ADOLESCENTS

What do you think's the difference between women's fear of being attacked and men's fears ?

I don't know ... you don't see many men getting raped do you !
When men get attacked they're just usually fist fights aren't they ?

This question, and its responses, came towards the end of a discussion session on gendered fear with girls aged 15-16[4]. The session formed one of many in a nine-month investigation (1991-1992) into gendered fear of crime among white, working class 11-16-year-olds in a north of England, state-run school; the findings of which will form the mainstay of this next section. The various methods employed, in the school based research, to explicate adolescents' construction of gendered fear will be detailed below; suffice to say that the discussants (above) had not been primed to talk about rape, and the intentional directness of the question, in seeking unfettered answers, simply allowed reference to sexualized and gendered fear with a matter-of-fact casualness. The above question and its responses are not an exception to the rule but neatly illustrate the standardized viewpoints which surround discussion of gender, fear and crime among the adolescents surveyed. To verify the wider applicability of such disparate comments a number of methods were employed to inform on the adolescent experience of fear: the questionnaire survey, discussion sessions and drama role-play.

In total, 663 children from one school completed a self-report, victimization survey-style questionnaire. Questions were asked with the aim of noting the diverse range of influences upon adolescent fear from peers, parents, school, the media, respondent victimization and their knowledge (witnessed or second-hand) of others' victimization in and around the housing estate where the research was located. This breadth of information reveals the extent to which gendered fear is the product of socialization processes that shape the biological changes, affecting both sexes at puberty, to their own ends. The respondent characteristics of sex and age formed the backbone on which the data was tested to determine, primarily, whether fear is gendered and whether it is age specific in the degree to which it is gendered. Cross-tabulations and references to statistical significance ensued from this wealth of information provided by the 243 variables available for analysis in each questionnaire. However, statistics only allow the researcher to view the world from one angle, so room was made for open-ended responses in the questionnaire, with blank pages at the end for respondents' comments on: "Crime: What makes you and other people worried or afraid, and what are your general feelings of safety around where you live?" The inclusion of qualitative response opportunities in the questionnaire reflects the other half of the research methodology: discussion. Single sex groups of six were taken from different school years to take part in semi-structured discussion, over a period of weeks, reflecting questionnaire subjects and issues independently raised by discussants. Quantitative and qualitative analysis complimented each other to present a balanced overview of socialization processes active in the creation of gendered values, and hence gendered fear, in the all important period of adolescence and puberty.

A central aim of the research's qualitative investigation is not simply to corroborate the "hard facts" of statistical analysis but to "tell it like it is"; to let the research participants lead the research through their own words. If the research had been solely questionnaire-based the neglected world of boys' fear would not have come to the author's attention. While the questionnaire was devised after consultation with its intended respondents on the appropriateness and comprehensiveness of questions, format and wording, and, while the questionnaire does provide an effective means of gathering large data sets, so much can be left unsaid because of the necessary restrictions imposed by its structured format. Similarly, discussion sessions provide insightful anomalies but, like the questionnaire, can be discursively viewed regarding their motivational aims. In other words, research should not be purely for the researcher's gain. Here the drama role-play comes into use as both a research tool and a practical means of working through gender roles. The drama workshop proved to be a fruitful exercise for both researcher and researched (the full scope of its usefulness and the applicability of various research methods must be left to another paper).

Now that the "where," "how" and even the "why" (the question in research that is so often left unanswered[5]) has been tentatively addressed, the chapter can return to some findings beyond the brief discussion extract cited earlier. Not wishing to dwell on the semantics of statistical inference too deeply in such a short chapter, reference will be primarily made to discussion sessions and then to questionnaire findings.

TELLING IT LIKE IT IS: SETTING THE SCENE

We're [males] afraid of being beat up and they're [females] afraid of getting raped.

(Boy, 13-14)

Once again, the above comment illustrates the nonchalant manner in which the reality of gendered fear, as a sexualized phenomenon, is expressed by adolescents. The boy's words can stand alone as a statement, but they are legitimated by the weight of evidence from other discussions and questionnaire findings. Gendered fear is based on a diverse range of influences from the internalized experience of personal victimization to the external influences of all-encompassing socialization processes. The following extract, from a discussion session with girls aged 15-16, encapsulates these multiple influences that are active in the adolescent's construction of fear and threat:

'Cos if it [crime] happens to your friends that makes you more aware. What your parents say. You're told to listen to them anyway.
You can't really miss violence and crime on television. Papers...every page you look at....
There's something happened to somebody. So I think it's all of it. You're just more aware because you can't really get away from it. It's everywhere.

Gender emerges from the research as the common denominator of fear, with age also revealing difference (but) within proportionally gendered confines. Fear of crime may be reduced with increased adolescent age, but girls' fear, over all, remains higher than that of their male peers. Class and race are homogeneous variables among the population sampled but this does not negate their role in the interpretation of results.   White, working class children living in a predominantly white, working class and geographically isolated northern British city, can not fail to be heavily influenced by the culture in which they find themselves.   This culture traditionally stresses patriarchal roles within the limited confines of any capacity for change or diversity (Campbell, 1993).   The image of "new man" or "career woman" is there on the television screen for adolescents to see but its potential for realization is, more often, an imaginary scenario; as two girls age 15-16 confirm during a discussion session:

> *I can't imagine a man stood at the kitchen sink with a pinny [apron] on ! [laughter]*

> *There's only me in my family.   There's me, my Mum and my   Dad and he even puts restrictions on my Mam ! Tells her what time to be in and "Do this, don't do that."*

The second girl's comments reflect the role of male protector for girlfriends, close acquaintances, and the women in a man's family. This is not a working class phenomenon but a late twentieth century version of female "chaperonage" which has its repercussions in the fetching and carrying, by car, of girls and women from middle class households. The need for females to be safe and to be "kept safe" cuts across class and is an implicit idea that both sexes become aware of from a young age.   This phenomenon is supported by Valentine's (1989) inter-class research on women's fear of male violence in public space and the impact this has on their lives, and their daughters' lives. Similarly, comments from Schlesinger et al.'s inter-class and inter-racial research, on women viewing violence, supports this idea of female "chaperonage" (1991: 49): "Well, it's an act of violence against a person where—it's awful. I've got a daughter of seventeen, so I can relate to that.   I mean she's not allowed out unless she's got a bodyguard with her."   The author's own research indicates the extent to which the protection of girls is a daily reality that inculcates lives. Girls learn to stay safe while boys learn to keep them safe (something which the majority of boys learn but which many fail to operationalize).

The only thing I worry about is my Mam and sister when they go round town because of the drunks.

(Boy, 13, questionnaire comment)

I have no problems alone at night but if I was with a female I would be protective after incidents in the past.

(Boy, 16, questionnaire comment)

As the earlier discussion extract illustrates, the forces shaping the socialization of gendered fear and (hence) appropriate gendered behavior are "everywhere." This all encompassing observation is not a crude generalization, as evidenced by the research which clearly states that: firstly, girls are more fearful than boys, secondly, girls fear sexual assault and rape more than boys, thirdly, girls fear males because of the threat they pose and, finally, this gendered fear is instilled from a range of socialized sources. Turning to some research findings, the following pages briefly illustrate these points only too clearly. Emphasis is placed on the socialization of gendered fear.

THE SOCIALIZATION OF SEXUALIZED FEAR

The questionnaire asks respondents if their parents do not like them to visit certain places (51.3% of boys and 67% of girls responded "Yes") and, if so, why they think their parents would not like them to visit these places; after which respondents are asked if and, if so, why they would not like to visit these places (55% of boys and 74.4% of girls said they would not like to). Analysis of the available response options to these questions, ranging from "Parents think you might get something stolen" to "Someone your age isn't allowed there," clarifies the centrality of the sexualized threat upon resultant levels of gendered fear. The responses "Parents think I might get sexually attacked" (11.6% of boys and 39.4% of girls) and "I might get sexually attacked" (9.4% of boys and 32.8% of girls) are the most statistically significant gendered responses at the 99.9% confidence level[6].

Placing statistical significance aside, the modal response to speculative parental reasoning and respondents' own reasoning,

regarding the above questions, is (respectively) for boys and girls—
"Parents think I might get beaten up" / "Parents think I might get
sexually assaulted" / "I might get beaten up" and "Parents will be
angry with me for going there." Parental restrictions emerge as
dominant in girls' own decision making factors, with concern for their
sexual and physical safety coming a close second (boys place parental
anger as second in their personal response options). These figures
indicate the important role played by parental restrictions, primarily on
their daughters', rather than their sons', lives. This gendered parenting
places particular limits on girls' free-range activities (Hart, 1979);
limits which are reciprocated over the generations, from mother to
daughter, in patriarchal society (Chodorow, 1974). The working class
boys and girls in the study appear to have greater free-range
opportunities than their middle class peers, but, these relative freedoms
remain proportionally gendered within class contexts. As the children
said:

> *Sometimes I get mad at my Mum 'cos I can't go to my
> friend's house by myself and so I say "Don't you trust
> me?" and she says "Oh, it's not you it's the people out
> there."*

(Girl, 12-13)

> *There's this lass [girl] round our end [street]. She's 14,
> nearly 15, and has to be in by 8 o'clock. Her Mam makes
> her. It's the Mams though ain't it. It's the Mams that let
> them [girls] out.*

(Boys, 13-14)

With increased adolescent age parental influence declines. Girls
continue to be told not to visit places by their parents, more than boys,
up to age 15-16, but this is perceived by girls (this age) to be of
reduced significance in their lives in respect of their burgeoning
knowledge on crime and fear:

> *I think when you're younger really it's your parents and
> then as you get older it's your friends [who inform you
> about crime]. 'Cos as you get older you don't see your
> parents as much and you're with your friends most of the*

*time and you listen to them more and you talk to them
more.*

(Girls, 15-16)

Declining parental influence reflects the development of
independence and young adulthood, but, it also follows a response
"pattern" that emerges through the majority of the questionnaire and
discussion sessions analyzed. While girls tend to demonstrate higher
levels of fear than their male peers, with an age breakdown, girls do
not reveal heightened levels of fear as they grow older. Both girls' and
boys' fear generally reduces with age while remaining proportionally
gendered. For example, when the questionnaire asks respondents for
their reaction to an imaginary newspaper headline declaring a city-wide
crime wave, 46.3% of boys and 73.6% of girls age 11-12 state they
would be "Afraid for [their] own safety" but, by age 15-16, these
percentages have steadily fallen to 17.9% of boys and 37.3% of girls.
The only explanation one can proffer for this negative correlation of
fear with increased adolescent age (an assumption heavily weighted on
the subjective analysis of discussion) is a sense of resigned acceptance.
One could read "apathy" for "acceptance" but the older children or,
more appropriately, these young adults, are simply displaying the kind
of attitude or "coping strategy" against fear which is demanded of
adults. Box says of girls, in relation to their blocked opportunity
structures, that they "have been socialized to endure the female's lot in
life" (1983: 180). This "lot" extends to the acknowledgement, by girls
age 15-16, of their future role as the "fearful" while boys must
recognize their place as the "fearless." (Among younger children the
construction of gendered fear is fresh and its boundaries, as yet, can
appear as fluid constructs). Adolescence is also characterized by intra
and inter-sex bullying and the fear this engenders (Slee and Rigby,
1994). However, this phenomenon does not equate with the underlying
construction of the more sinister threat that lies for girls in the guise of
the rapist or sex attacker. The realization that fear is sexualized and,
therefore, gendered, tends not to be openly stated at any age. The
accumulative experience of girls' heightened fear transposes itself into
adulthood, while those against whom fear is directed, men, are not
explicitly referred to as the instigators of fear.

The author's research indicates that parents, peers, and the media
instil "information" on the gendered nature of crime which boys and

girls implicitly translate to offense, offender, and victim status. This
"reality" is tinged with generalizations, stereotypes, and
misinformation, as the following discussion extract illustrates:

When you watch Crimewatch [television programme] and all
that . . .
It's nearly always women that get attacked i'n it.
Raped and just dropped off on a motorway.

                                                    (Boys, 13-14)

Sometimes "who" children are afraid of (usually men) is directly
referred to.   However, the meaning behind this directness (the
patriarchal construction of fear) is often lost within the quagmire of
having to cope with its reality. It is easier to say "I'm afraid of the
bogey*man*" rather than admit "I'm afraid of the *man*." As one 15-
year-old girl aptly demonstrates with the comment she adds in brackets
at the end of her questionnaire:

Seeing people (mostly men) on a night time makes me on
edge very much.

Boys are also afraid of the bogeyman as aggressor (rather than
sexual assailant) but, with age, they learn to drop or hide their fear to
a greater extent than girls do. One is able to state, with statistical
support from the research questionnaire, that fear does appear to
decline amongst boys with age; for example, when asked the question
"Have you been worried or has something made you feel 'on edge'
when outside?," the number of boys responding "Yes" steadily declined
from a high of 72.2% at age 11 to a low of 29.7% at age 16 (in
comparison, the number of girls responding "Yes" was 57.9% at age
11 and 68.3% at age 16). For boys, the question of disappearance or
non-admittance has to equate with the social requirement that boys
become "male" as they grow older. The following comments highlight
the social instigation of machismo which is more readily paid lip
service to in working class communities if not, in actuality, any more
stringently enforced than by middle class society.

'Cos they [boys] feel pansy [pathetic/feminine] if like they
meet their Mams, or if their Dad comes to pick them up

from somewhere. They feel "Oh, I'm not gonna tell me mates, or they'll think I'm a poof" [homosexual].

(Girl, 12-13)

I'd go anywhere. I'd go through all of them [different city locations] though I don't like 'em.
I'd go all over the place.
I'd go anywhere.

(Boys, 15-16)

Boys can readily state "I'd go anywhere" because they are relatively free from fear of sexual assault and rape. For these reasons, in combination with their burgeoning machismo, boys can express much lower levels of fear in the public domain than girls. For example, in response to the question (cited earlier) "Have you been worried or has something made you feel 'on edge' when outside?," 46.5% of boys and 72.2% of girls responded "Yes" (statistically significant at the 99.9% confidence level). Both sexes highlight "people" and "badly lit areas" (which these "people" might frequent) as mainstays of their fear. More girls than boys refer to "people" as a cornerstone of their fear, a finding corroborated by responses to the question "When you're outside do some people make you feel worried or "on edge"?, with 74% of boys and 88% of girls (statistically significant at the 99.9% confidence level) confirming this to be the case. What is most interesting is "who" the sexes are afraid of.

Consider those saying that "people" rather than "things" made them afraid when outside. This group was provided with a list ranging from "boys your age" to "old people" and "druggies" from which they can select any number of groups which instil fear in them. While boys' fear of "older boys" emerges as a statistically significant gendered response (at the 99.9% confidence level), with 48.3% of boys and 28.5% of girls referring to this category, the finding has to be weighted against other response options. Fear of "older girls" is selected by 20% of girls and 4.2% of boys (statistically significant at the 99.9% confidence level) but, aside from intra-adolescent conflict, fear of "men" emerges as the only other significantly gendered response at the 99.9% confidence level, with 21.2% of boys and 42.6% of girls selecting this category. The fear engendered by men is further corroborated when one turns to those most fear-evoking categories for both sexes: "drunks" and "druggies." Girls' and boys' fear of these groups ranges from 64.9% to 83.4% when one accounts for all respondent ages, 11-16. When pressed to examine the characteristics of such "undesirables" during discussion sessions, discussants tend to paint a gender specific picture which they view as stating the obvious (Quote: "They're men of course !"). Herein lies the male threat that is couched in terms of atypicality and the imagery of the bogeyman.

With fear firmly established as gendered one can turn to respondents' most recent experience of victimization to ascertain the extent to which this is gendered. The questionnaire asks "Has anyone in the last few weeks done or said something to worry or scare you when you've been outside?" The study indicates that 21.4% of boys and 34.2% of girls have recently been worried or scared by someone (significant at the 99.9% confidence level). This finding tells us quite a bit—more girls than boys claim to have been recently victimized—but at the same time it tells us very little. While information is gathered on incident characteristics and the relationship of victim to offender, the method of investigation is fundamentally flawed as it does not account for previous experience of victimization nor can it ascertain the profile of those who were willing to respond in the affirmative (to name but a few objections). Emerging from the incident details, the "respondent /aggressor" scenario reveals the significance of intra-adolescent bullying, with half of girls recalling same-sex confrontations. The figures on recent victimization, however, fail to live up to the numbers (74% of boys and 88% of girls) who are able to state that, when outside, some people make them feel "on edge"; these people characteristically being adult males.

Without denying the fundamental impact that bullying has on many adolescents and the resultant fear it produces, one can perceive a deeper strata of fear that lies with the sexualized male threat and the socialization of female vulnerability. The adolescent "in fighting" of teenage girls is a real problem, but one that is left largely behind as adult roles are adopted. A significant minority of the girls surveyed revealed instances of sexual victimization, by male perpetrators, in the past. These incidents were written or talked about because of their impact. Girls who had not been sexually victimized were all too aware of this danger. One 15-year-old girl wrote on the back of her questionnaire:

The only things that scare me are being raped and having to walk pass noise crowds of (many) youths or people who seem to be causing trouble.

Her initial fear embraces her second fear as the "umbrella" threat that is at once recognized and at the same time denied. Women and girls handle their fear (essentially their fear of men) in this way to avoid the hard-hitting reality of gendered threat. Having said this, a number of queries can be levied at the gendered nature and implications of this research.

REDUCED TO GENDER ? CRITICISMS AND NEW AVENUES

The previous section might read like biased selection of data for the confirmation of a self-fulfilling prophecy. While the author freely admits that the data was *selected* and the responses to it *subjective*, the initial aim of the research was such that a "simple" hypothesis had to be tested by retaining a clarity of vision among a sample population which was neither multi-class or multi-racial. Ultimately, the reader should not be shocked to find support for the origins of gendered adult fear amongst adolescents. The adolescent experience is not that dissimilar from the adult's and, with this realization, barriers can be lifted to let in new research agendas. However, if nothing "new" has actually been said, the accusation of essentialism could be levied at the research, as yet another example of a one-dimensional, that is "gendered" or more appropriately "female-centric initiative," that claims to speak for "everyone."

The research requirement was to examine adolescent gendered fear. This was achieved by studying one homogeneous group of adolescents. However, homogeneity does have its problems of non-comparability and, hence, its ready critics. To pre-empt negative criticism of the research the author considered the enrolment of a number of schools to account for some of the diversity of class and race found in Britain. With severe restrictions on finances (a fact all too common in research!) it was decided to conduct a detailed investigation of gendered fear in a single school. This is not a justification of the work's limited appeal but more a reality of factual provisos. If anything, the few pages of results outlined earlier should provide the reader, if not the author, with new channels for investigation.

Gender, as the core variable discussed in the research, opened up findings not only on girls' socialization as the "fearful" but also on boys' socialization as the "fearless." It is the boys' absence or denial of fear, with age, that needs to be contextualized in their lifestyle as white and working class. To explicate the *reality* of male fear from its early childhood confines or the academic appraisal of masculinity, one can insert conflicts surrounding class and race as catalysts to the male experience of fear. If the boys in the research were living in multi-racial London one might have gained insight into the world of "legitimized" fear focused on racism. The same can be said of girls but, with females socialized into the ready admittance of fear, the context of race can do more to understand the expression of racial violence and fear among males. While adolescent boys may find it difficult to acknowledge and talk about the fear they do possess, this sense of having to be "male" might prove to be a useful tool when discussing the violence and fear surrounding racial conflict. Class may also instil a sense of "difference" which can lead to conflict and the ensuing threat and fear of violence. A middle-class youth who suddenly finds him or herself on "the wrong side of town" can be all too aware of possible danger and (hence) fear. But, as the victimization survey has revealed, most actual crime is intra-class and intra-race while it is fear of crime that crosses the class boundary.

While inter-class and inter-racial conflict is important in forming one's social identity, it is the acceptable limits of behavior within a class or a race that largely determines appropriate action and reaction to crime and fear. Regardless of class or race, females have a heightened sense of fear because of the sex crime threat; but, their resultant lifestyle reaction to this threat may be markedly different as a reflection of their income, where they live and (perhaps most importantly) how the wider society perceives them. Working class and middle class women might be equally fearful of male attack when leaving a friend's house at night, but one can afford a car or taxi home while the other is consigned to the riskier and less desirable mode of public transport or a walk. These economic restrictions reflect the wider limits that patriarchal society places on women and which have their secondary hierarchies in class and race. Males define the appropriate female role, and women, as socialized beings, tend to corroborate this. Gender appropriate behavior is contextualized by one's class and race. Individuals may cross the threshold of categorization—an Asian woman may become a successful lawyer—but she runs the risk of multiple victimization and the fear this arouses because she is a target on the grounds of her race, her sex and her wealth. Her position brings her some security against victimization, particularly in economic terms, but she has to confront threat and fear from a range of sources.

To step outside the norm of expected behavior appropriate to one's gender, race and class is to challenge the doctrine of patriarchal society. Working class boys, as Lees (1983) and Heidensohn (1985) note, "slag off" girls and threaten them with the label of promiscuity in order to locate them within their feminine role. Working class girls do the same while the sexuality of their male peers is left relatively unchallenged. Those males who do question male sex and (hence) gender roles—homosexuals—are heavily punished by a society which frowns on any act that isn't "healthily" heterosexual. The middle classes may appear to afford their daughters greater freedom than their working class peers, but, political correctness aside, one can determine the markers of gendered sanctions which are barely disguised behind the rhetoric of keeping women "safe." The question "safe from whom —other women ?" needs to be asked. Yes, girl gangs are a significant feature in a *minority* of girls' lives (Campbell, 1995), but one has to weigh this against the level of fear that males can induce in women with the fear of rape and sexual assault.

Again, the discussion should not be reduced to essentialism. Gendered fear does not simply refer to the experience of male versus female, rather it implies the multiplicity of the gendered experience for both sexes. The fear sensed by the Asian girl from an inner city, working class district can not hope to speak for her peers of sex and age who comes from a middle class, white background in the heart of rural England. The list of variables that could potentially influence the experience of fear is seemingly endless. This does not mean that criminological research should limit its scope to "all or nothing," but it does call for an acknowledgement of peoples' diversity and, having done this, the discipline must require that the tenets of race, gender, class and age be firmly embedded in future initiatives. Mere tokenism will not do.

CONCLUDING COMMENTS

Gendered fear of crime has repercussions across class and race; its roots lying deep in a global culture of patriarchy. Fear of sexual assault and rape impacts significantly on women's lives while it labels men as "aggressors." Recognizing that the gendered experience of fear is a socialized phenomenon, research must acknowledge the role that childhood and, particularly, adolescence has to play in its creation. Society's emphasis on the individual as "sexual being," from puberty onwards, needs assessment as a distorting tool of gendered socialization. Examining adolescence and the myriad of its expressions as "the fearful" and "the victim" can help criminology to focus its attention on these most common and essentially gendered experiences of crime.

The above research has touched on gender and class and can only make suggestions for further research which can expand on these findings while incorporating the wider experience of adolescent fear— particularly as it relates to race. More children in many more schools, and other settings besides, need the opportunity to discuss their fear of crime and "tell it like it is."

NOTES

1. Women tend to focus their fear on "stranger danger" in the public domain. Reasons for public place fear can be legitimized on a number of levels: as a reaction to a real threat, as a coping strategy against an all-pervasive fear, as the end product of media propaganda, as a subconscious diversionary tactic away from some "home truths." Whatever the causes, women's focus on public place danger has to be recognized. For these reasons (alongside the difficulty of obtaining information on children's fears at home with the prior approval of parents) the research documented in this chapter examined gendered fear in the public domain.

2. The racial categories referenced here are those defined by the I.C.S. authors.

3. The I.C.S. revealed a negative correlation between high levels of harassment and increased respondent age with women, generally, experiencing higher levels than men. This gendered harassment was particularly marked amongst the 16-24 age group. Women in this group consistently revealed higher levels of fear than men;

however, between the three ethnic groups surveyed there was a marked disparity, with (respectively for males and females) 21.8% and 60.9% of Whites, 43.3% and 72% of Afro-Caribbeans and 33.3% and 42.4% of Asians citing harassment. Clearly, racism and lifestyle, within the specific gendered constraints of culture, goes some way towards explaining these intra-gender disparities.

4. Discussion groups were held according to school years and, as discussants were not asked their exact age, the findings can only refer to age bandings e.g. 11-12, 12-13, 13-14 etc. Questionnaires do provide an exact age match for each respondent; this allows for the division of age into bandings of 2,3 or 6 for the purpose of comparative statistical analysis.

5. College students are frequently interviewed by researchers, often for the reason that both parties are conveniently 'on campus' (though often no reason is given). White, working class children from one school were selected for the current research because of the clarity of causal variables this facilitated in the assessment of fear and because the author could gain relatively swift access to the school in question.

6. The research employed the chi-square test and looked for statistical significance at the 95% confidence level and above. In other words, relationships were sought with the statistical indication that they were occurring by chance less than five times in every one hundred cases. The statistics cited in this chapter were occurring at the 99.9% confidence level and were, therefore, highly significant.

REFERENCES

Anderson, S., Kinsey, R., Loader, I., and Smith, C. 1990. *Cautionary Tales: A Study of Young People & Crime in Edinburgh.* Centre for Criminology: Edinburgh University.

Anderson, S., Smith, C., Kinsey, R., and Wood, J. 1990. *The Edinburgh Crime Survey.* Scottish Office Central Research Unit Papers.

Aries, P. 1973. *Centuries of Childhood.* Jonathan Cape: London.

Barclay, G. (ed) 1993. *Digest 2: Information on the Criminal Justice System in England and Wales.* Home Office Research and Statistics Department: London.

Blitzer, S. 1991. They Are Only Children, What Do They Know ? *Sociological Studies of Development*, 4: 11-25.

Boers, K. 1991. *Fear of Crime — An Explanatory Model*. Paper presented at 1991 British Criminology Conference: York, U.K.

Box, S. 1983. *Power, Crime and Mystification*, Tavistock: London.

Brownmiller, S. 1975. *Against Our Will*, Penguin: London.

Burrell, I. and Brinkworth, L. 1994. Sugar N' Spice but Not at All Nice. *The Sunday Times*, U.K., 27th Nov.

Burt, M. R., and Estep, R. E. 1981. Apprehension and Fear: Learning a Sense of Sexual Vulnerability. *Sex Roles* 7 (5): 511-522.

Campbell, A. 1995. Media Myth-Making. *Criminal Justice Matters*, 19 (Spring): 8-9.

Campbell, B. 1993. *Goliath*, Methuen: London.

Chodorow, N. 1974. *The Reproduction of Mothering: Psychoanalysis and the Sociology of Gender*, University of California Press: Berkeley.

Connell, R. 1987. *Gender and Power*, Blackwell: Oxford.

Finkelhor et al., 1983. *The Dark Side of Families*, Sage: Beverly Hills, pp.119-130.

Gordon, M. T., and Riger, S. 1989. *The Female Fear*, The Free Press: New York.

Hall, S., and Scraton, P. 1989. Law, Class and Control, in M. Fitzgerald, G. McLennan and J. Pawson (eds.) *Crime and Society*, Routledge: London, pp. 462-483.

Hanmer, J. and Saunders, S. 1984. *Well-Founded Fear: A Community Study of Violence to Women*, Hutchinson: London.

Hart, R. 1979. "Children's Experience of Place," Ph.D. thesis, Environmental Psychology Program: City University of New York.

Heidensohn, F. 1985. *Women and Crime*, Macmillan, London.

Hough, M., and Mayhew, P. 1985. *Taking Account of Crime: Key Findings from the 1984 British Crime Survey*, Home Office Research Study No.85, H.M.S.O: London.

James, A., and Prout, A. 1990. A New Paradigm for the Sociology of Childhood ? in A. James and A. Prout (eds.) *Constructing and Reconstructing Childhood*: Contemporary Issues in the Sociological Study of Childhood, The Falmer Press: New York, pp.7-35.

Kelly, L. 1987. The Continuum of Sexual Violence, in J. Hanmer and M.Maynard (eds.) *Women, Violence and Social Control*, Macmillan: Basingstoke, pp.46-60.

Kennedy, H. 1992. *Eve Was Framed*, Vintage: London.

Kinsey, R. 1984. *Merseyside Crime Survey: First Report*, Merseyside County Council: Liverpool.

Lees, S. 1983. How Boys Slag off Girls. *New Society*, 13 October.

MacLean, B., Jones, T., and Young, J. 1986. *The Islington Crime Survey*, Centre for Criminology: Middlesex Poly.

Maxfield, M.G. 1984. *Fear of Crime in England and Wales*, Home Office Research Study No.78, H.M.S.O: London.

Qvortrup, J., Bardy, M., Sgritta, G., and Winterberger, H. (eds.). 1994. *Childhood Matters*, Aldershot: Avebury.

Russell, D. 1982. *Rape In Marriage*, Macmillan: New York.

Schlesinger, P., Dobash, R. E., Dobash, R. P., and Weaver, C. K. 1991. *Women Viewing Violence*, Broadcasting Standards Council: University of Stirling.

Schwendinger, H., and Schwendinger, J. 1975. Defenders of Order or Guardians of Human Rights?, in I. Taylor, P. Walton, and J. Young (eds.) *Critical Criminology*, Routledge and Kegan Paul: London, pp.113-146.

Slee, P.T., and Rigby, K. 1994. Peer Victimization at Schools, *Australian Journal of Early Childhood*, 19 (1) : 3-11.

Smart, C., and Smart, B. (eds.). 1978. *Women, Sexuality and Social Control*, Routledge and Kegan Paul: London.

Stanko, E. A. 1985. *Intimate Intrusions*, Routledge and Kegan Paul: London.

Stanko, E. A. 1990. *Everyday Violence*, Pandora: London.

Taylor, I., Walton, P., and Young, J. 1974. *The New Criminology*, Routledge and Kegan Paul: London.

Valentine, G. 1989. *Women's Fear of Male Violence in Public Space*, Ph.D. thesis: University of Reading, U.K.

INDEX

McDermott, M. J. 81, 82, 88n, 220, 245n
McDonald, David 214n
McDonell, Dennis M. 160, 192n
McKay, Nellie 19, 26n
McKenzie, Doris 162, 187n
Media iv, 86n, 105-118, 120-123n, 207, 273, 275, 281, 288, 290
Melville, S. 80, 88n
Menzies, Robert 59, 69n
Mercy, James A. 57, 69n
Merton, Robert 17, 26n, 55, 69n
Messerschmidt, James 4, 5, 8, 19, 26n, 33, 44n, 56, 61, 69n
Michalowski, Raymond 144, 157n
Miller, Jody v, 219n
Miller, Susan 30, 47n
Mills, C. Wright 6, 15, 26n
Milovanovic, Dragan ii, vi, 4, 25n, 26n, 45n, 49, 67-70, 74-76, 78, 84, 87n, 88n, 144, 157n, 241
Minorities 7, 10, 27n, 120, 141, 143, 146, 149, 150, 167, 221
Mooney, Jayne 52, 60, 69n
Moral panics 105, 121-123n
Morgan, Jenny 168, 188n
Morra, Norman 58, 69n
Morris, Allison 58, 68n, 219, 243n
Morrison, Toni 8, 23n, 26n
Morrissey, Marietta 5, 26n
Morse, G. A. 163, 190n
Muncer, Steven 167, 187n
Murray, Charles 157n
Murray, Susan 248-251, 258, 260, 261, 263-265n
Myers, Martha 45n
Nasar, Sylvia 147, 157n
National Campaign About Drug Abuse 176, 190n
Neil, C. 177, 190n
Nelson, James 13, 27n
Nelson-Kilger, Shirley 220, 221, 245n
Newsmaking criminology iii, iv, 86n, 121, 122n
Newton, Phyllis J. 249, 265n
Noble, Amanda 133, 139n
Northern Territory 210, 216n
Nunez, Santiago 25n